* "nothing human is alien to me!"

Our Stories
Matter

What?

So what?

Now what?

Studies in the
Postmodern Theory of Education

Shirley R. Steinberg
General Editor

Vol. 446

The Counterpoints series is part of the Peter Lang Education list.
Every volume is peer reviewed and meets
the highest quality standards for content and production.

PETER LANG
New York • Washington, D.C./Baltimore • Bern
Frankfurt • Berlin • Brussels • Vienna • Oxford

Robert J. Nash & Sydnee Viray

Our Stories
Matter

Liberating the Voices
of Marginalized Students
Through Scholarly
Personal Narrative Writing

PETER LANG
New York • Washington, D.C./Baltimore • Bern
Frankfurt • Berlin • Brussels • Vienna • Oxford

Library of Congress Cataloging-in-Publication Data

Nash, Robert J.
Our stories matter: liberating the voices of marginalized students
through scholarly personal narrative writing / Robert J. Nash, Sydnee Viray.
pages cm. — (Counterpoints: studies in the postmodern theory of education; vol. 446)
Includes bibliographical references.
1. English language—Rhetoric—Study and teaching. 2. Academic writing—
Study and teaching. 3. Autobiography—Authorship. 4. Narration (Rhetoric)—
Psychological aspects. 5. Social justice—Study and teaching (Higher)
6. Minority college students—United States—Attitudes. I. Viray, Sydnee. II. Title.
PE1404.N384   808'.0420711—dc23   2012045355
ISBN 978-1-4331-2114-2 (hardcover)
ISBN 978-1-4331-2113-5 (paperback)
ISBN 978-1-4539-1050-4 (e-book)
ISSN 1058-1634

Bibliographic information published by **Die Deutsche Nationalbibliothek.**
Die Deutsche Nationalbibliothek lists this publication in the "Deutsche
Nationalbibliografie"; detailed bibliographic data is available
on the Internet at http://dnb.d-nb.de/.

The paper in this book meets the guidelines for permanence and durability
of the Committee on Production Guidelines for Book Longevity
of the Council of Library Resources.

Contents

Acknowledgments   vii

Foreword: Wind Paz-Amor, *i am poetry*   ix

1. The Who, What, and Why of Scholarly Personal Narrative Writing   1

2. SPN Empowerment for Marginalized Writers: Our Lives Signify!   10

3. Exploring the Three Metaphors of Oppression in the Academy   24

4. How Stories Teach Theories: Sydnee's Personal Reflections on Social Justice Themes   35

5. Introducing the Ten General Guidelines for Writing Scholarly Personal Narratives   43

6. The Four-Fold Path to Liberation in SPN Writing: Generation, Percolation, Translation, Publication   69

7. The Writer's Toolbox: Practical Tips and Questions for SPN Writers: Part One   82

8. The Writer's Toolbox: Practical Tips and Questions for SPN Writers: Part Two   97

9. Four Authors Who Have Lived on the Margins— and Written about It on Their Own SPN Terms: Part One   113

10. Four Additional Authors Who Have Lived on the Margins— and Written about It on Their Own SPN Terms: Part Two   147

11. Robert's and Sydnee's Closing Invitation to Our Readers   171

Afterword: Jacob Diaz, *Learning to Trust My Voice*   177

Bibliography   183

Acknowledgments

First, I cannot express strongly enough how much my co-author, Sydnee Viray, has meant to me and to our writing project. Our collaboration on this volume produced some of the most enjoyable and inspiring co-authoring moments I have ever had. She is brilliant, funny, creative, insightful, and incredibly understanding. After all, if she could put up with all my authorial quirks and quibbles during the months we worked together, then she's got to be the kindest, most compassionate person at my university.

Second, I want to thank my partner, Madelyn, for always supporting me during my writing projects, many of which have consumed entire summers. She has been patiently there for me through the countless articles, chapters, and books that I have written during a 45-year career in higher education. I am just so grateful to her in a way that words are unable to convey. During the upcoming year that will see the publication of this book, Madelyn and I will be celebrating our 50th wedding anniversary. For me, the co-incidence of these two wonderful events speaks volumes about the richness of our lives together.

Third, I want to thank by name the authors who contributed SPN reflections to this book. My co-author and I are extraordinarily proud to include their work here. In alphabetical order, they are: Amarildo Barbosa, Tamara D. Brown, Fieh Chan, Jacob Diaz, Kyle Dodson, Maria Dykema Erb, Vanessa Santos Eugenio,

Amanda Flores, Robin Hood, Jennifer Jang, Khristian Kemp-DeLisser, Leslye R. Kornegay, Stacey A. Miller, Modou Ndione, Michiko Oishi, Wind Paz-Amor, Alvin Sturdivant, and Candace J. Taylor.

Fourth, I wish to thank my former co-author, and dear friend, Dr. Richard Greggory Johnson III, for his continuing support of all my work. His influence has been integral to our publishing this book with Peter Lang.

—Robert J. Nash

First, I would like to thank my co-author, Dr. Robert J. Nash. He has made this writing project and process an incredible learning experience, as he would say, "from the inside out." I will always remember our countless conversations, playful debates, outrageous metaphorical analyses, and—lest I forget—our endless pints of ice cream sprinkled with philosophical learnings, socio-political observations, and religio-spiritual interrogations. He has helped me to see who, what, where, when, and why a writer is. I am forever grateful and honored to share in this opportunity.

Second, I would like to thank my family: Nanay ko, Susan Calderon Viray, tatay ko, Lawrence Francis Parker, my adoptive father, Dale Lawrence Wood, my stepmothers, Debi Parker and Carol Wood. I would like to thank my partner, Vanessa Santos Eugenio, for her love and support. I feel so blessed to have an orchard, not just a single tree, of supportive sisters (Mary Ann Viray Alfaro, Priscilla Andrews, Erica Sylver, Ashley Parker) and brothers (Jeremy Parker, Jeramey Regimbald, and Jeffrey Regimbald). I am forever grateful for our laughs, our tears, and, most important, our shared stories. And to my family and growing orchard in the Philippines, all of you are in my heart and embedded in my spirit. *Ibigin isa sa bawat at lahat ng inyong. Ka sa akin sa espiritu ng nakasanayan. Maari mong bawat mahanap ang inyong personal na pagpapalaya sa lahat na ituloy mo. Mahal na mahal ko kayo.* (Translation: I love each and every one of you. You are with me in spirit, always. May you each find your personal liberations in all that you pursue. I love you very much.)

Third, I am deeply grateful to all of our contributors. Each of you has eloquently anchored this book with your stories of surviving the academy. Your liberation stories are heroic in terms of personal honor, being emotionally raw, and inspiring. SPN is a young genre, and we are making it one word at a time. No one shall box us into the margin, because our stories are now being set free. Thank you, thank you, thank you!

—Sydnee Viray

Foreword

Wind Paz-Amor, *i am poetry*

I understand.
How a voice trembles.
How thoughts can race.
How easy it is to doubt your very own words for fear that what you have to say or write
doesn't matter to anyone else.
I understand.

If I am honest, I will say that I was afraid to hear my words out loud, let alone see them on paper. I knew that if my words existed anywhere else but inside of me, I would run the risk of being told that something I enjoyed so much, something I believed in so much, might not have meaning. Or worse, that it just might not be good enough. My identity as an Afro Latina Lesbian is something that I didn't often hear or see represented in higher education; my lens, my identity, is a felt experience, one I have learned carries great importance and impact, especially in Historically Predominantly White (HPW) universities. All voices belong within these walls, including my own. My writing, my poetry, my voice *was* vulnerability for me and became an extension of my identity; it's what I knew and know for sure to be mine. Speaking it, writing it, sharing it, is what became the risk. How does one become so afraid of one's voice? And how does one find it again?

I can best explain my perception of higher education at the time by comparing it to a federal bank or some kind of corporate conglomerate that had the *power* to give *power* only to those deemed worthy! It was like an entity guarded by sky-high iron gates, with gatekeepers and all. Even if I got past the gates, how was I ever going to find a sense of place in it? Was I smart enough? Would I be laughed at for asking stupid questions? I wrote poetry but believed the honorable title of *poet* was one I did not have "the right" to take on. Outside of "creative writing," or English courses, was the use of poetry appropriate or acceptable in other areas of writing in higher education?

Poetry helps me to give voice to the unexplainable in my life and in the world: the racism, sexism, sizeism, homophobia, classism, ableism; the deep, dreary dark and the radiant light. I cannot separate poetry from me without risking my survival. I have been taught to grow amid the consistent unraveling. For many queer women of color, this is a shared experience. Some of us have broken our codes of silence. Some of us are desperately trying to find self in between the unsaid rules of "keep it together" and "hustle." At times this is a disjointed yet fully lived experience.

I remember the aching feeling and the anxious anguish I experienced when I decided to read one of my poems in my first graduate course, Scholarly Personal Narrative (SPN) writing, with Dr. Robert J. Nash. Just the thought of it rendered a dry, bitter taste in the back of my throat. Although fear clung to my voice and made my mouth as dry as the Sahara desert, I spoke and read to a room of students, writers, and colleagues . . . shaky voice and all.

Awakening
Awoke feeling my ancestors swimming through my blood stream
Felt every cell and pulse taken over by memory.
I heard drums in the distance and felt ceremony approaching.
There I was naked and awaiting in prayer
The burning scent of frankincense and myrrh in the air
Showered by holy waters of rain
In between silence and stillness
I was born.

When you are children you are taught to "use our words" to ask for what you need or to describe what you see from the "I" perspective. As you transition toward entering school, you're taught to never, under any circumstances, use the "I" in your writing. Your story, your experiences seem not to have a place in your education. Inevitably, somewhere along the line, you forget that you have something inherently wise and "all your own" to contribute. It becomes easier to believe that your story has no bearing or place in the academy. And, like a volume dial on a radio, you run the risk of your voice growing quieter and quieter and eventually becoming mute.

Did you know that voice has power—that writing allows you to keep testament and that sharing your story has the ability to help another? What I discovered is that voice has the power of tidal waves; it can illuminate the night sky like a lightning storm, and it can captivate a room when spoken from a place of personal truth. For the first time in my educational career I concretely believed that what I had to say undoubtedly mattered. More than that, I knew Scholarly Personal Narrative would help me carve out my own authentic place in higher education. I was beginning to crave the sound of my own voice. The more I spoke and shared, the more I heard and listened, the more I felt a force, a surge happening inside. It was courage.

Courage is born and passed along through sharing stories; within the hymns and psalms of every story sung and told, underlying every voice was the courage to speak. Courage is both the innate and the learned ability to bend when all forces of gravity say you should have broken. Courage is the moment in between choosing what you think you know and what you hope will all be worth it "in the end." The voice of courage can be as soft and subtle as a whisper or as textured and deafening as a pounding drum. It can echo and reverberate between your skin and bones, enough to make your teeth chatter; or it can appear as ghostly and as faint as a muffled memory. It's as powerful as a waterfall washing over you that moves you to act, even if that act is standing still.

Clearly
Everywhere I go I look into the eyes of the people around me clearly.
Moment past moment
Catching deep seeded empty glances;
Tired eyes;
Engraved worry lines.
All around faces are telling the stories that voices gone silent cannot.

People walking around
Forgetting why they are so special
So critically important
So bright
Forgetting we are a piece of each other

I have learned that Life is harder when you believe you have nothing to offer.
Love is hard to feel when you don't believe you deserve it
Peace is hard to find when you don't take time to breathe deeply and quiet your mind
And happy is hard to be when you're taught to find it outside of yourself.

I've learned that family is an unwritten testament that we were here
And that sadness when ignored leads to hopelessness

The woman in the store today carried eyes sunken low behind carvings of disappointment
And although directly in front of me she seemed so distant.
So distraught
In that one moment when our eyes met,
I wanted to send love
You pretended to stare blankly through me.
I panicked from within and tried to look away.
But my heart felt what your eyes and voice denied me.

I am still crying the tears and stories you store inside.

What stories have you been storing inside? Has the silence served you? What is your authentic voice? These, and many similar questions, were what the methodology of Scholarly Personal Narrative forced me to ask myself. Finding scholarship that supported my experience, or echoed my lens and voice, was where the liberation in the methodology began for me—as Dr. Nash says, in the "Me-Search." SPN writing gave me entrance into higher education through a door wide open instead of through a latched back window. My thoughts, my narrative, my writing felt welcomed. And, in turn, I found "place" where I once only saw "gates."

SPN allowed me to use my authentic prose-poetry lens and voice and use it in my writing while at the same time researching supporting scholarship that echoed my experiences. This gave me the confidence I needed to become familiar once again with the sound and depth of my voice, my story, and my writing. Again and again, I experienced affirmation. Finally, here was a methodology through which I could bring my full self, all of my intersecting identities, "to the table" and weave it with my own scholarship—supported by educators, philosophers, artists, activists, leaders, and authors who came before me. Courage and a sense of home and voice were the unanticipated brilliance that emerged from diving into the depths of SPN writing. With it came the ability to own and speak the experiences that fight against the act to desperately cling to the fringes of silence. The piece of us that holds our stories—all of our stories—is the piece that irrevocably moves us to share what we have witnessed and experienced, and from which we have resiliently bounced back. To say SPN is healing would be an understatement. I would say it allows one to rebuild a life.

i am poetry
I started by saying that I didn't think I could take on the word poet.
Scholarly Personal Narrative taught me that one doesn't take on the title of poetry.
But rather one is poetry.
I am poetry.

The SPN writings that you will find in this book are exemplary of just how distinct and dynamic Scholarly Personal Narrative can be. The heart, the head, and the scholarship move the soul, and the writers in this book bear witness to that soul. My journey with the methodology of Scholarly Personal Narrative with both Dr. Robert J. Nash and Sydnee Viray has been transformative. Like a blueprint, SPN leads students, human beings, back to themselves. Here are two authentic educators who lead with reflexivity and invoke authentic, "meaning-full" dialogue *with,* not *for* or *at,* students.

So,
Dearest Reader,
Use your voice.
Feel your courage.
Share your stories.
And know.
You are the scholar we have been waiting for.

All of my love,
Wind Paz-Amor
(Wind Paz-Amor is Assistant Director of the Living/Learning Center, University of Vermont)

The Who, What, and Why of Scholarly Personal Narrative Writing

Opening: Who We Are as Persons in Higher Education

Each of us, in our own way, has experienced marginalization and underrepresentation in the halls of academia. Thus, our empathy for marginalized students is based on our own unique life experiences. Robert Nash, raised in the Boston housing projects, is one of six sons of two orphaned, blue-collar parents, neither of whom finished high school. In addition to being a first-generation high school graduate, he is also a former community college student. Sydnee is a Filipina American immigrant who was raised by adoptive parents when she immigrated to the United States. She has worked with, and on behalf of, the most disenfranchised Americans as a trained social worker. Currently she counsels marginalized students who are without federal aid and could not otherwise afford a secondary education.

Each of us has experienced first-hand the upside and downside of being an outsider in higher education. Because of this, each of us is able to identify, both emotionally and intellectually, with the marginalized students we advise and teach every day at our "public ivy" university. Each of us knows what it means to overcome obstacles in order to survive and thrive in a prestigious academic environment. And, more to the point of our book, each of us has benefited from the opportunity to tell our stories by composing scholarly personal narrative manuscripts. As practitioners and scholars, we have, in a phrase, "liberated our voices." Moreover, we have lived, and continue to live, many of the stories that our students tell about their own feelings of marginalization and "outsiderness." Each of us has experienced, in our own way, the challenges that our student-authors write about in Chapters 9 and 10 of this book. Like them, each of us has sought self-validation, self-empowerment, authenticity, liberation, resiliency, reconstruction, and, at times, resistance. In writing ourselves as scholars, we, like our students, are in the process of creating lives of passion, courage, and faith.

What Is the Attraction of SPN to Marginalized Students?

Since its introduction at the University of Vermont (UVM) and its spread throughout the country, SPN has been the first choice of scholarly research for large numbers of underrepresented, marginalized students. Hundreds of undergraduate and graduate students of color at UVM have written SPN manuscripts dealing with several issues of social justice. Among these are social class difference, religious diversity (including non-belief), race and ethnicity, GLBQQ (gay, lesbian, bisexual, queer, questioning) orientations, international differences, disability, gender expression, and gender identity. In addition, marginalized students have written about their relationships to feminism, critical race theory, and queer theory.

As co-authors, we have heard time and time again from our underrepresented students that Scholarly Personal Narrative writing legitimizes the first-person, singular perspective on the pressing social justice issues facing all of us today. In particular, our marginalized students, representing a variety of identities, have been profuse in their praise of this style of writing. We often hear variations on the following comments:

- "For the first time in my educational life, I've been able to write a paper from my own perspective, and, what's more, SPN lets me express my views proudly."
- "Because of all the times that I have been told *not* to include the personal pronouns 'I,' 'my,' 'me,' or 'mine' in my academic writing, I have had only one opportunity to write a paper in my own, unique, personal voice. Even in my own culture we avoid using 'I.' My SPN thesis has honored my particular take on my topic and even my own experience of my culture."
- "In many of my undergraduate and graduate courses, I've been encouraged to choose a social justice theme as the focus for my papers. However, I must keep my personal views out of my writing. In contrast, SPN has freed me from becoming nothing more than an academic parrot. It allows me to report the literature and use my own story

as an example and/or a counter-example."

- "Why must I always swear allegiance to objectivity, dispassion, and abstract analysis whenever I write academic manuscripts? Why can't I do more SPN types of writing where, at least some of the time, I can be subjective, passionate, and personally invested in my analysis of a topic?"

- "So many of my professors tell me that unless I can weigh, measure, interview, or quantify my research, then it is impossible to arrive at a defensible, Upper-Case 'Truth.' Isn't exploring the life that I have actually lived an equally important way to arrive at some defensible truths? What is this so-called 'Truth' anyway, if I am unable to understand and express it through the lens of what I believe, see, hear, feel, and how I live? SPN writing helps me to examine my topic from the inside out, rather than from the outside in, in order to arrive at a set of sustainable, lower-case truths for living my life in the best possible way."

- "I'm convinced that the best way to connect with my readers in my writing is to tell stories. Stories are the common experience we all share, no matter how different we might be. SPN writing is all about telling stories—big and small, secular and spiritual, and personal and interpersonal. What better way is there to make my points and to draw conclusions than to frame them with my stories? With SPN, I can be out of the closet with my stories, which allows me to connect with others through personal experience. These are the stories that make me unique while still allowing me to bond with others."

To summarize, we have gained the following insights from teaching disenfranchised students how to craft SPN writing:

- Disenfranchised students are grateful to discover that, for the first time in their education, a scholarly writing methodology can be freeing in the sense that it teaches them that their stories matter and, what is more, that their stories can be important to others. No longer do disenfranchised students feel the guilt, shame, and judgment of being "The Other." Now underrepresented students can position themselves at the center of scholarly discourse rather than always at the edges.

- There is a common need that everyone shares, and this is the need to "validate the self." This universal need motivates students to tell their personal stories of resistance and resiliency, of failure and success, of despair and hope, of descent and transcendence, and of powerlessness and empowerment.

- Whenever educators allow students to tell their individual and group stories, the students, in turn, are able to empower others to tell their stories. Thus, a community is born and bound together by the need to understand the stories of others. The result is often the discovery of narrative overlaps, no matter how different the individual/group stories might be.

- SPN writing honors the experiential and intellectual resources of marginalized individuals. In fact, our students gain strength as they recount their personal stories, their family histories, and their community traditions.

- Students gain a newfound sense of pride and ownership of the worth of their own stories and the validation of their own experience. They feel authentic in their writing. They use the writings of others to deepen, enrich, and enlarge their own stories. No longer do students feel that their perspectives and experiences must always give way to the dominant model of scholarly discourse in their respective fields. They now understand the validity—indeed the necessity—of incorporating themselves into the dominant scholarly discourse. Now students become powerful because their own views have the potential to deepen, enrich, and enlarge the findings of the dominant scholarship. Students are able to see themselves as being able to augment and illustrate the more objective research of the experts.

- Students realize that the primary purpose of all scholarly writing is to give a fair hearing to diverse voices and views. No perspective, on principle, is to be marginalized, rejected, or denied a hearing. In fact, what critical race theorists call "counter-narratives" are pivotal methodological tools for arriving at multi-dimensional and multi-intersectional truths about the human condition and the individual.

A Brief Postmodern Introduction to Scholarly Personal Narrative

We are unapologetic postmodern thinkers and writers. We believe that there is no such thing as an immaculate perception, or reception, of the "world out there." We are realists, however, in the sense that we do not deny the existence of an external, physical world. This would be foolish. We are postmodernists, though, in postulating that what matters most in SPN writing is the meaning that authors impose on the "world out there." Thus, personal interpretation, perspective, translation, and construal are at the center of how the author "sees" and understands the world.

This is why SPN writing puts the *self* of the scholar front and center. The best SPN "interview" is the scholar's self-interrogation. The best analysis and prescription come out of the scholar's efforts to make narrative sense of personal and cultural experience. All else is commentary—significant to be sure, but commentary nonetheless. The ultimate intellectual responsibility of the SPN scholar is to find a way to use the personal insights gained in order to draw larger conclusions for readers, possibly even to challenge and reconstruct older political or educational narratives, if this is an important goal for the researcher.

As postmodernists, we see this type of self-agency as a key ingredient of identity liberation within Scholarly Personal Narrative. Rather than directly challenging the mainstream, normative story, SPN writing describes the multidimensional personal qualities scholars need to make meaning of their lives within a heterogeneous society. This discharges the grandeur of the political debate and allows for scholarship to reshape the mainstream discourse by letting go of the bias judgment from outside of, and within, these marginalized communities.

Early in his career, Jerome Bruner, a Harvard University psychology professor, wrote a book, *The Process of Education* (1977), that changed the face of K–12 pedagogy throughout the United States. In the decades since, Bruner has undergone what he calls a "narrative turn" in his thinking. He self-identifies as a "narrative constructivist." For him, in the social sciences, "the truth that matters is not empirical truth but…the *narrative* truth." An empirical, cognitive psychologist for several decades, Bruner has since come to believe that the best way to understand the "self" is to think of the self as a storyteller, "a constructor of narratives about a life." In fact, for Bruner, there is no fixed, hidden entity that one calls a "self." Rather, the self is really a multiple telling of narratives. The self is a "distributed self, enmeshed in a net of others," whose primary task is to make meanings through narration.

What exactly is Bruner saying here? If social scientists want to understand human behavior in all of its complexity, then Bruner is urging them to begin with the stories that people tell about themselves and about their involvement with others. According to Bruner, "self" is nothing more than a narrator's creative construction, not some incontrovertible essence that makes each one of us truly unique and special. "Self" is whatever story we construct about who we are, depending on whom we are with, and who we would like to be, at any given time. The best way to think about the "self," then, is as a storyteller who needs to narrate a number of stories in order to create meanings. If this is an accurate depiction of Bruner's latest thinking about the "self," then, by extension, ethnographic interviewers will need to learn new ways of coding people's stories. "Distributed," changing personal narratives do not fit conventional scientific categories.

We strongly recommend Jerome Bruner's wonderful book *Acts of Meaning* (1990) for beginning SPN writers. This book is Bruner's official rejection of a concept of mind as "information processor" in favor of a new concept: *mind as a creator of narrative meanings*. This is where Bruner the constructivist "comes out" as a postmodernist for the first time in his scholarly career. Thus, like Bruner, we think of the SPN author as neither a strict constructivist nor a strict objectivist. Constructivists are people who approach the world as a phenomenon to be studied primarily from the inside out; objectivists approach the same phenomenon from the outside in. Constructivists tend to ask: What meaning lies *inside* of you, and how can you best narrate it? Objectivists ask: What meaning lies *outside* of you, and how can you best prove it? In reaction to this overly facile dichotomy, though, we believe that at some level we are all both constructivists and objectivists. So, in a sense, we are all postmodern constructivists and objectivists, often at the same time.

We in the university, whether we like it or not, are of mixed intellectual temperaments to some extent or other. Some of us are more *dominant* in our constructivism; some are more *dominant* in our objectivism. But none of us is ever completely free of the opposite, *dormant* perspective on the world, nor should we be. As authors and teachers, we like to think of ourselves as both *dominant* and *dormant* in our constructivism and objectivism. At times we are both story teller and story verifier; narrator and analyzer; values seeker and facts finder; inside the text and outside the text; humanist and social scientist.

In the pages ahead, we spell out in greater detail the practical writing implications for what we have just said about constructivism and objectivism. We also ask several underrepresented students to illustrate these principles in a series of original SPN written reflections. These reflections explain how SPN writing has freed them to express their voices in their own unique ways. By extension, they also instruct readers on how to add the first-person voice to academic writing without losing either scholarly rigor or vigor.

Why SPN Now?

We are convinced that what is necessary at this time is a book that explains and exemplifies the methodology of SPN for marginalized/underrepresented/previously "disappeared" students at all levels of higher education. Our book speaks to students who are majoring in the arts, humanities, social sciences, cultural studies, and in many of the professional schools such as education, social work, business, clinical and counseling psychology, educational leadership and policy studies, and several others.

Presently there is not a single book on the whys and hows of scholarly personal narrative writing that focuses on this particular audience of underrepresented students. We believe that SPN is a methodology of academic writing whose time has finally come in the academy, especially for marginalized students whose voices have been silenced. SPN writing, as we will point out, has its origins in early slave narratives; 1960s feminist liberation stories; religio-spiritual autobiographies; existential, postmodern, and postcritical theory; and memoir/autobiographies of victimization and victory. These latter include the stories of Jewish holocaust survivors, as well as the personal accounts of liberation and empowerment of those who have been the victims of discrimination and bias based on gender, sexual orientation, disability, and a host of other identities.

Our book attempts to fill a huge vacuum in the literature on the art and craft of personal narrative writing for undergraduates and graduates, because it appeals to a hugely expanding, previously underrepresented audience. It also provides faculty with a substantive pedagogical rationale, and writer's guide, for teaching this kind of scholarly research—not just to underrepresented students but to *all* students who are ready to tell their stories in their own original, creative ways.

Each of us as co-authors has had a variety of first-hand experiences with SPN writing, in particular the teaching of disenfranchised students about its benefits and promises. Robert is an older, White faculty member, raised in a blue-collar, working-class family. He has taught thousands of underrepresented students for over 45 years and has introduced SPN to a multiplicity of diverse audiences (including administrators, faculty, and students) throughout the United States. Sydnee is a Filipina American student services professional who immigrated to the United States in the late 1980s. She has worked with, and on behalf of, the most disenfranchised members in the United States as a trained social worker. Currently, she counsels both traditional and non-traditional students who are without federal aid and cannot otherwise afford a secondary education.

In the chapters that follow, each of us describes our respective takes on Scholarly Personal Narrative writing. We ground our understandings in the early—and still developing—relevant literature and knowledge base. In addition, we tell about our personal experiences with SPN writing, both as writers and as educational practitioners. We work hard to keep our language direct and clear at all times, and, whenever we can, we try to make accessible the technical, and sometimes esoteric, language of the academy. Above all, we strive to be practical in our writing instruction, and we offer several examples of actual SPN writing done by students at all levels of higher education. Finally, we are candid in sharing both our successes and our failures in teaching this methodology of writing to marginalized students.

What Readers Can Expect from the SPN Journey Ahead

We have taken great pains to write a book that is succinct, accessible, inspiring, and, most of all, engaging and informative. We hope that our book will do the following:

- Become a "how-to" resource for readers to understand, and to practice, SPN writing.
- Discuss, with specific examples, how SPN writing is both liberating and empowering.
- Develop a powerful rationale for encouraging marginalized students to write in the SPN methodology. This will include an explanation and analysis of such concepts as social location, social situation and social construction, under-representation, marginalization, counter-narratives, individual stories of resistance and resilience, liberation and transformation, and academic memoirs.

- Describe the important steps to take in presenting the non-traditional SPN method-ology to all constituencies on a college campus, including faculty and academic administrators who are most likely to be critical of this type of personal scholarship.
- Include a number of practical vignettes, case studies, and writing scenarios to illus-trate in a concrete way how to use SPN writing in a variety of educational settings, and to construct a number of counter-narratives on a college campus.
- Encourage a representative group of marginalized SPN writers to actually write about their first-hand experiences with this methodology of writing—their successes and failures, their opportunities and challenges, and their disappointments and sat-isfactions.
- Illustrate how SPN can "shatter" complacency, challenge the dominant discourse, and further the struggle for social reform. By constructing counter-narratives, the SPN writer emerges from the marginalized dormant narrative and is now able to strengthen the importance of particular rituals and traditions. In other words, SPN allows the freedom for writers to interpret the data in such a way as to validate the writer's par-ticular background of difference.

In each chapter of the book we provide several specific examples of SPN writ-ing done by our students (and by ourselves) based on our personal experiences and augmented by the relevant scholarly literature. Also, at the end of some chapters, one or the other of us includes a personal reflection on the main themes of the chap-ter. The writing style of our book is, in part, in the format of Scholarly Personal Writing; thus, in a sense, we practice what we preach.

Closing: Who We Are as Professionals in Higher Education

Two-and-a-half decades ago, Robert J. Nash began the process of creating a research methodology called Scholarly Personal Narrative (SPN) writing. Since then, Robert has taught dozens of courses on this methodology. He has also published widely on the topic, including two best-selling books, *Liberating Scholarly Writing: The Power of Personal Narrative* (2004), and, with DeMethra LaSha Bradley, *Me-Search and Re-Search: A Guide for Writing Scholarly Personal Narrative Manuscripts* (2011).

Robert has been a professor in the College of Education and Social Services, University of Vermont, Burlington, for 44 years. He specializes in philosophy of education, ethics, higher education, and religion, spirituality, and education. He directs the Interdisciplinary Master's Program, and he teaches ethics, religion, higher education, and philosophy of education courses, as well as scholarly personal narrative writing seminars, across four programs in the college. Since 1996 he has published 13 books, several of them national award winners, along with over 100 articles, numerous book chapters, and several book reviews. In 2003 he was named the Official University Scholar in the Social Sciences and the Humanities at the University of Vermont, only the third faculty member in the history of the College of Education and Social Services to be so honored.

Sydnee Viray is a highly respected student services administrator at the University of Vermont. She is a consultant/scholar in the areas of diversity and inclusion and financial management for mission-driven non-profits and for government bodies. She has served on several non-profit boards of trustees/directors. Her interests are broad with regard to diversity, multiculturalism, and social justice. Specifically, she is skilled in understanding the interplay between various interpretations of social justice while still maintaining respect for each person's self-determination in a learning process. Her multiple identities reflect the critical importance of respecting the various touchstones of intersecting identities where privilege and oppression can interface. She has spent the last 10 years as a community social worker advocating for, and with, economically and racially marginalized community members. She is the author of an SPN graduate thesis and has written several SPN manuscripts featuring a number of diversity themes. She is currently a Scholarly Personal Narrative writing co-instructor (with Robert) at the University of Vermont.

2

SPN Empowerment for Marginalized Writers

Our Lives Signify!

Introduction

We like what the postmodern writing specialist Vivian Gornick (2001) means by the term "signify":

> A serious life, by definition, is a life one reflects on, a life one tries to make sense of and bear witness to. The age is characterized by a need to testify. Everywhere in the world women and men are rising up to tell their stories out of the now commonly held belief that one's own life signifies. (p. 23)

For us, as teachers and authors, scholarly personal narrative writing starts with the *writer's* life rather than with the lives, thoughts, and activities of others. A life that signifies is a life that matters. SPN is self-reflective writing. It frees up the author, whether a scholar or an ordinary woman or man, to "testify," to bear personal witness to present and past events. Many students in our classes are confident that they can write a term paper, a research paper, or a literature review, as some say, with their "eyes closed." They know the templates for these conventional types of manuscripts by heart, because they have done so many of them throughout their years in formal education. They know from practice that it is mostly just a matter of understanding how to fit some new pieces of the knowledge puzzle into the old research templates. But telling a personal story about one's individual, cultural, and social history in a classroom setting, with the professor present, is hard for most students. Writing one's personal story in a creative way is even more difficult.

Perhaps the most difficult challenge for our students, though, is to believe deep down that, indeed, their lives do signify. We both work very hard to convince our students that even "marginalized" people have the ability, and the right, to create new knowledge about the societies they live in. Moreover, they have the responsibility to critique, and reconstruct, new ways to understand the customs, values, and history of their social groups. This type of reconstruction was unthinkable for some disciplines a generation ago. It no longer is, however, because more non-scholars, as well as academicians, are asserting their right to look critically at their socio-historical contexts. These writers know, indeed, that their lives signify. They willingly embrace the right to position themselves at the center of their inquiries. They know that self-signification adds creative vitality and personal relevance to social knowledge.

SPN writing aims to teach others in some way. When done well, it conveys both personal and intellectual meanings to readers. SPN writing benefits readers by touching their lives, by informing their experiences, by transforming the meanings of events, and—in Gornick's telling phrase—by "delivering wisdom." All of this is the SPN author's expressed outcome, not just for the writer, but for the reader as well. Gornick punctuates this give-and-take, this to-and-fro between the writer and the reader of personal narratives, by saying that, in the end, what simply *happens* to the writer is not what truly matters. What matters is the "large sense" of meaning that the writer is able to convey both to self and to readers about what simply happens.

What follows in the next section is a series of statements written by disenfranchised students who have taken Robert's course in Scholarly Personal Narrative (SPN) writing. All of them later wrote an SPN undergraduate honors thesis, a master's thesis, or a doctoral dissertation. (Some faculty members of color who also took the course have gone on to write articles, memoirs, and books using the SPN writing methodology.) Each of the excerpted statements in the next section speaks to the need for marginalized students to seek empowerment by writing their stories in such a way that their authentic voices get heard. In short, they want their words to "signify."

Listening to the Liberated Voices of Students Writing Themselves as Scholars for the First Time

Here are the words of Amarildo Barbosa, a Black student affairs professional, who explains why he chose to write his graduate thesis as an SPN manuscript:

I had planned out in my mind how I would approach this writing project over one year ago. There were several issues that clouded my ability to finally make a decision on whether or not SPN was something I wanted to do. I had written some small papers focused on the experience of Black men in higher education based on the research of prominent scholars who have done incredible amounts of work in this particular area. In thinking about how I could provide new insight into this field, I struggled to find a qualitative research topic that would allow me the opportunity to deliver the message about the plight of young Black men in a manner that would be significant. I was not sure as to which aspect of this subject area I could make the most meaningful impact. It was at this point that I began the debate between embarking on a qualitative ethnographic research project or writing in Scholarly Personal Narrative (SPN).

I was concerned with creating something that would be considered valid in the world of academia. I came to understand that there was a significant amount of pushback in certain circles when SPN was discussed in the context of scholarly work. One text in particular provided me that much-needed moment of clarity. In writing her book In My Place, *Charlayne Hunter-Gault is able to tell her story from childhood through her personal experiences in higher education at the University of Georgia. Her book provoked within me some debate and introspection. I took a step back and considered my options. Qualitative research, at times, is not generalizable. Its value is in the insight and understanding gained through formal interviews between the researcher and the participant.*

On the other hand, scholarly personal narrative inquiry allows the participant to share a personal story; here the story and personal perspective of one's life has tremendous value. Hunter-Gault's vivid accounts of what life was like for her growing up in Due West, South Carolina, and integrating the University of Georgia during a racially turbulent era, has been invaluable to my educational experience as a Black male navigating his way through higher education. In that same respect, I find that my story will be of value to others.

In the end, I became convinced that the best way to offer original insight into the challenges facing young Black men today in higher education is to tell my story. For me, SPN was the best platform to communicate the value of my experiences. Writing in SPN has proven to be a process filled with reflection and fulfillment upon completion. I feel as though, for the first time, I have written with a purpose, leaving behind bits of wisdom for others to unearth.

Listen to Michiko Oishi, a Japanese immigrant and author of an SPN thesis:

I employed the Scholarly Personal Narrative (SPN) methodology in writing my thesis. I first encountered SPN 6 years ago in my initial graduate class at UVM. I remembered the nervousness I felt on the first day of the class, since it had been 20 years since I graduated from a Japanese college. The author, and instructor of the class, Robert Nash, said this in his book Liberating Scholarly Writing: The Power of Personal Narrative: *"There is genuine wisdom and meaning in the unique life you are creating for yourself and for others." I was so encouraged by reading this, because I realized, for the first time, that all of my life experiences do matter in academia as well as in my immediate family and sphere of friends.*

I was encouraged to look back on my journey—my secondary education in Japan; my experience of living life by serving other people in the developing countries of Thailand and Laos; my position as director of a world peace center; and the realization of my dream of having a family and raising children. I was encouraged to see, and reconfigure in my writing, all of these experiences as genuine wisdom. I immediately knew that this was the way that I would like to write. I came to that first class just to check the water, to see how it would be to take a graduate course. Before long, I ended up applying to Robert's graduate program in Interdisciplinary Studies. Throughout my graduate classes, I have experienced that a personal narrative approach, which is closely tied to scholarly writing, can give learners the deepest engagements and understandings of the topics being taught. I am so proud to have produced an SPN thesis that received wide acclaim throughout the college.

Here is Fieh Chan, a Chinese high school math teacher, who included in his thesis the following observations about SPN writing:

I have dealt with issues of race and socio-economic class (class) since my birth. The fact that my skin is yellow and my eyes are slanted makes my non-Whiteness obvious. It is the first thing I see in the mirror each morning and it is what the outside world uses to judge me. It is what the majority of that critical first impression is based on. It is something that I am unable to hide.

Unlike my race, my social class is something that has been in flux over time and is able to be masked, although my actual success in masking my class in the past is debatable. If so much of me is so obviously foreign, how is it then that I have been able to whitewash my life's account for the better part of 35 years? When pressed, I often explain by saying it was an attempt at putting those asking at ease, but I question now whether I was really trying to put myself at ease.

Whenever I am asked about my family and our story I always give the same account. I recount how my parents and three brothers immigrated to America in the early 70s with only two hundred dollars in my parents' pockets. I explain my father worked for the former CIA director William Casey under the Reagan administration and that my father took care of his home, ironed his clothes, catered his parties, and essentially fulfilled the duties that the fictional character Alfred did for Bruce Wayne in the Batman comics.

I have chosen to write an SPN thesis because it allows me to most accurately recount the defining moments in my life. Robert says it is all about the S-cholarship, the P-ersonal, and the N-arrative. By writing from the "I" and the "me," I am bringing legitimacy and value to my personal narrative for myself and for the academic community. SPN allows the writer to create new scholarship that lives symbiotically with the traditionally accepted scholarship of academia. Whereas most graduate degrees are meant to legitimize the receiver and serve as official evidence the student has done due diligence and successfully completed a master's program, it is my intent that this thesis can serve as a way for the scholarship produced by my life to legitimize and give meaning to the Interdisciplinary Program at UVM and to the graduate degree I will receive.

Consider the comments of Maria Dykema Erb, a high-level administrator in a diversity center on a North Carolina campus, reflecting on her Korean-Asian background and what the SPN writing methodology has meant to her:

I am a Korean adoptee who grew up culturally as a Christian Reformed, Dutch American on a dairy farm in North Ferrisburg, Vermont; I am also a first-generation college graduate.

Statistically, I shouldn't have even been in college, let alone graduated with my bachelor's degree. Almost half (45 percent) of first-generation students who began higher education in 1989–1990 had not obtained a degree or certificate and were no longer enrolled by 1994, compared with 29 percent of non-first-generation students (Nunez & Cuccaro-Alamin, 1998).

My Mom, Wilma, and my Dad, Cornie (Cornelius), emigrated from the Netherlands when they were children. They met in New Jersey, were married, and started their dairy business in North Ferrisburg, Vermont. My Dad's brother and his wife, Henry and Cora, who were Christian missionaries based in Guam, adopted two daughters from a Korean orphanage during their time overseas. My Mom and Dad were excited about the prospect of adopting their own daughters, and in January 1972, I arrived at JFK International Airport at 10 months old (my younger sister, Janet, was adopted separately 3 years later). I would learn later in life that my parents chose to adopt baby girls over boys because their chances of surviving in South Korea were very slim. Girls lived on the streets as beggars, became prostitutes, or worse yet, died. I am most grateful for this blessing, for without my parents adopting me, I would not have the abundant life and existence that I experience today.

Fortunately, after taking three courses with Robert using the SPN methodology for writing our papers and reflections, and authoring an SPN thesis, I have a much better understanding of the value and importance of personal narrative research and scholarship in higher education. I have come to appreciate how privileged I am to be part of a national (and perhaps international) movement that is on the cutting edge of transforming academia using SPN as an alternative means to share research findings. Making research relate more personally can help readers find the common themes that may apply to their lives, and ultimately make a scholar's work more accessible to a broader audience.

Finally, read the comments of Amanda Flores, a Latina woman raised as an immigrant child of migrant farm workers, about the value of SPN writing for her thesis.

When I was in the third grade, the only thing I desired to be was a member of the University Interscholastic League (UIL) Storytelling team; little did I know this experience would foreshadow my choice to present my master's comprehensive exam in scholarly personal narrative (SPN) form. Storytelling, in the terms of UIL, is the process of retelling or recounting a story after it has been read to you with your emotional interpretation. In the case of SPN, storytelling is recounting what you have experienced. My story is best said through my words, and my words best describe my reality, and my reality best represents my experiences. Despite what felt like never-ending mountains, I found the courage to continue on with my success through inspirational and motivational quotes, stories, and leyendas. These parables help me make meaning out of my life's struggles and life's darkest moments. I know this is the best way to share my story and inspire others to share their stories. After all, as Robert has written, "good teaching, good helping, and good leadership are all about storytelling."

Scholarly Personal Narrative (SPN) is an alternate form of scholarly writing that grounds its scholarship in the author's story. As Robert says, it starts with the "I" and proceeds outward to the "you" and the "they." I consider SPN to be an art form, and like art, it allows me to paint my life as a living portrait. And like music, I will compose my own life where successes echo crescendos and obstacles emulate decrescendos. Music is my life and primary form of spirituality, and I am the marcher to my own beat. SPN uses the writer's narrative as a form of teaching, informing, advocating, and transforming. It requires that the author's narrative be central to the universalizable themes discussed and be interwoven with existing literature that echoes the validity in their truth. After all, the best way to make sense of the "truth" is through the construction and telling of stories, both to ourselves and to others.

This SPN thesis will reveal my trials and triumphs as a migrant farmworker student breaking institutional stereotypes and paving new roads. I choose to share my story in SPN because it is through this form in which I will be able to write without the limiting constraints of a quantitative or qualitative paper. It is a way for me to make my thoughts become realities; a way for me to release my most inner thoughts; a way for my truth to be read, my voice to be heard, and my emotions to be felt. As you read my story, I hope you will want to take inventory of your own early lessons about the world, your hopes and fears, your life's themes, and your sense of calling. You might even consider tackling a short autobiography about how you came to be who you are today.

SPN: Expressing the Resonant Sounds of the Writer's Voice

As all of the above excerpts suggest, whenever our underrepresented students do scholarly writing, there needs to be a way for them to freely express the resonant sounds of their personal voices and to proudly tell their own, unique stories of meaning. These stories represent who and what they are, and, in a sense, they are a declaration of refusal to abdicate these essential dimensions of themselves. We urge our students neither to conceal nor to deny the diverse identities that make up themselves. We encourage them to proudly express their storied voices and their multiple social identities. We want them to let their stories ring out loud and clear throughout their research.

Ralph Waldo Emerson once said that it is impossible to utter even two or three sentences without letting others know where you stand in life, what you believe, and which people are important to you. Voice in SPN writing is the unique tone and style of the author. It's the "you" whom you are choosing to tell your story. It's the recognition that you can never be fully outside your writing. As an author, you are always an insider: not omnisciently removed from what you write, but caught up personally in every word, sentence, and paragraph; in every statistic and every interview; in every comma and period. Your writing, at some point, will always give away your personal story, even when you attempt to cloud it with the thick idiom of academese and objectivity.

SPN is about giving yourself permission to express your own voice in your own language; your own take on your own story in your own inimitable manner. SPN is your grand opportunity to practice listening to the sound of your own voice. Find your special sound and style, and you will find your story. Lose these, and you will continue to be silenced. Writing will be impossible—if not now, then soon, and probably forever. During the semester when we co-teach our SPN writing course, we often hear from students that they are grateful for the chance to express their own, unadulterated personal voices on the scholarly topics that mean the most to them.

Just how important is the personal *voice*, not just for our students, but also for those literary and rhetoric scholars and professors who, having been trained in traditional models of objectivist scholarly writing, have actually begun writing in a personal narrative style? Listen to three scholars writing in Gil Haroian-Guerin's (1999) book on personal narrative writing. Here is Maria-Cristina Kirklighter:

> I've been told that personal essays count for very little in enhancing my vitae. I've been told that critiquing academia through personal essays is risky business. In other words, I've finally been told that these words are to be divorced from my experiences if they are to hold academic ivory value. So here I sit as a disrobed, ivoryless, and Honduran/Southern Angla contemplating these conflicting values....But I also know that the only avenue I have for reaching a non-Honduran/Southern Angla audience and making them see what some of these words mean to me is through the personal.

Deborah Mutnick reacts in this way:

> The personal narrative allows me to penetrate what often seems like a shield of impersonal, often jargon-ridden, formulaic prose, which we use at least in part to cover up our insecurities, and to contribute substantively to the construction of new knowledge about everyday life.

Finally, hear the words of Louise Wetherbee Phelps:

> Among other reasons, I write personally to dramatize the living moment of thought and portray it as passionately felt; to make intellectual life and academic work intelligible as experience, embedded in and reflecting daily life and personal identity.

What our SPN students through the years all have in common, despite their many salient differences, is the similar conviction—expressed by the scholar-teachers above—that *their lives truly matter. They signify. Their voices are resonant and important.* Their personal lives are not lived in a vacuum but rather in a series of overlapping, concentric circles with others. They affect, and are affected by, the actions of others. Our SPN students are in the process of continually learning how best to share their most cherished meanings with others in mutually respectful, written exchanges. Our students want permission to write about their lives in their own voices; moreover, they want to include all aspects of their identities as well as express all their multiple intelligences and perspectives in their writing.

Most important, though, our students believe deep down that they have earned the right to put themselves into their scholarship. They know that writers are always an integral part of what they observe, study, interpret, and assert. The inclusion of the self in research and scholarship is inescapable, even more so when writers try intentionally to excise the self from their research. The "I" voice always has a way of seeping into an "objective," third-person text. Our students have learned to accept this subjective seepage—indeed, even to celebrate it. We are pleased when they do.

The denial of the value of the self's stories in an academic setting is born in the command all of us have heard in school at some time: never use the "I" in formal writing. The "I," we have been told, is incapable of discovering and dispensing wisdom without the support of the "Them," the certified experts. Messages like these leech the fascinating, storied self out of the budding writer, leaving only the clichéd, and often pinched, stories of experts to recirculate over and over again. Our first order of business in encouraging personal narrative writing is to let our students know that the search for meaning is very difficult unless they can write personally about their quests. We need to let our students know that their personal stories count.

And so, in order to prepare our students for personal narrative writing about meaning, we challenge them to dare to stand for something in their writing. We ask them to try to take a position on something with strong conviction and with a display of palpable affect in their language. We give them permission to allow their authorial voices to be clear, distinct, strong, and, above all, personal. We tell them to resist the conventional academic temptation to be "objective": stoical, qualified, subdued, abstract, and distant. We fully acknowledge that at times it is okay, even desirable, to try to be detached or dispassionate, and at other times even scientific and objective. But it is also okay, particularly when writing about topics that are vitally important to the author, to be fully engaged and excitable, to be transparent and vulnerable.

A Personal Reflection on How SPN Writing Liberated One Graduate Student's Voice

What follows is a personal reflection by a recently graduated master's student whose life was greatly enriched by her SPN writing process. Tamara Brown is a woman who has seemingly lived a lifetime in only 32 short years. Almost every sentence in her writing expresses the "resonant sounds of her own, liberated voice." We asked Tamara to write this particular piece because it illustrates the central themes in this chapter: liberation, empowerment, transparency, vulnerability, and authenticity.

Tamara Brown: I am originally from Buffalo, NY, but I have made many homes across three states including Richmond, VA; New York City, NY; and Burlington, VT. I currently live in Shelburne, VT, where I share a home with my wonderful partner, Dan, and our two puppies. I hold a B.F.A in Theatre Studies from Niagara University, with a concentration in Musical Theatre and Theatre History. I earned my master's degree in Interdisciplinary Studies at the University of Vermont, where I defended my thesis titled Education Through Meaning-Making: An Artist's Journey from Quarterlifer to Educator.

I am a professional mentor in the TRiO/Student Support Services Program. I feel that I "fight the good fight" every day in the name of social justice and student advocacy. I serve students who fall under one or more of the follow criteria: (1) limited-income students, (2) first-generation college students, and (3) students with disabilities. I act as a liaison for these sometimes silenced students, and I help nurture and guide them throughout their college journey. I love my job and my students.

My first identity is Artist. Music, Theatre & Dance drive my soul. Then I would say that I am an Educator. I like to call myself an Artist-Educator. I would then go on to identify as an African-, Dutch-, French-, Native American; a 32-year-old (who looks 25 or younger); extremely positive; middle class (soon to marry into an upper-class family); a loyal, loving partner; an ex-non-wounded Black Roman Catholic; extremely spiritual, universe & nature loving; able-bodied; highly educated (high school, college & graduate degrees); resilient woman.

I am very much a pluralist. I enjoy trying to always see things from each side of the coin. I do this to almost a fault, but it is so much of who I am that I have learned to embrace it. The way in which I feel the most comfortable expressing pluralism is through storytelling. It's easier to understand where someone different from me might be coming from by telling each other stories and trying to find some commonality within those different stories.

An Artist-Educator Tells Her Story

Tamara Brown, Academic Advisor for Student Support Services, TRiO Program, The University of Vermont

"Thank you so much for allowing me to tell you my story. I believe that simply by telling our stories sometimes it awakens within us what it is that we truly need and desire in life."

The above quote is the concluding line from a letter I wrote to Robert J. Nash over four years ago while I sat alone at a coffee house on 9th Street and 2nd Avenue in Manhattan. I sat on that open-air back patio, and I wrote my heart out onto the page to a man I hardly knew. Granted, he was a man whom I would soon call my friend, my mentor, and my confidante, but at that point he was a stranger who wanted to know my story. My story. Not someone else's account of the world. My story. The above quote is also the center and heart of this piece of writing. I believe that allowing myself to tell my story opened a gate that surrounded my soul. Telling my story opened my heart to what I really wanted in life. Telling my story made my desires and truths real. On that day, I began my journey of being honest with myself and finding my true path in life.

As I sit here at my desk, I can't help but smile when I look back on the past four-and-a-half years: I left a lucrative career in finance and a very socially comfortable lifestyle in New York City to move to Burlington, Vermont; I wrote a Scholarly Personal Narrative (SPN) thesis and successfully defended it; I directed a college production of *The Vagina Monologues*; I graduated from my master's program at the University of Vermont (UVM); I performed in the musical *Hairspray* at the Flynn Theatre in Burlington; I met a wonderful partner, and we are currently building a life together; I have an amazing career working with, and advising, marginalized college students. I'm basically living out the dream that I had over 4 years ago.

But it didn't come easily. I mean, sure, it's pretty easy to make the above list and set out the milestones of my late 20s like they are points on a "things to do" checklist, but the actual *doing*—now that was a journey. I mention all of this because I want my reader to understand that none of these goals seemed possible to me until I dared to *name* my dreams. I believe that it is when we see where we have been, and name where we want to go, that the magic begins. In the letter that I wrote to Robert, I told him my story. I told him how unhappy I was at my job in finance in New York City. I told him that I had tried graduate school before, and that I was afraid to try again. I told him that my first passion was (and still is, and always will be) theatre. I told him how terrified I was of my passion and dreams, and he told me to write about it. Robert gave me a gift when he told me to write my story. He gave me the gift of SPN. SPN writing was almost like a spiritual awakening for me. It allowed me to get my thoughts together, tell my stories, unpack them on paper, and then rebuild them again into lessons I can use for the stories I tell tomorrow.

I used SPN to compose my graduate thesis. I wrote my SPN thesis about how to help college students find meaning and purpose in their lives. I believe that in order for educators to help their students find purpose in their lives, educators must find purpose in their own lives as well. In order to practice what I was preaching, I chose to dive heart-first into my own meaning-making process and explore what gives my own life meaning and purpose. I wanted to write about educators, artists, and meaning-making with college students. I had a lot to say before I started writing, and I am no stranger to telling my story, so at first when I was introduced to SPN I thought it was going to be an easy writing process. And was I wrong about that! During the writing process, I was terrified that the world would know I was a phony. I remember making statements about students, educators, and artists that I don't think I would have had the strength to say had it not been in the context of SPN writing. I am a marginalized student—who wanted to listen to me? What did I have to say that was so important? Who am I to say that I know what college students need? Who am I to identify myself as an artist? What do I know about being an educator?

Every day these questions and negative thoughts would enter my mind telling me that not only can't I do this, but I do not deserve to be writing like this. How am I an artist? Sure, I have my undergraduate degree in Theatre Studies, and I've acted professionally for a few years, but who am I to say that I am an artist? What if my friends or colleagues who actually *are* artists see this writing and call me out as a fraud? And this whole educator identity: I've never taught a course in my life. I don't have enough legitimate student contact to call myself an educator. What if the real educators read this and declare me a fake? I had nightmares in which my thesis chairman would stand up and interrupt me at my defense and say, "Excuse me, but will the real Artist-Educators please stand up." Yeah, it was bad.

But I had to get through those negative moments. I had to ignore those voices for a little while in order to get through the process. And how did I do that? Well, honestly I had to *fake it so that I could make it*. Seriously, that was my tactic. I know it's not a very technical or philosophical remedy, but it really worked. I told myself that I am an educator. I am an artist. I do know what college students want and need. SPN writing allowed me to make statements that I wasn't sure others would agree with, and sometime during the process I realized that I actually believed those statements. Also, I had to look at the knowledge and experience that I *did* have. Sure, I might not be on Broadway or a member of the Actors' Equity Association, but I do live and breathe theatre as an art form. I may not have ever taught a course in my life at the time, but I did have several students who looked up to me and viewed me as their mentor. Some educators may be offended that I dare call myself an educator; but I had some innovative ideas about how educators can find meaning in their lives and help their students find purpose as well. I had stories and depth, and it was time for them to come out.

Writing an SPN thesis gave me the space to name my own purpose and dreams. I used this form of writing to explore where I have been in my journey so far. I got to look at my choices with a fine-tooth comb and decide what I was going to do with those choices. Writing an SPN thesis also gave me the opportunity to forgive myself and begin a healing process. I had been trapped by my mistakes and misfortunes. Writing allowed me to free myself from the past by carefully looking at it and accepting it as lessons and triumphs.

Make Them Hear You

As I explained earlier, I wrote my SPN thesis about how to help college students find meaning in their lives. I believe that by helping them to find what really gives their lives meaning, they will be more successful during their college career and beyond. I explored the idea that before educators can help their students find meaning in their own lives, educators must first discover and name their own personal meaning. During my exploration of my own purpose and meaning, I defined myself as an artist-educator. I told many stories about my journey to this self-identification. The following excerpt is one of my favorite pieces that I included in my SPN thesis. I believe that it truly defines what education and art mean to me and why, for me, the two can never be separated.

> When I was in graduate school (that is, the first time I took a crack at getting a master's), I was an actor in a local children's theatre company called Theatre IV. We would travel all over the state of Virginia and perform historical and educational shows for students grades K–12. I remember being welcomed and appreciated by many audiences of young people, but there were several times when we did not feel very valued by some of the students. The students who thought that it was more amusing to make fun of the visiting troupe and the performance were very cruel, indeed. I remember coming off stage once after being laughed at right in the middle of a monologue. I instantly felt ashamed, hurt, and angry. I didn't want to go back out there and perform for those brats. Who do they think they are? Don't they know who I am? Oh, I'll show them, alright! I thought to myself.
>
> Their cruelty clearly struck a chord with me. But before I'd let the immaturity of teenagers at least 10 years my junior take my professionalism and pride down with them, I'd stop myself and take a deep breath. I would return on stage with this one single thought: I need to do my best performance for the little me that is out there dying to hear what I have to say. Yes, there is always a younger me out in every audience who, unlike his or her taunting peers, is actually interested in learning, or in theatre, or maybe even just sees me as a positive role model—a young woman in her mid-20s going after her goals and doing what she loves for a living.
>
> As soon as that image of myself at that age comes into my head, all the hurt and anger at the kids disappears, and I'm left with compassion and a fire that pushes me to perform even stronger for the audience. The same emotion goes for my feelings on education and meaning-making. I needed to write this thesis for me—the little me in the classroom who needs to see a role model who says, Hey there early quarterlifer, it's ok to be an artist. I am. Or it's ok to be

an athlete, or a doctor, or a teacher (or whatever your dream is); I did. I went after my goals and dreams, and you will too.

In the Broadway musical Ragtime *there is a moment in the song "Make Them Hear You," sung by the character Coalhouse Walker, Jr., where he calls out to all men and women to tell their stories and to use those stories to ensure the future of our young people. The lyrics and melody of this song comfort me when I am clouded with doubt about my vocation in education. In the musical, Coalhouse is a Black man struggling for equality at the turn of the century. It is the first decade of the 20th century, and Henry Ford's Model-T has made freedom more accessible for middle-class Americans who had previously had little mobility. Freedom as a theme follows Coalhouse during the whole play. Although he is a free man constitutionally, he still suffers prejudices and racial slander in his life. His new Model-T is vandalized by local White men who want to ensure that Coalhouse stays in his place as a middle-class Black man. As a result of the combination of this event and the unfortunate death of his wife, a raging anger builds in him, and he embarks on the journey of a champion to fight injustices.*

Unfortunately his efforts eventually become very violent, and he is killed as a result. Before his death, he acknowledges that violence may not have been the best option, but he has no regrets. He felt that his fight was a worthy cause, and he was willing to die for it. He sings "Make Them Hear You" just before he dies. As the song progresses, he has a realization that his fight was not in vain and that there is something to be gained from making sure that his story lives on. He sings, "Go out and tell our story to your daughters and your sons/ Make them hear you.../ Proclaim it from your pulpit, in your classroom, with your pen/ Teach every child to raise his voice and then, my brothers, then/ Will Justice be demanded by ten million righteous men" (Ragtime, *"Make Them Hear You").*

This moment in the performance ignites my heart with pride. It reminds me that I have a purpose and a responsibility to these young people. My fight may not be for justice, as it was Coalhouse's, but I think there is something very unifying between what he was fighting for and my own journey in higher education. Those words inspire me to, in fact, teach every child to raise her voice for the purpose of finding her voice, her calling, her meaning in life. A large part of creating meaning in her life is finding her voice in order to use that voice and stand up for her convictions.

Experiencing musical moments like these taught me to seek my own voice and create my own meaning. My meaning-making process has pushed me to want to bring meaning to students and help them to seek their voices and their meaning. My calling is to perform—or teach—for the "little me" that's out there in the audience and in my classroom.

Several educators disagree with me when it comes to this notion of using our own meaning and journey to help our students find their purpose and voice. But in my non-conformist way, I challenged them in my thesis anyway. I still believe that this is one of the best ways to reach our students. Today I live and breathe the statement that I made in the above excerpt from my thesis. I am a higher education professional working for a program called Student Support Services (SSS). SSS is a program under the Department of Education's TRiO programs. SSS supports underrepresented students, particularly students who come from limited-income families, students who are first-generation college students, and students with disabilities. I am extremely proud and honored to say that I serve and advise marginalized college students.

In my work with students, I have found that the most powerful meetings occur when I tell my students about my own journey. My heartache, my mistakes, and my personal path are the things that speak to them the most. It's that one time I was lost and didn't know what my next step was that my students respond to. My mistakes and journey resonate with them because they see a successful, professional Black woman sitting at the desk across from them who "made it." I, too, was a marginalized student. I know what it's like to be judged before you walk in the door. I know what it's like not being able to afford what my more affluent friends and classmates could easily afford and trying to pretend that I wasn't poor.

I know what it's like not being able to talk to a parent about where to buy my books on campus, because he didn't go to college and would look at me with confused and sad eyes because he could not help. Also, I know what it's like to be excommunicated from a group of my childhood friends who didn't go to college because they thought I believed that I was better than them now. I've been there, and what's more important is that I'm not afraid to talk about it to my students. I found my voice so that I could help them find theirs. SPN writing possesses a special magic: It restores the resonance and power of one's own voice. Now, at this time in my life, I express my voice whenever and wherever I can, particularly with those I love and with those who come to my office each and every day—students and colleagues alike.

3

Exploring the Three Metaphors of Oppression in the Academy

Introduction: How Metaphors of Oppression Result in Voicelessness, Spacelessness, and Facelessness in Higher Education

In the section that follows this introduction, we will define and unpack the meanings of three metaphors: *marginalization*, *disenfranchisement*, and *underrepresentation*. For us, these metaphors are the precondition for, and the sum total of, what we call "oppression." We will not only define these terms, but will also give some real-life examples of how these metaphors show up in the 21st-century classroom as well as in scholarship. We will explain how these metaphors create strata of students. We will also describe how these three phenomena result in voicelessness, spacelessness, and facelessness for hundreds of thousands of students in American colleges and universities.

Toward this end, you will read a couple of Sydnee's SPN reflections about the unwritten rules that regulate the behavior of "outsiders" within the classroom. You will bear witness to the struggles and confusions of individuals like Sydnee, who try to deal with their outsider experiences whenever they attempt to transgress and transcend the fixed boundaries of academia. We hope you will recognize the irony in these unwritten rules for marginalized outsiders. At least in principle, it is the institution of higher education that forcefully advocates for a variety of liberties: freedom of speech, freedom of expression, and freedom of thought. And yet it is the same American university that unwittingly violates these freedoms with its unquestioning loyalty to centuries-old academic traditions and practices.

We believe that in higher education oppression can be especially cruel, because it is more subtle. The American university is conformist, and, in the name of "academic rigor," it can often be rigid. Marginalized students who refuse to conform to its centuries-old norms are often forced by the system to opt out. In this way, higher education becomes a sorting machine whereby only mainstreamers survive. The rest are silenced, or worse, eliminated. One of the major themes throughout this book is that SPN writing can help all of us—faculty, staff, and students alike—to overcome the three metaphors of oppression by giving us permission to write our way into integrity, dignity, liberation, and authenticity. But before this can happen, higher education needs to become far more pluralistic in its thinking about what constitutes acceptable scholarship.

In the mid-19th century, Horace Mann championed public education because he believed that the success of the country depended on "intelligence and virtue in the masses of the people." Later, John Dewey argued, "If we do not prepare children to become good citizens...then our republic must go down to destruction". He believed that democratic movements for human liberation were necessary to achieve a fair distribution of political power and an "equitable system of human liberties."

However, some philosophers of education have criticized the distortion of Deweyan approaches to teaching and learning, especially the way these are practiced today in many elite private and public schools. These schools are frequently racially, ethnically, religiously, and economically segregated. Therefore, efforts to develop genuine democratic classroom communities ignore the spectrum of human difference. This ignorance leaves a continuing imprint on society's attitudes toward race, class, ethnicity, gender, social conflict, and inequality. At all levels of education, both teachers and students suffer the consequences.

In addition, because of the pressure on students today to achieve high scores on standardized tests—because of such federal mandates as "No Child Left Behind"—many public school teachers feel compelled to maintain an undemocratic level of control over the classroom. They teach first to the test, and only afterward (if at all) to what might be relevant to students' needs. Universities and colleges are not immune to this level of control. In higher education, the ultimate measure of success is for students to score well on standardized tests, get high grades, prepare for careers, write carefully controlled research papers, and passively absorb the knowledge of the experts. Paulo Freire (1970) calls this type of education the "banking model." Students become mere depositories of knowledge, and teachers are always the depositors. Knowledge in…knowledge out…knowledge forgotten.

As has been argued so often today by such scholars as Louis Menand (2010), Mark C. Taylor (2010), and Myra H. Strober (2011), higher education is really a euphemism for career education. Teaching is little more than telling and selling—a form of wheeling and dealing narrow, technical knowledge. Scholarship is all about deferring to the voices of mono-disciplined experts. And, above all, research always checkmates "me-search," especially when grant money and institutional prestige are at stake. The sad truth is that philosophers, creative writing teachers, theatre arts professors, and other humanities scholars need not apply to the professoriate today. In fact, positions in these (and related) fields are fast drying up—or moved to the ranks of lecturer, adjunct, or visiting faculty—as tenure slots continue to disappear whenever senior faculty retire. Sadly, some of these disciplines get discontinued because of low student enrollment. And, because the humanities and the arts seem so out of sync with the career-driven mission of American higher education today, and with the STEM (science, technology, engineering, mathematics) research mandate that fuels academia's obsession with external grant funding, self-expression of any kind is under suspicion. Robert remembers a colleague in his department making this sarcastic statement to him: "I never heard of SPN helping anyone to acquire grant money. So why bother?" Why indeed!

Marginalization, Disenfranchisement, and Underrepresentation: Metaphors of Oppression

Marginalization is a metaphor used in sociology to describe a phenomenon where people are systemically and socially confined to the fringes and margins of society. This term originated with Robert Park's (1928) concept of "marginal man," a term he coined to characterize the lot of impoverished minority ethnic immigrants in predominantly White, Anglo-Saxon, Protestant United States. Particularly in Latin America, "marginal man" was a term that captured the supposed "backwardness" not of immigrants in *developed* countries, but in *developing* countries. These are marginalized people who fail, or are prevented from participating in, the economic, political, and cultural transition to modernity.

Disenfranchisement is a metaphor roughly equivalent to not being able to vote; not being able to give voice to your deepest beliefs and convictions regarding the "franchise" you own. In the United States, disenfranchisement was highlighted during the early 1900s Women's Suffrage Movement. In a sense, then, disenfranchise-ment—a legal term—has the potential to silence the voices of whole groups of peo-ple, as actually happened before African Americans achieved full voting rights. Today we are witnessing the early *en*franchisement of gays and lesbians, as six states officially recognize same-sex marriage (a number of other states recognize same-sex relationships through domestic partnerships or civil unions).

Underrepresentation is a metaphor closely related to disenfranchisement in that a potential voter is denied a voice in the choice of a political candidate. "No taxation without representation," a political slogan first used by Reverend Jonathan Mayhew in 1750 and later supported by John Patrick Henry, is a demand that even today is a living metaphor for marginalized, disenfranchised peoples. Increasingly, underrepresented peoples want to have a role in the decisions that will affect their lives. For example, in academia, they want their full presence acknowledged dur-ing a classroom "roll-call," in a literature review, in a Citation Index, or even in a Wikipedia entry.

Finally, we understand and use the metaphor of *oppression* somewhat differently from most mainstream, multicultural writers. We follow the lead of the feminist scholar Sharon D. Welch (1999, 2000). For Welch, and for us, the legacy of oppression, especially during the long history of racism, homophobia, and sexism in the United States, is still alive and well. Only nowadays, instead of finding expres-sion in explicitly dramatic acts of violence and cruelty against minority groups (such as outright subordination, or lynching, torture, enslavement, and imprisonment), it takes a different form. Oppression, especially in higher education, is the *suppres-sion* of personal voice, personal herstory/history, personal resistance, personal belief and critique, and, above all, creative self-expression of all kinds. Subjectivity is ruled out of order; objectivity—in all the disciplines—is the exclusive rule of the day in academia. Oppression, from our vantage point in the halls of higher education, occurs whenever and wherever faculty forbids the full expression of the self in teach-ing and learning. We believe that the suppression of the personal voice is much more than simply a "micro-aggression." In fact, it is a "macro-aggression." Such suppres-sion unravels and disintegrates the fabric of individual difference in education.

Thus, SPN has the unlimited potential to become a liberating force. Whenever our students can talk and write openly about their personal experiences with mar-ginalization, disenfranchisement, and underrepresentation, then they are able to come face to face with the day-to-day realities of oppression in the 21st century. In short, oppression in higher education results in the obliteration of the *self* in groups and, by implication, the obliteration of *groups* in the self. Both the individual and the group history of the individual disappear. We hold that access to the voice of the self is the precondition for all other types of open access in a genuinely democratic society. This is the wonderful payoff of "writing the self as a scholar" in academia. SPN gives the term "access" a new, richer, and more grounded meaning.

Sydnee Viray's Personal Reflection—Part One

In this section I reveal, through my own SPN account, how these metaphors of oppression actually play out in the academic setting. Although my reflections are personal in nature, there is universalizability (generalizability) in my experience with these organized systems of oppression. Thus, be ready for the subtle, at times embarrassing truths that will emerge via one person's actual experience in a college classroom.

My First Computer Science Class

Sydnee Viray

> You'll never silence tha voice of tha voiceless
> —RAGE AGAINST THE MACHINE

I arrived at my computer science class and found that I joined 13 others in the class. I had to do my usual head count: How many Asians are in this class?—not because it was a computer science class—but because I was enrolled at a public ivy university in the northeastern region of the United States where Asian students were few in number. So I counted…one, two, three. Wow! And I make four. Thirty-three percent is a significant number. We had four White American women, a single African American male, and the rest were White American males. I found a seat behind the only other Asian female and the African American male, and I sat next to two of the White American women. For me, picking a seat was always nerve-racking. It felt political. I thought…If I sit here, will I be noticed, and will that affect my grade? How about if I sit here? If I have to do a group project, will I be able to work with these classmates? No one I know is in this room; how will I ever fit in? Maybe I don't belong here; who the hell am I kidding?

I take my seat with trepidation. Surely the seat I choose will likely be the one that I will sit in each and every class, as I have been trained like a dog to be socially responsible. I know from experience that once I have been accepted this far into the classroom, I shouldn't rock the boat by engaging in a weekly game of musical chairs. I get the friendly eyebrow raise from the Asian American woman, but the rest lower their heads as I make my way to my seat. I unpack my notebook and my mechanical pencil and wait with the rest of my classmates for our professor.

She arrives. A middle-aged White woman swiftly enters the room with a laptop and a folder with papers in it. She glances at the clock, while I think to myself, "She's late." She looks up at the class. We quiet our conversation from the murmur to silence. She has taught this introductory programming course for over 20 years, she says.

"Does that surprise you?" she asks, as she examines our facial expressions.

I think: "Twenty years?! That's impressive. Honestly, I didn't even think women were allowed to touch computers that long ago. But way to go! Pioneering the way for women to sit in this room."

She then proceeds to do roll call. Students shift in their seats. I start to perspire a little. Because I am an anxious sort, I always perspire when I fear the worst. "How is she going to pronounce my name? And which name is she going to say?" You see, I go by two names. I have a legal name, and then I have a chosen preferred name.

She begins. "Abigail?!"

"Here."

"Tony?!"

"Here."

"Kee-Shhji-exe-uhn??? Or is that Shee-wahn?? Oh, I can't pronounce this. Are you here?"

In the back of the room, a man of Chinese descent speaks up with a thick Mandarin accent, "I am Qi-Shi Xia. Do you mean me, professor?" He seems bright and wide-eyed and eager to please.

"What about you?" She points to the other Asian man in our class sitting to his right, "What's your name?"

Asian man to the right responds in a very clear American English accent, "I am Hyun-jun Hwang."

"Ok. So you both are here."

"Wow, did she really just say that? One guy is totally and obviously Chinese, and the other is totally and completely Korean. "WTF"? I think I can imagine the worst, but really? These are my thoughts as she breezes through the list and continues to stumble on the "foreign" names.

And let's not forget about the African American male whose name is as American as it gets, "Joseph Smith." She pauses on his name for a few moments to be sure he really is *the* Joseph Smith on her list.

My first day in this computer science class repeats itself daily in most of our 21st-century American collegiate classrooms. I remember learning about how the United States was a melting pot and a salad bowl, but who knew that in today's classrooms the melting pot spits out the letters X, Q, and Z? Whenever this particular combination of letters does not roll off the average American professor's tongue, then faculty are confounded. This is just one part of the experience of being marginalized. For some it starts with a name. Would the instructor call on the student based on where s/he is sitting? Not in my class! Sadly, being called upon was always based on whether or not the instructor could remember how to pronounce a student's name. Let me just say that I was barely called on in that computer science class during an entire semester.

There were also other ways that voices disappeared in that classroom. Of the 13 registered students, we had 4 White males. A couple of these guys owned the spotlight. They were seen walking into the classroom with the instructor several times throughout the semester telling jokes and connecting on the hometown experiences they had in common. Meanwhile, the rest of us would be waiting much like we did on the first day of class. But there was one White guy in particular who left an impression. He always sat in the front seat, and, arrogantly, he would tell us, his classmates, his answers to the homework the night before. Yet he, too, had his marginal role to play in our classroom. You see, he was a bit overweight, had unkempt hair, and wore a black *Rage Against the Machine* T-shirt that read: *You'll never silence the voice of the voiceless....Rage against the Machine,* and he wore it defiantly several times during the course of the class.

Ironically, in the accounts above, I am able to *see* the voiceless experience in action. Even a student sitting in a classroom can be consciously or unconsciously marginalized. For example, the metaphor of marginalization affected how I chose my seat, how I participated in roll call, and how I engaged with other students. As a result, I disengaged for the entire semester. Although I was a straight-A student in this class and had a natural talent in computer technology, I never chose to take another computer science course. My personal account reflects just one of the countless stories that get played out in the college classroom throughout the United States each and every day. Through stories like these, the three metaphors of oppression are woven throughout the American educational fabric.

Sydnee Viray's Personal Reflection—Part Two

Clinging to My Piece of Debris

Sydnee Viray

> What is the appropriate behavior for a man or a woman in the midst of this world, where each person is clinging to his piece of debris? What's the proper salutation between people as they pass each other in this flood?
> —BUDDHA

These metaphors of oppression exist not just in the *psychological* realm, but also in the *physical* realm. In the following reflection, I self-disclose my own insecurities regarding body image by "clinging to my piece of debris" concerning what I have been conditioned to believe is aesthetically acceptable in Western culture. What I have learned from this reflection is "a [my] slow humility" hopefully leading me to discover "the palm of [my] repose."

The overweight White guy who wore the *Rage Against the Machine* T-shirt was voiceless in the way that a penny gets overlooked in a change purse. While he spoke often, many people in the classroom discredited his voice because of his appearance and, specifically, because of his size. I say this because I judged him. I judged him as not belonging, not fitting into this adult playground we called a classroom. But of course he had every right to be there. He had a rightful stake in this franchise called higher education. He was paying just as much as I was to learn from others and to be free to learn in his own way. Yet I judged him, because the truth was I was just as acutely aware of my body in the space of the classroom as I was of his body in the classroom. The way I dressed to be on a college campus was deliberate, so for me to notice another body in the room that did not match my expectations meant I succumbed to the voice of judging. I was asking: "Are you in or are you out? Where did you come from?"

bell hooks reminds us: "It was really clear that the space of high culture was where he was in mind, and the space of street and street culture was where he felt he could be most expressive of himself within the body." This is how I read my White classmate's T-shirt. He sent me a message by expressing that he felt voiceless at times.

> . . . because to remember yourself is to see yourself always as a body in a system
> that has not become accustomed to your presence or to your physicality.
> —BELL HOOKS, *TEACHING TO TRANSGRESS* (1994, P. 134)

Yet I have had White professors of thin body types walk into a classroom out-fitted in denim pants that were dethreading and fraying at the bottom; with pockets so worn that the blue denim had faded to a soft white; and with open-toed sandals. Some of these White professors wore T-shirts and displayed unkempt hair. Did I judge these *academics*? No. I deconstructed their bodies to only include their minds. They filled the air with their ideas, theories, speculations, and unarguable, *objective* truths. Or shall I say that what I really wanted to hear from them was their ideas, but then be given permission (and encouraged) to judge for myself whether their truths were objective and relevant to my experiences.

In a counseling class I recently took, the professor prompted us to "socially locate" him within the social context of our classroom. "Interesting," I thought. It brought awareness directly and sharply to my judgments and expectations of where I thought he ought to be. My classmates and I inventoried his attire: cashmere scarf, open-toed sandals, glasses [no wedding ring despite having a partner]. And then his actual physical appearance: longer hair, his white skin, etc. I had, in my own mind, decided he was not a professor.

So, I had to ask myself how does a professor show up in the classroom space in the context of his students? For some, he fit the picture of what I had come to expect. It didn't matter what he wore but where his mind was. I realized that I measure professors based on how they use their minds, yet this measurement did not apply to my peers, and I lost out because of this. Naively, I had already narrativized my professor's entire life before he even opened his mouth, whereas with my classmates, I narrativized my social location based on a competitive frame of reference. Thus, I lost out on two counts: One, I had already pre-judged the intellect of my professor to be worthy…indeed supreme; and so I missed out on making a genuine human connection with him. He was the authority, and I was the lowly learner. Two, I failed to see that my classmates and I could become an interdependent community of learners and scholars, because I was playing into the metaphor of a "culture of vultures." I saw my classmates as cut-throat competitors for such scarce academic resources as high grades, awards, a front seat at the academic table of expertise, and campus-wide recognition.

My take-aways from the experiences I describe above are many, but my primary insight is this: I, a woman of color, an out-lesbian, and a Filipina immigrant, am also a woman of aesthetic privilege. Because I am lean, athletic, and an Asian woman considered attractive by Western standards of beauty, I find myself unconsciously judging others when it comes to body image. I act, and think, out of my aesthetic privilege. It hurts me to admit that I, too, can be marginalizing, disenfranchising, and underrepresenting. Obviously, I am not proud of this.

However, it is because of this personal realization that I have worked so hard to become an effective social justice advocate at my university and in the state of Vermont. How so? Because I am acutely aware that, when it comes to the privilege of meeting certain cultural standards of beauty, even I have the potential to be the victimizer and not the victim. I believe that all of us—whether advocate or adversary—contain embarrassing contradictions in our personal narratives of social justice. I am Exhibit A when it comes to being a living container of contradictions. I am so grateful that SPN writing has helped me to identify, and to work through, these harmful inconsistencies in my beliefs and behaviors. SPN gives me permission to write my own story of accountability and privilege…alongside my story of social justice advocacy and personal shame.

← judgement and categorization seperates us .

"Deep Down within My Inner Space, I Am the Same as You." Together, We Can "Shatter the Darkness"

> The objective of the learning process is to liberate the participants from their external and internal oppression; to make them capable of changing their reality, their lives, and the society they live in.
> —Ray Bradbury, *Fahrenheit 451*

Recognizing Commonality in the Voices of Others

The quoted words in the section-heading above are those of the poets, Benjamin Zephariah, and Langston Hughes. Before we close this chapter, we will talk about how the three metaphors of marginalization, disenfranchisement, and underrepresentation do not have to apply only to one particular group of outsiders. "Deep down in our inner spaces," we are similar. Knowing this, together we can "shatter the darkness." As Sydnee has pointed out in her personal reflections, to some extent we are all "oppressed." In a metaphorical sense, at some point we have been pushed to the margins, we have found ourselves positioned outside of the majority, and we have suffered major disappointments because of our social positions. Moreover, in academia, each of us has experienced the silencing of our voices because they are "small" compared to the "big," authoritative voices of the "experts." Sydnee, a visible member of a minority group, has talked about her own experience with marginalization, and also with marginalizing. So, too, has Robert, a visible member of a majority group. The three metaphors play no favorites. Or as both Welch (1999, 2000), and Freire (1970) would say: It is inevitable that eventually the oppressors will become the oppressed, and the victims will become the victimizers.

Ironically, the first step toward recovering the truth of our individual voices is to recognize the truth and the overlap in the voices of others who, on the surface, might look and sound different from us. For example, Sydnee tells the following story about herself and her broken dream.

> *I was crying. My eyes were red and puffy, and I held in my hand calculations of how my dream was now a fading bad thought that had turned into a nightmare. The piece of paper was drenched with my tears of sorrow and not as comforting as a tissue would have been in that moment. I had just left the Financial Aid office. I found out that I could not afford to go to medical school despite my competitive GPA, my service-stocked resume, and my deep passion to heal others. I couldn't afford it! And, moreover, I had to deliver this news to my family. I did not want to disappoint them, but the numbers screamed too loud. TWO HUNDRED THOUSAND DOLLARS! I couldn't even conceive in my mind what this number looked like. All I knew was that I didn't have it. I didn't even have a percentage significant enough to attempt enrollment. My dream was dead. Now what?*

In writing her personal reflection about her broken dream, Sydnee, a financial aid professional, is better able to see her *self* in others and others in her *self* as she goes about her job each day. She works with hundreds of limited-income students of all sizes, shapes, skin colors, social classes, and ethnic backgrounds. Each of her students has a central life-dream. Each has a vested interest in their education. Each has a set of career goals, life ambitions, and revered families to make proud. Each has experienced disappointment, shame, and the devastating loss of a long-sought-after dream. SPN writing delivers a format for the writer to connect with the "inner space" of others. It enables the writer to "break the shadow" of silence. And, at its universalizable best, SPN writing can induce others to change their reality, their lives, and, even, the society they live in. The ultimate purpose of all research is to motivate people to take action. SPN writing is a call to action that combines both re-search and me-search.

Sydnee's personal story exemplifies all three of the axiomatic SPN questions: What? So What? Now What? These are the simple questions that "shatter the darkness" of our private, ongoing stories and connect us to the private, ongoing stories of others. Sydnee's "what" is the broken dream of not being able to afford a medical school education. Sydnee's "so what" is the emotional fallout that occurs because her long-sought-after dream is unattainable. Sydnee's "now what" is her personal call to action. In her professional work with limited-income students, SPN allows her to share the story of her own personal disappointment, and ultimate resilience, with others. Some may ask, "Couldn't Sydnee be this type of empathic professional without SPN?" In response, we say: "Yes, of course. But we maintain that the opportunity to do SPN writing is more likely to give a voice, face, and space to what lies within her. Why? In short, this type of writing de-marginalizes, enfranchises, and represents the untold stories of the academy!"

4

How Stories Teach Theories

Sydney's Personal Reflections on Social Justice Themes

Introduction: Breaking the Silence

As academics working with students on a daily—and often on an hourly—basis, we sometimes turn to identity development theories and models as we facilitate a conversation about their identities. Often, as their narratives unfold, we hear about how social structures like racism, classism, heterosexism, and sexism influence their development. Our guiding mantra is this: "Without the basic dedication to equal rights for all students, many of our youth will continue to be forced to live within the margins of the classroom" (DeSurra & Church, 1994).

Throughout recent history, feminist, queer, and critical race theorists have used narrative to create visibility for the underrepresented; to break the silence and shame surrounding the identities of the "outsiders"; and to promote a collective voice among "outsiders" in the academy. These theorists hope to encourage dialogue across identities both marginal and dominant. In this chapter, Sydnee will draw upon her personal narrative to dramatize key concepts and themes of each theory. Her objective is to exemplify how SPN writing can liberate the voices from the margins. In her personal stories, Sydnee will illustrate, with real-life examples, the meaning of such technical concepts as "counterstorytelling," "naming one's own reality," the "multiple lenses of gender," essentialism, White privilege, microaggression, performativity, heteronormativity, and the empathic fallacy. Sydnee's SPN writing will demonstrate how story can often be the best way to teach complex, sometimes abstract, concepts and themes.

*are students the outsiders?

Sydnee's HERstory

The Many Waves of Feminist Theory

Sydnee Viray

The noun *history* derives from the Latin word *historia,* which has been defined as "narrative of past events, accounts, tales, and stories." But the word is also rooted in the Greek *historia,* defined as "a learning or knowing by inquiry." Thus, SPN is a combination of both narrative storytelling and narrative self-interrogation. On another level, the term *history* contains two words that are easy to pick out—*his* and *story.* From this vantage point, we can derive even more meaning.

So, what is my "herstory"? This question plagued me as an undergraduate who had boldly enrolled in my very first Women's and Gender Studies course at a predominantly White research institution of higher education. I listened to the White, female-identified professor assert that we all have a "herstory," and we would be cross-examining the herstories of the various waves of feminism (at that time we were only at wave 2.5 or 3). I remember leafing through my textbooks on violence against women, and mothers and daughters of the 20th century. But my favorite book, edited by Cherrie Moraga and Gloria Anzaldúa, was *This Bridge Called My Back* (1981/2002)—one of the most cited works in feminist theory. This wasn't even a book that my professor assigned; it was among the recommended readings found in the back of my syllabus that year. What I loved about this work was that Moraga and Anzaldúa collected and edited an academic-worthy text that contained prose, poetry, personal narrative, and scholarly analysis by African Americans, Asian Americans, Latinas, and Native Americans. The edited volume contained six sections, each uncompromisingly defining and personalizing feminism by womyn of color in the United States.

As I reflect on that reading and learning experience, I am reminded that in her book *Feminist Theory: From Margin to Center* (2000), bell hooks makes the point that "the problem that has no name," as heralded by Betty Friedan in *The Feminine Mystique* (1963/2001), describes the conditions of women who are college educated, middle and upper class, married, and White (hooks, 2000). However, hooks asserts that it is important to recognize that there is no one "feminist" perspective or position. There are multiple "feminisms" that have relied on narrative approaches to open up the discourse to many types of feminist voices. What hooks has done is to help *all* womyn, regardless of their social membership, to name their realities.

During the second wave of feminism, a new language emerged that unveiled sexual and equality disparities of the time. hooks reminded us that second-wave feminism boxed womyn into the traditional empirical research model so popular in the academy. I remember reading hooks's work and finding my breath again. I had always wondered, "What if my voice, my story, is not feminist enough? How can I—a living, Asian American, female-identified, androgynous, exploring human being—feel validated if I have other womyn defining my legitimacy as a feminist?" hooks made room for me, and I am grateful for it.

I remember sitting in the Women's Studies classroom when the discussion of high heels came up. I was angered by the *discourse*, and I thought, "I wear high heels. So what? Now, I am not a feminist? Wait a minute! Didn't second-wave feminism demand skirts in the boardroom, not womyn wearing pantsuits?" I was deeply offended by this portrayal of what feminists looked like in that classroom and by the ideological slant of the discourse in general. Can men be considered feminist, too? Of course. We see young men wearing pink shirts that are labeled "this is what a feminist looks like." From this vantage point, there are many feminist voices. The narrative has enlarged to include male-identified feminists and men who support the current feminist narratives—and maybe even men who have created their own narratives. For example, Robert gets infuriated whenever people accuse him of being partial to smaller women of color because they are "cute." As a result, Robert has created his own feminist narrative as a counter-narrative to judging a woman's intelligence (and worth) by her aesthetic profile. And he always makes a point in class to examine the history of the word "cute." It has evolved over time from meaning "pretty" and "attractive"—in a somewhat dainty way—to meaning "artificial," "contrived," and "'cutesy,'" in order to charm or seduce others.

Sydnee's Queer Story

The Fluidity of My Gender Expression

Sydnee Viray

Indiana gas station, 2003: "Excuse me, you are going into the wrong bathroom. The men's bathroom is over there," shouted a Caucasian woman who had cropped, permed, gray hair. She wore a fanny pack on her waist that read: "God Bless America." She was behind me as I approached the bathroom labeled for females—a bathroom that I felt accustomed to and felt entitled to enter without permission. That is, until this woman imposed her guidance. I then realized she could only see the back of my body. I am a barely five-foot, one-inch tall, brown-skinned Filipina. I had very short hair at the time and was wearing a black baseball cap that had rhinestones stuck to it and that read: PRINCESS. I wore a pair of tan corduroy pants and a tight-fitting, mauve, long-sleeve shirt with a black fleece. When I heard her pronouncement, I looked back at her. I gave her direct eye contact to see if she was speaking directly to me. I also furrowed my brow as if to question, "Are you talking to me?" She then read my hat and furrowed her brow right back at me. I then looked at her fanny pack and said, "Well, 'God Bless America'…after you ma'am." I let her pass me and enter the bathroom. I stood outside the door and waited for the bathroom to be vacated. When she came out of the bathroom, I smiled at her, and she gave me a polite pursed lip, which I interpreted as a smile. And then I proceeded into the female-designated bathroom.

Why did I say that? Why did I say, "God Bless America?" I asked myself this, and even now, I wonder what was going through my mind. This person did not know my gender, my name, or my age. But she knew that I didn't fit the look of somebody who could use this bathroom. My feminine performance (what queer theorists call "performativity," as in playing a particular gender role) did not qualify me to use the bathroom—which only she was entitled to use. Ironically, yes, when I think about the image of Jesus Christ, I can't help but think of how His image doesn't fit the look of a man. He has long hair. He wears a robe that reminds me of the latest *haute couture* trend coming out of Italy. His sandals remind me of the gladiator sandals I saw in Macy's the other day. These sandals were being sold and marketed to womyn not men.

So, I wondered if this woman would ever tell Jesus Christ which bathroom was for men and which was for women. I said "God Bless America," I think, to let her know I am a believer, too. I do not believe in heteronormativity (compulsory gender roles and behaviors). Nor do I believe in sexual binaries (either-or biological sex distinctions). I do believe that there is fluidity in gender expression. I believe that I can have all my female sex organs and yet shave my head and wear clothing traditionally marketed to men. I believe that when someone decides to tell me which bathroom is for men, and which is for women, I think their purpose is to tell me that my options are limited and that there is a right option and a wrong one. In a country where shopping is a recreational pastime because there are endless options for things like deodorant, types of pasta, colors of socks, and brands of butter, why do I only get two options of gender-specific bathrooms?

In queer theory, liminality (dwelling on the "border" or "threshold") is the kissing cousin of marginality. I found my options to enter a bathroom restricted to whether I identified as a man or a woman. I believe, also, that the academy has practiced this duality of restriction in its own work—the need to fit each scholar into a specific discipline box—whether female or male. Interdisciplinarians need look elsewhere for legitimacy. For example, Robert is the director of a graduate interdisciplinary program in educational studies at his university. And even though the program is one of the largest in his college, as well as one of the fastest growing, many of his colleagues just do not know how to take it seriously. For them, interdisciplinary studies is liminal (marginal) at best, and "soft" at worst. Why? Because the program resides in the "in-between" of the disciplines—homeless, helpless, and hapless.

Likewise, whenever a womyn consents to so-called "gender-bending" (behaving androgynously), she is often greeted with discomfort at best, and cruelty at worst. This tension seems to be a reflection of an all-pervasive insecurity in the academy, which at its core is an either-or knowledge factory. I remember hearing in a classroom recently the long, seemingly endless acronym LGBTQQAAI....So many of my classmates were perplexed and troubled because (a) they did not know the meaning of all the letters, (b) they were impatient because the acronym just never ended, and (c) they wondered why, in the name of "political correctness," every identity needed to be accounted for. Such is the mono-normative bent of so much that takes place in higher education today, including research, teaching, and internecine disciplinary politics.

Here is a recent quotation I read in a textbook: "I walked into the archivists' office, mentioned that someone had once told me that Miriam Van Waters was a lesbian, and asked, rather naively, 'Was she?' An archivist responded—I paraphrase slightly—'We don't say that about anyone without proof.' The implication, in tone and words, was that I was making an unpleasant accusation" (Black, 2001, p. 52). Each time I sit in a classroom and read the assignments for the course, I can't help but think about the author's gender identity. I especially started thinking this when I read that many females of the early 20th century used masculine pseudonyms to ensure that their words would be published. I can't help but think to myself, "Do I really need proof about a scholar's orientation or gender expression?" Perhaps I don't need the proof, but I would at least like to have the option of learning from scholars who are successful at performing within cisgendered ways, as well as from those who can perform in a transgendered experience. If nothing else, this would give me full access to my academic options.

Sydnee's Amerasian Story

Salvation through Love

Sydnee Viray

> *I was born under a mango tree*
> *that sat on an island in the great Pacific ocean,*
> *below the crescent moon and stars in the vast sky.*
> *My family is a mix of Tagalogs, Iloconos, and Spanish.*

I eat rice with my hands and, when satiated, my smile
can light up the darkest of rooms.
I migrated to the US when I was young.
I have enjoyed and benefitted from the riches of a nation,
where God is printed on its currency.
I carried with me a rosary and was baptized as a Catholic.
I'm here to learn, love, live and to tell my story of my journey
To this country through my multiply intersecting identities and my vantage points.
As a womyn I believe in something greater out there,
And, therefore, I have found something greater within.
Sit down and let's get to know ourselves now that my pen is down.
—SYDNEE VIRAY (2012)

The salvation of man is through love and in love. I understood how a man who has
nothing left in this world still may know bliss, be it only for a brief moment, in the
contemplation of his beloved.
—FRANKL (1959)

I was born out of the Amerasian movement of the 1980s. This was a time when young American servicemen were dutifully serving their great nation in Asian countries such as Thailand, the former South Vietnam, Japan, South Korea, and, most notably, in the Philippines, where the largest U.S. air and naval bases outside the U.S. mainland were established. These men served their country while impregnating the local, impoverished Asian women in their leisure time. In Olongapo City, my birthplace, and Pampanga, Philippines, there are over 50,000 Amerasians. It is a "dream come true" to the child and the child's family if the sperm donor actually stays to father the child, but many Amerasian children have lived without ever once meeting their donor.

In 1983, my biological father, a 20-year-old U.S. Navy man, met my mother, a 20-year-old Filipina, in a dance club. According to both, they "fell in love" with each other. Their consummated relationship resulted in my mother's pregnancy with me. And here is where my plot began: After 8 months in my mother's womb, my father decided to leave. He decided that donating his sperm was the best he could offer his impoverished girlfriend. He left my mother, my birth arrival, and my country. My father's irresponsible action in leaving issued from advice given to him by his ship's traditionalist Christian chaplain. The Navy chaplain reminded my father that he had a greater vocation beyond raising a Filipina child. The only "salvation" that the Chaplain offered to my father was to move on and forget about this "puppy love" and child. In my opinion, what resulted was my father's greatest damnation: he stole my mother's primary hope of escaping the poverty and starvation of her own reality.

Everything can be taken from a man but one thing: the last of the human freedoms—
to choose one's attitude in any given set of circumstances, to choose one's own way.
—FRANKL (1959)

Much like Dr. Viktor Frankl, the survivor of four Nazi death camps, my mother refused to accept this prescriptive reality. She dreamed, at the age of 7, that she would move to the United States and provide the salvation that her family so much desired. Later, she maintained her vision of her beloved, my father, and focused on doing whatever it took to travel to the United States. She made the most devastating sacrifices: she used her body, her mind, and her heart to cultivate what her soul most craved. In December 1983, only months after my birth and 7 months after having a piece of her heart drift out to sea, she arrived in America. She left me in the arms and care of her *kuya* (older brother), my *ya-ya* (governess), and my *lola* (my grandmother). 8 years old.

Within a couple of months, she married another Marine, whom she met in the Philippines. She traveled over 8,300 miles to Vermont to learn the strange ways of her new country and culture. In 1986, she was reciting the American Oath of Allegiance to become a naturalized citizen of one of the richest countries in the world. This also afforded me my own naturalization by 1991. However, when I was reunited with my mother, she was reminded of her mission to find her beloved. So she searched, and searched, and searched. She searched even herself; "Did this man really exist? God, my daughter looks just like him, doesn't she? Okay *na*, I know he exists but *saan* (where)?" She would tell me, "His name is Lawrence Lee Parker. He is from New York. White Plains…no…Brownsville. His mother was Elizabeth Carol, or was it Carol Elizabeth?"

The truth is that my mother's vision did not have to be bionic. I look just like her beloved. Every day my façade grew to reflect my mother's salvation through love and in love. Every day she prayed and took on an attitude that this man would someday return to our lives.

Then, on March 23, 2009, I received this email:

Sydnee,

My name is Lawrence Parker (Bud). I would like to know if you are the daughter of Susan Viray from Olongapo City. I know that she had a daughter that was born on June 20, 1983, and that baby girl was my daughter as well. The name I was told that was given to this child was Princess Laine Viray.
Please reply to this email address if you would like.

The angels are lost in perpetual contemplation of an infinite glory.
—FRANKL (1959)

Or, as my mom said to me when I delivered her the news, "Amen, Princess, God does exist. Thank God." So, beginning on March 23, 2009, I began a process of rediscovering my meaning. I became lost in "contemplation of infinite glory" learning about my father, my mother, and myself. I began a relationship of almost instant connection and bonding. The meaning of my life became "infinite," yet also finite, in stories of my parents' choices. It is here that, for the first time in my life, I learned how to love a man so deeply.

In this particular reflection, I am asking my readers to empathize with (and not judge) the love I feel for a man I now affectionately call my "bio-dad." I am fully aware that there is an "empathic fallacy" operating in my story. My bio-dad is seen as a military hero by his country, but how can a "hero" desert both his lover and his daughter? He hurt and betrayed my mother. He abandoned me because of the advice given him by a Christian clergyman. I ended up in the United States with an adoptive father. For 26 years, I longed for the father I never knew. It is true that my story alone will not change the official foreign policy of the American government that denies citizenship rights to the abandoned offspring of the military in the Philippines. However, I hope that my personal story will help readers to understand that there is "salvation in love" and "in hurt," and there is an element of universalizability in this truth for everyone. It is possible for love to grow out of hurt, for right to emanate from wrong, and for choice to replace chance. I made the conscious choice to rewrite my father-daughter narrative.

Please know, however, that even though I am an "essentialist" in thinking about my Amerasian identity (for example, I and my Amerasian friends have suffered similar macro- and micro-oppressions), I also realize that we differ in certain "essentials." Not all of us live in comfortable homes and eat nutritious food on a daily basis. Not all of us find our birth fathers. Not all of us have citizenship. Not all of us go on to earn multiple degrees in higher education. Not all of us have the privilege of sharing our stories with trusted others. And yet I hope that, through my SPN writing, I can convey one "essential" insight that might ring true to my readers: Even though I was *left behind,* I can choose not to have my story *left out!* While I am on the margin, I can still choose to be on the page! I can choose to re-narrativize my story. I can choose to transform my story of loss into a tale of salvation through love.

5

Introducing the Ten General Guidelines for Writing Scholarly Personal Narratives

Responding to the Concerns of the Beginning SPN Writer

Before we present the ten general guidelines for writing SPNs, we want to describe, and respond to, the four most common concerns that come up whenever our students attempt this type of personal narrative writing for the first time.

The First Concern: Please Help Me to Understand the Similarities and Differences between SPN and Like-Minded Types of Scholarly Writing. Will This Help Me to Earn the Respect of My Peers and Professors If I Choose to Write an SPN?

Every year, without fail, our marginalized students come to us with some fundamental concerns about writing in the first-person singular voice. Few, if any, are confident at the outset that they are capable of writing in this genre, because they have never done it in a course. Most are not really sure what the lure of SPN is, because they might have heard negatives about this writing methodology from friends, instructors, or advisors. Some graduate students have been told that SPN is actually the court of last resort for those students who are ABD or ABT (all but the dissertation, or all but the thesis).

Some of these students might actually harbor a certain degree of skepticism about the worth of SPN writing in an academic setting. It just sounds too easy to them to do this kind of writing and still be able to call it "serious scholarship." Most don't want to be seen as taking the easy way out in order to produce, and finish, an undergraduate or graduate thesis or dissertation. And yet, in spite of this fear of being seen as lesser "experts" than their peers for choosing to do an SPN writing project, they are still intensely curious about this methodology.

The first step in responding to our students' initial fears is to help them to understand the similarities and differences between the SPN methodology and a few other, more acceptable research methodologies that also emphasize personal scholarship. What follows are the distinctions we make for our students between and among SPN, memoir, autobiography, autoethnography, and self-authorship. These distinctions help us to pave the way to a greater understanding and acceptance of SPN in relationship to more established scholarly writing genres.

Memoir
Similarities: As in SPN, a *memoir* starts with the *writer's life* rather than with the lives and activities of others. It is up to the writer to make sense of the raw data of life by looking inward, not outward, at least initially. Notice, too, that the major truth criterion for memoir writing, as with SPN, differs drastically from more empirically based forms of research and scholarship. Memoir writing is "true" whenever writers work hard to make personal meaning of the raw material of their day-to-day experiences in a way that enables readers to actually believe it and, ideally, identify with it.
Differences: Memoirs tend to be more informal and less scholarly than SPN. A memoir is literally a "mining of the writer's memory" of past events, people, and strong personal feelings. In contrast, in SPN writing, authors make a concerted effort to *thematize*, and then *universalize*, their unique narrative truths. SPN writers use the events and people in their personal lives to exemplify and explain the larger ideas/concepts/constructs that bind together human beings everywhere, in spite of their differences.

Thematizing also entails SPN writers showing how their personal truths might have universal value. In other words, for memoirists, the personal story is central. For SPN writers, the larger, universalizable meanings implicit in the personal stories are central. So, too, are the ideas. Some of our students will start with personal memoir writing (undertaking a kind of confessional, personal exploration), gradually expand it into a more reflective, conceptual essay, and eventually convert it to a full-fledged SPN document.

Autobiography

Similarities: An *autobiography* and an SPN put the author's *self* (the Greek *autos*) at the center of the writing. Both tell stories. Both take artistic (stylistic) risks, and the writer's personal voice is always clear and distinct.

Differences: Autobiographies are more chronological and linear in structure and format than SPN. They are also more historical and sweeping. Autobiographies have a recognizable timeline that includes a beginning, middle, and end. Sometimes autobiographies follow clear and distinct formats that strive to produce a type of historical objectivity rather than authorial subjectivity. In short, autobiographies feature an A-to-Z review and summary of the entire trajectory of an author's life.

In contrast, SPN writing is more episodic, selective, and personalized. An SPN, in the words of Anne Lamott (1994), is a "series of one-inch picture frames" of the writer's life. And the writer's inner life is always front and center. However, in SPN it is important to remember that the major purpose of all the one-inch picture frames of this "inner life" is to deliver a thematic payload. This payload answers the always-present SPN questions: "What?" "So What?" "Now What?" The SPN writer needs to keep three key inquiries in the direct line of vision: What relevance does my story have for readers? What are the take-aways that will benefit my readers' personal and professional lives? How can I make my story resonate in some way with all the varied, unique stories that my readers will bring to my text? In the words of the noted autoethnographer Heewon Chang (2008), SPN writing, unlike autobiographies, is "self-infused scholarship" that is central to academic writing. It is as much introspection as extrospection.

Autoethnography and Self-Authorship

Similarities: *Autoethnography*, like SPN, is concerned with three elements: culture, self, and others. Unlike SPN, however, autoethnography's primary goal is to shape a self-narrative in such a way that it becomes a text through which the socio-cultural understanding of self and others is illuminated. Like SPN, though, autoethnography is all about telling stories, constructing selves, elaborating pivotal themes, and eschewing the strict, traditional interpretive styles that dominate the social sciences.

Self-Authorship has much in common with SPN, including one of its main existential goals: learning how to create sustaining beliefs in one's life by becoming the author of one's own life. Similarly, SPN is all about meaning-making and self-creation. SPN emphasizes the power of the writer's voice in the construction of individual and group identity. And SPN is also liberating, empowering, and self-clarifying.

Differences: The major difference between SPN and autoethnography and self-authorship is in their discipline-based approaches. Autoethnography is grounded in the techniques of ethnographic (anthropological) analysis and interpretation. The focus is always on the self's ongoing relationship with the culture. The ideal outcome of autoethnographic research is to use the self as a lens primarily to understand the socio-cultural context that forms the background for the emergence of the self. SPN, however, is unconstrained by any specific research method or perspective.

While the underlying intent of SPN and self-authorship makes each cousins of the second order, the major difference between the two lies in their respective intentions and goals. Self-authorship is rooted in student development theory. Moreover, it has an overarching professional aim: to help students in a higher education setting answer these developmental questions: "How do I know?" "Who am I?" and "How do I want to construct relationships with others?" SPN is much less developmentally focused and professionally applied. While SPN enthusiastically values these meaning-making questions, it comes at them in a different way. SPN gets at the construction of personal meaning through self-narrativizing, essaying, self-interpreting, describing lived experience, re-creating the self, investigating key life-themes, universalizing, and, most of all, by assiduously avoiding simplistic research formulas and questions that are one-dimensional.

The point we are trying to make with our students who wonder about the academic credibility of SPN writing is that they need to understand the similarities and differences among similar scholarly methodologies. This is important if they want the respect of those who might favor one or the other of these genres. SPN writers who can point to the overlaps among the personal narrative writing approaches will be more able to legitimize SPN as a scholarly writing choice.

Alternative research approaches like SPN take a great deal of time to pass the traditionalist muster of academia. In spite of its own claims, the American university has never been known for its progressivism in the ways it pursues new knowledge. Research orthodoxy continues to rule the day. Data collection, measurement, analysis, and validity are the "rigorous" code words of scholarly choice. Older, quasi-science approaches to truth-finding die hard because, when it comes to research, academia is tenacious in its commitment to what has been, rather than to what might be. But we are confident that change is inevitable. Already, the voices of marginalized student-scholars are growing louder, stronger, and more insistent. As academic pluralists, we welcome them.

In the end, however, we honor all approaches to research and scholarship, and this includes the four types that we have described in this section. What we are saying here is that scholarly personal narrative writing can take many different forms. While it is personal, it is also social. While it is practical, it is also theoretical. While it is self-reflective, it is also public. While it is local, it is also political. While it narrates, it also proposes. While it is self-revealing, it also evokes self-examination from readers. While it is subjective, it also respects the objective studies of researchers and often cites these when appropriate. Whatever its unique shape and style of communicating to readers, SPN's central purpose is to make an impact on both writer and reader, on both the individual and the community. Its overall goal is to encourage all writers to discover and cherish their own richly textured voices in order to communicate their insights and values to others with force, integrity, dignity, style, and grace.

The Second Concern: What's So Interesting about My Puny Little Life? Who Really Cares Enough to Read My Personal Narrative?

Many of our marginalized students don't think they have anything worthwhile to write about. "What's so interesting about my puny little life?" is the message they convey, without exactly using these words. "I've got nothing 'big' to offer. So why should I embarrass myself?" This type of self-abnegation always makes us wince. Why? Because we know from years of personal experience with underrepresented students that every life is a story, and every story has the potential to teach. As Richard Rhodes (1995), a two-time winner of the Pulitzer Prize, says, "If you speak [your story] with passion, many of us will listen....Yours enlarges the circle" (p.1). Our own circles are visibly enhanced every time we teach our students how to write SPNs. Why? Because no matter our individual age, stage, and wage, we are always inspired by the fact that we have more in common with one another than we might think.

Walt Whitman wrote something that we quote to our self-deprecating students at the beginning, middle, and end of every writing course we teach: "I am large. I contain multitudes." Each of us has minutes, hours, days, weeks, months, years, and decades of life-experiences to draw upon—whether we're teen-agers, old-agers, or all the ages in between. We are all grappling, each in our unique way, with the irrefutable, existential enigmas of human existence. These include the quest for meaning and purpose, identity awareness, significant relationships, vocational fulfillment, religio-spiritual insight, and educational growth. Perhaps the most important enigma for all of us to grapple with, however, is to learn how to get along with those who are different, or "other." The "other" threatens our tribally conditioned certitudes about anything and everything that we deem to be sacrosanct. The more frequently we remind one another in our writing of the commonalities amidst our differences, then the more likely it is that we will be able to live with one another without fear and suspicion, which lead to all-too-predictable outcomes of conflict and violence.

Often our students will ask if their voices are worth being heard in response to these huge existential challenges. We sometimes reply to them in more poetic terms by quoting Henry David Thoreau. He said that the "squeaking of the pump sounds as necessary as the music of the spheres." In other words, we tell our students that their little squeaks, like ours, have the power to carry equal weight with the cosmos's music. It all depends on their vantage point, their self-confidence, and their power of discernment. Thus, we encourage them always to let their stories squeak in all their splendor. Their individual and group stories will teach, but only if they have the courage to put them into words and to narrate them with pride and enthusiasm.

The denial of the value of the self's stories in an academic setting is born in the command all of us have heard in school at some time: Never use the "I" in formal writing. The "I," we have been told, is incapable of discovering and dispensing wisdom without the support of the "Them," the certified experts. Messages like these leech the fascinating, storied self out of the budding writer, leaving only the clichéd and often pinched stories of experts to recirculate over and over again. Our first order of business in teaching about SPN is to do what we think of as "courage encouragement." We let our students know up front that constructing an SPN takes courage, and every single one of them has found the courage to survive some of the most difficult circumstances.

Once our students are convinced that their stories count (and this often takes some time), they can begin what are actually the major challenges for SPN writers. These challenges include identifying and embracing these stories, telling them with gusto, and discerning their meanings for themselves and others. And when they are finished, they must learn to let the chips fall where they may. In this regard, Phillip Lopate once said something very wise about writing an essay: "To essay is to attempt, to test, to make a run at something without knowing whether you are going to succeed...." Essaying, we tell our students, is a lot like living a life: full speed ahead, and let the fallout take care of itself...as it usually does.

The Third Concern: How Will I Ever Learn How to Write an SPN When I've Never Been Given an Opportunity to Write in This Way?

The vast majority of our thoroughly schooled-up undergraduate and graduate students will often say that they have rarely, if ever, written in an SPN genre. Will it be possible, therefore, for them to learn the SPN writer's moves that promise success? Many will comment that they can write a term paper, a research paper, or a literature review with their "eyes closed." They know the templates for these conventional types of manuscripts by heart, because they have done so many of them throughout their long years in formal education. They know from practice that it's mostly just a matter of understanding how to fit some new pieces of the knowledge puzzle into the old research templates—a matter, if you will, of knowing how to pour new research wine into the same old format bottles.

Tried-and-true research formats are good, of course, particularly when scholars are aware of both their strengths and limitations—what they can and can't do. But SPN is a methodology without a well-established research template in higher education. We tell our students that we will pretty much be making up the genre as we go along. In fact, most of what we've learned about SPN writing has come from our work with students. We quote the Talmud here: "Much have I learned from my teachers, even more from my colleagues, but from my students, most of all" (Ta'anit 7a).

Although it is true that we can learn a great deal in class from reading published personal essays, autobiographies, memoirs, and other like-minded documents, SPN writing nevertheless begins with a nagging need on the writer's part to tell some kind of truth. And the best way to tell a truth is to tell a story. A story is always profoundly personal and unique to some degree, never replicated in exactly the same form by anyone else. Your truth may be very different from mine, and vice versa. But if I can hear your truth within the context of your own personal story, I might be better able to find its corollary in my own story.

Anyone who has ever managed a childhood, intimate relationship, education, job, or parenthood can tell a story. Anyone who has ever been a sibling, teacher, friend, or boss can tell a story. Anyone who has ever suffered or rejoiced can tell a story. Anyone who has ever been betrayed by someone, or has been the betrayer, can tell a story. Anyone who has strong (or even weak) political, moral, or religious convictions can tell a story. Anyone who has ever felt marginalized, alienated, discriminated against, judged, or bullied can tell a story. All of this is simply to say that anyone can narrate a story by virtue of having lived a normal life. And, if you can tell a story that is honest, trustworthy, revealing, and close to the core of your own experience, then you can most certainly write one.

Why is it, for example, that many of us feel so comfortable when telling our stories in an email, in a text message, on a Facebook page, or in a blog? The writing flows easily. We are not even thinking consciously about our style or format. We are simply talking in print, telling tall and small tales, composing our lives in a communication medium that allows us to be ourselves. We narrate in these different media formats in order to record the ups and downs of our existence; in order to scream, or to whisper—I am alive, and I matter, and my stories matter, and you matter, too. It's easy and it's fun. Our casual musings in the social media carry the promise of creating an intimate tie that binds author and reader, sender and receiver, if only for the moment. Why can't academic writing do the same thing without compromising its fundamental, intellectual values?

In our opinion, no writing is ever wasted. All of it is practice, the rehearsal for the more formal production of composing acceptable scholarship. What we can put into a relaxed email or informal blog can also be put into a fresh, academic prose style. For example, we have used several of our old emails, phone texts, and Facebook updates to jump-start our thinking about a complex issue that we want to explore in depth in more formal manuscripts. We often revisit our written responses to students' manuscripts over the years that we save in a file. Somewhere in the tens of thousands of words we have written to our students lies the inspiration we need to jump-start our thinking about our own manuscripts.

For example, this chapter is the direct outgrowth of the four most common concerns that our students have when first introduced to SPN writing. Many of our students will email us to make sure we are aware of their fears. We make it a point to save all our emailed responses to students in a file we call "Inspirations from the Marginalized." This file actually freed us up in this chapter to respond directly to students' fears more empathically, and to use a less stilted, academic language— a language that students at every level of higher education can understand, because this is the way they write. This file helped us to respond with both our heads and hearts and to write more clearly and more pungently…or at least we hope so. It forced us to be more honest, less pretentious, and—most of all—more understanding of the difficulties that all of us face whenever we sit in front of a blank computer monitor and try to summon up the nerve to type words that mean something.

Having said all of that, however, we also need to be mindful of the no-nonsense fact that all writing must start with the motivation and the self-discipline to actually begin to write. After you finish telling yourself again and again that you are smart and brave enough to write an SPN, and that there is, indeed, material in your life that can edify or instruct others, then you need to begin the task by actually sitting in a chair to write. Goethe put it this way: "Whatever you can do. Or dream you can do. Begin it. Boldness has genius, power, and magic in it. Begin it now. Now. Now. Now." Robert often says that in writing, the most important part of the human body is not the head, hand, or heart; it is the butt. Before any writing can get done, each of us must put our butt in a chair and get started. He reiterates these words over and over again—too frequently in the estimation of some students. Still, most students need to hear them: "*Butt* to chair, and no *buts* about it!"

The Fourth Concern: What If I Don't Want to Open "Pandora's Box" When I'm Doing Such Personal Writing? How Can I Avoid "Bleeding" All Over the Page?

Last week, during our first SPN class of the semester, we asked our students to talk about one major fear they had about embarking on writing their manuscripts. The most common response went something like this: "I don't want to bleed my personal issues all over the page. I'm really afraid that once I open Pandora's box, I will lose control of my censoring mechanism. I don't want to subject my readers to the pain of my pathetic, little broken life. This feels self-indulgent, self-pitying, and even mortifying. Everyone's got ordeals to contend with; why do they want to read about mine? Furthermore, why would I want to open old wounds and subject myself to so many painful memories? Doesn't memory repression sometimes work for the good? Doesn't it protect us from having to undergo constant soulache, heartache, and headache?"

These fears are reasonable. Who wants to write about unpleasant "downers"? Who wants to bring to the surface what has been repressed for such a long time? Who wants to spend time dwelling on the past? In the end, doesn't excessive bleeding lead to death—both literally and figuratively? What can possibly be uplifting about one writer's personal struggles? Isn't the major purpose of SPN writing to educate, explicate, and exemplify? How can pain and suffering inspire anyone? How on earth can "letting it all hang out on the printed page" be a work of serious scholarship? Shouldn't I be accentuating the positive rather than dwelling on the negative?

Even in our own SPN writing, there are times when we wonder if we should reveal as much as we appear to be doing. We also wonder why it's necessary for us to relive all the old hurts and failures. Robert frequently quotes Nietzsche on the dangers of fixating on the suffering self: "If you stare into the abyss long enough, pretty soon the abyss stares back at you...and then you have to decide whether or not to jump." After all, who wants to spend time staring endlessly into our own hellish abysses while we write?

We fully understand that self-disclosure can be threatening, not just to the self-disclosers but also to many readers and listeners. But painful self-disclosures need not be so negative and hopeless. Remember Joseph Campbell's counter-advice to Nietzsche's staring into the abyss: "As you go the way of life, you will see a chasm. Jump. It is not as wide as you think." Or as Audre Lorde said: "Pain is important: how we evade it, how we succumb to it, how we deal with it, how we transcend it." Staring into one's abyss can produce insight, faith, hope, resilience, even joy.

Or it can produce their opposites. Most likely, though, it produces more than a little of both.

One of our devout Christian students put Lorde's aphorism in perspective for some of us. He said: "In my religion, there can be no resurrection without the crucifixion. There can be no salvation without the suffering. There can be no wisdom without the ignorance. Actually I am proud of writing about my mistakes, because it gives me a chance to see what I've learned from them." To which we say, yes, but it all depends on your perspective. And, as we remarked earlier, one of the major purposes of the SPN writer is to present an alternative perspective on the world, and then to suggest the possible, generalizable implications of that perspective for the rest of us on how to live a life of meaning and purpose.

Also, who says that SPN writing has to concentrate exclusively on the downsides of a writer's life? A life genuinely lived, and fully experienced, includes both pleasure and pain, happiness and sadness, insight and oversight, opportunity and risk, and wins and losses. Balance is the key. We have supervised, advised, and read hundreds of SPN manuscripts. Each and every one of them is unique in its self-revelations. Some writers live their lives red-hot, some live them ice-cold, and some live them lukewarm. Some focus on the hard-won wisdom they discover in life's trials and tribulations; some focus on the failure in order to activate the success; and some focus on the challenges that each and every one of us must face, and overcome, in order to become a fully authentic human being. Whatever their different foci, however, what all our SPN writers have in common is their willingness to search for, and eventually uncover, the nugget of gold that lies hidden in the litter of their lives.

And so we remind our students that in classical Greek mythology, Pandora, the first woman on earth, did indeed accidentally release all the world's ills from her box (actually a jar). But both she and Zeus were confident that eventually what lay at the bottom of the jar—the virtues of hope (Elpis), faith, and possibility—would also find their way into the world. Thus, Pandora's box was not meant simply to be a curse on humankind; rather, it was meant to signify the hope and optimism that makes our lives both bearable and inspirational. While it is true that self-exploration in writing can sometimes be difficult, we believe, with Lourde, that the payoff is well worth it. Understanding and learning from our pain is one of the best ways to achieve wisdom, and even transcendence. All of us have the choice to open Pandora's box. In SPN writing, we have the choice to write about all the ills that emanate from that box. Or we can choose to emphasize the insights that we have gained from looking deeply and honestly into our lives.

An Introduction to Ten General Guidelines for Writing SPNs

In this section of our chapter, we will present ten introductory guidelines for writing an SPN. These will be mostly explanatory, because we intend to be more practical in the next chapter regarding specific tips and tools for SPN writing. Please keep in mind that these guidelines are still evolving because, relatively speaking, SPN writing is in its infancy as a research methodology. At this particular point in its evolution, SPN is the unfinished product of Robert's teaching a course on personal narrative writing; his supervision of scores of publications, dissertations, and theses; and his having countless discussions with authors about scholarly writing. Both he and Sydnee have also read widely on the topic of writing, and this background reading has enriched their thinking over the years about how to construct an SPN with integrity and verve. Finally, we ourselves have begun to write books and articles in this genre, including the volume you are reading at the present time. (Some of these general guidelines appeared in Robert J. Nash's [2004] *Liberating Scholarly Writing: The Power of Personal Narrative.* He has reconfigured and re-interpreted them in what follows.)

Guideline 1: Know the Importance of Your Central Questions, Organizing Themes, and Engaging Hooks

Many students have come to us over the years with this complaint: "I can't get started on my SPN. I want to, but I'm like a boat without a rudder. I'm stuck, and going around in circles." What we hear in the subtext is the sound of a would-be writer without an identifiable point to make; not exactly sure of what story to tell, and why, and from what perspective; and bereft of any organizing theory or concept—a steering mechanism, if you will.

It is important to remember that all points of view start with *questions.* No questions, no positions; no questions, no stories; no questions, no SPN manuscript; no questions, no answers, no matter how tentative. *Themes* stake out the territory you will cover in your SPN. Will you be advancing a special agenda? Will you be constructing an extended argument on behalf of a particular perspective: an ideology, a philosophy of social justice, a way of living, a cause, an ethic, a religion or spirituality?

A literary *hook* is a special device—a lure—that will draw your readers into your narrative and keep them there. A theme is a conceptual guide that keeps your reader focused on the overall point of your narrative. You design a hook, however, to capture your reader's attention. For example, in rock music a hook is a repetitive instrumental passage, a refrain, that gives it immediate appeal and makes it easy to remember. Half a century ago, Elvis Presley's and the Beatles' songs all had memorable "hooks." More recently, Michael Jackson, Whitney Houston, Lady Gaga, and The Black Eyed Peas have been wonderful "hooksters" in their music. In an SPN, provocative themes can hook. So, too, can skillfully told stories. Memorable characters and a narrative arc that keep readers thoroughly absorbed can hook. A critical incident around which to build a story can hook. Authentic dialogue can hook. Sometimes a simple and clear writing style can hook. Other times it might take a more elegant writing style. It all depends on your SPN's goals.

Anyway, a good, clear statement of what you believe at the outset both focuses and hooks. William Zinsser says that the two most important sentences in any piece of writing are the first and the last. We agree. The first sentence entices the reader to spend some time with you. It also gives you, the writer, at least a tentative direction in which you can travel. The last sentence means that you have stayed the course and completed the journey. You are there at your endpoint, and with luck, the reader has arrived with you. The last sentence is your final opportunity to convince your reader, and yourself, that the trip has been worthwhile. For an author, the last impression, not the first impression, is the most enduring impression left on a reader. But, you can't hook unless you focus.

Guideline 2: Move from the Particular to the General, from the Me to the We, and from the Theory to the Practice, and Back Again— as Often as Possible

Have you found the most salient mix of particularity and generality, concreteness and abstractness, practice and theory? Try to avoid emphasizing only *whats* as a way to engage readers. This is the way that too many empirically grounded researchers and scientists tend to write. Concrete examples and details can be fascinating, to be sure. But in an SPN, every *what* needs a *why*. Every fact needs a hypothesis. Every phenomenon needs a purpose. Most data need insights. Actions need reflection. And they all need honest, poignant personal stories to deliver them cogently. It is the stories that draw in the reader and humanize the writer. This is why first-person, self-help books, memoirs, and novels always outsell, by a huge percentage, third-person, nonfiction books written by discipline-based experts who are doing empirically based, socio-scientific "studies." Stories sell. They are the goldmines of the publishing industry. And yes, even the hard-core empirical researchers have stories to tell that we believe can only deepen and enrich their "objective" data collections and analyses.

By the same token, however, avoid emphasizing only *whys* in your writing. This is the way that too many philosophers and intellectual pundits tend to write. As a result, some of their writings get lost in the academic stratosphere, as do their readers. Generalizations, abstractions, and theories need particulars, concretes, and details to support and exemplify them. Professors of writing often tell their students not to write about humanity; instead, write about one human being. We would also add this suggestion: Write first about your own humanity (or lack of it), and then if you're lucky, you might have something important to say about the humanity of others.

Or as Juvenal, a 1st-century A.D. Roman poet, once said: "Nothing human is alien to me." How so? We strongly believe that there is not a single human action, judgment, or feeling that all human beings throughout the course of history haven't experienced (or at least imagined) in their own unique ways. And so at the core, we are all more alike than unalike. In fact, each of us, regardless of race, religious or political creed, age, sexual orientation, social class, gender, and so forth, is marginalized in some way. Who among us has not experienced at least a moment or two living on the margins of what society deems conventional and acceptable? The truth is that each of us lives our life in the existential particulars, and it is here that we are able to connect with marginalized and non-marginalized people everywhere.

What is the universal appeal in your writing? SPN writing is about thinking globally but writing locally. It's writing that begins from the inside out rather than from the outside in. However, it eventually needs to work its way to the outside. If it doesn't, then it becomes merely self-serving: confessional and apologetic, perhaps a bit solipsistic. But when SPN writing is both local and global, it invites the reader to make comparisons and draw contrasts. The key is to practice moving from the provincial to the cosmopolitan, and back again, in your writing. Sometimes these moves can be subtle, sometimes obvious. But as a writer of SPNs you must always be on the move between two destinations—the particular and the general— if you are to speak with special resonance to your reader.

Notwithstanding the value of moving back and forth between particulars and universals that we've talked about above, readers will still need something with a little more staying power to hold on to after they've read your story. Most of the time readers do not want to disappear into the moments and particulars of our, or their, lives. All of us at some time seek the comfort of the large idea. We want to live life big, not small. We seek universal meaning that transcends the insular. We live our lives in the years and decades as well as in the minutes, hours, and weeks. We need markers, reference points, and compasses to keep us on track. Thus, SPN writers will need to identify an occasional universalizable marker as they tell their stories.

Guideline 3: Try to Draw Larger-Life Implications from Your Personal Stories

This guideline is closely related to the previous one. Aim for larger-life implications whenever appropriate. While you will be telling some pretty revealing and provocative personal stories about your life that will hook the reader, don't just stop there. Use your personal story hooks as a pretext for exploring bigger educational, social, cultural, and political issues. Suggest deeper implications, not just for individuals but possibly for cultures, groups, corporations, even nations. This might sound grandiose. But, paradoxically, one of the reasons for going *inside* of yourself in an SPN is so that—at least some of the time—you can get your readers to go *outside* of themselves in order to see their external worlds in a different way.

Some marginalized SPN writers of a more political bent might take this opportunity to analyze and/or critique what they see as injustices, misconceptions, follies, and self-deceptions in the social world around them. Of course some readers might not agree with these critiques because they are based primarily on the story of the world that the critics prefer to tell. But in the interests of scholarly integrity, you will at times need to develop the broader, "real-world" (whose "real world"? you ought to be asking) implications of your personal stories. This might entail constructing a social critique whenever it is relevant. It might also entail developing a social action statement, a code of ethics, a political commentary, or an educational policy.

Guideline 4: Whether You Know It or Not, You Possess a Vast Store of Background Knowledge and Scholarship. Use It in Your Writing...Selectively

During the last few decades, personal narrative writing has found a home in such disciplines as multicultural studies, women's studies, religious studies, postmodern philosophy and literature, and certain types of composition and rhetoric studies. Many feminists, social justice activists, and postmodern authors feature fresh new types of me-search in order to emphasize the lived life of the writer-scholar as the major source of questions, perspectives, and methods. For oppressed people of color throughout the world, personal narrative scholarship has given them long-overdue permission to insert their own authentic voices into their writing.

During the past decade, so many of our own students of color have enthusiastically welcomed our invitation to write in a way that blends their stories, interpretations, theories, and universalizable themes. For these students, the personal element of scholarship is inseparable from the impersonal. As one of our graduate students put it:

> SPN writing has given me long-overdue permission to express my own voice in my own unique way. I have been encouraged to tell my stories as one way to express my truths. My master's thesis is the best writing I've ever done, because I arrived at what I think are defensible generalizations about race, oppression, and privilege through my personal narrative as well as through my background knowledge and scholarship. When I enter my doctoral program next year, I will be able to summon up the courage to insist that I include myself in all my writing. I will do this because I have a strong case to make, and story to tell, that no knowledge, scientific or otherwise, transcends individual or social perspectives.

Having written the above, however, we also believe strongly in citing the ideas/studies/theories of the research "experts" in SPN writing. We remind our students never to shrink from their own store of formal knowledge, or apologize for presenting the insights of thinkers who are smarter than they are, or who make their point better than they do. Both our undergraduate and graduate students already know a lot about several academic disciplines, either through formal training or through personal interest. Therefore, we encourage them not to be afraid of drawing generously from as many of these bodies of knowledge as they can whenever they tell their stories.

Here are the words we use to challenge our students to be proud of their hard-won background knowledge and scholarship: "Try to cross several disciplinary boundaries whenever you think these border-crossings will enrich or expand your story. What you know intellectually can only make your personal story stronger, because your intellect is integral to your personal story. What you don't know can only make your story weaker. Don't mind showing off your knowledge a bit, in just the right places, but never try to make your readers feel stupid. There's a happy medium between intellectually overwhelming and underwhelming the reader, and it lies in enticing the reader to keep on reading because some of your ideas may actually be useful.

"Try to use your background knowledge to challenge readers to keep up with you, or, maybe, to accumulate some new knowledge along the way. The academic disciplines, when relevant, give personal narrative writers a special credibility in the academy, as well they should. The disciplines have the potential to organize, deepen, and upgrade personal stories. They provide the conceptual cement for creating stories that are intellectually sound, cohesive, and lasting. One question to ask yourself regarding the academic disciplines when you write an SPN is this: Are you disseminating even a little bit of discipline-based knowledge in the story you are telling about yourself and others?

Guideline 5: Use Scholarly References Whenever Appropriate, but Studiously Avoid "Reference Overload"

Lace your SPN with appropriate allusions to cherished texts and quotations. Think of these as your signature scholarly references. Learn how to avoid using too many, or too few, of them. Alluding to too many sources means that you actually have very little to say on your own. Alluding to too few means that you have no background in what others have said about what you want to say on your own. The *on-target* scholarly reference provides a context, deepens your writing, extends its implications, grounds its insights, and, most of all, explicitly acknowledges the contributions of others to your thinking. No author is an island, ever. No author is above needing a little help from others every now and then.

To some extent, writing is about recirculating others' ideas within the framework of the personal narrative that only you are living and narrating. If you are truly honest with yourself, you know that, at most, you will be able to circulate and describe no more than one or two original ideas in all the writing that you will do for the rest of your life. Try to do this with creativity, style, insight, and verve; but also look to the wisdom of others *at strategic intervals* to update and revise your recurring thematic motifs.

The *off-target* scholarly reference, however, cheapens your writing because it is little more than spurious padding, a distraction from the larger argument of your narrative. Avoid the temptation to sprinkle your manuscript with gratuitous quotations from every expert under the sun in order to show off your brilliance. Work instead to achieve the best balance between expressing your own ideas and referring to others for support, clarification, and improvement. Too much academic writing is nothing more than an excuse to drop names for the sole purpose of showing off one's scholarly pedigree. This is always a bore. If you really want to know the truth, most of your readers (yes, including even some of your professors) will take only a quick glance—if that—at the lit reviews, the endless research studies, the footnotes and endnotes, the longer-than-necessary bibliographies, and the show-off, sometimes irrelevant, quotations. If we are being honest with ourselves, we know that reference overload serves mainly to "legitimize" a piece of writing that deep down we think is too weak to stand on its own.

Guideline 6: Always Try to Tell a Good Story

David McCullough (2003), the Pulitzer Prize-winning historian, says: "There isn't anything in this world that isn't inherently interesting—if only someone will explain it to you in English, if only someone will frame it in a story." An SPN is most worth reading when it engages, or regales, or persuades, or inspires, or teaches, or pleases. Good stories told in simple English can achieve all of these goals. At the very least, your writing needs to make a powerful claim on your readers' distracted and busy minds to pay attention for even an hour or two. So tell them a story; better still, tell them several stories. The results are guaranteed.

Your story needs to have a plot, colorful characters, suspense, a climax, a denouement, and some significant lessons to be learned. While writing, you need to remind yourself constantly that as interesting as you think your life is, you have to work very hard to make it interesting to others. The best way to do this is to tell a story with some suspense and conflict to it. Try whenever possible to add narrative tension. Keep the reader guessing for a while. You don't need to give everything away in the first few pages or even in the first few chapters.

As teachers, we are convinced that no hook hooks the reader (and student) as powerfully as a story—or better still, a series of stories. This might be because some socio-biologists think the narrative sense is hard-wired into our brains. If this is true, then we are hard-wired to make meaning of our lives by imposing stories on our worlds. The etymology of the word "narrative" is revealing. It refers to the ancient Sanskrit "*gna*," which means "to know"; it also refers to the Latin "*narro*," which means to tell. From a socio-biological perspective, telling stories is one of the ways we have survived the test of human time. It is through our stories (religious, political, nationalistic, and so on) that we make sense of our lives, because they give us a meaning to live for. It is also through our common stories that we create families, tribes, and other homogeneous groups of belonging that bind us together in loyalty against those we consider the "other." The more allies we create, the less we have to fear from our perceived "enemies."

Thus, narratives are instruments that help us to know about ourselves and others and to solve problems; they are also tools for us to tell others about our experiences. The reason why these instruments are part of our brain's structure is probably because they have conferred survival benefits on human beings since the beginning of human time. The use of stories as tools has allowed us to become problem solvers, communicators, and survivors. Stories inspire. They also motivate, captivate, and, in many cases, activate us.

Guideline 7: Show Some Passion, but Be Sure Your Passion Is "Cool"—Not "Red Hot"—and Humble

Etymologically, the word "passion" means both pleasure and pain, agony and ecstasy, and cool and hot. As a social justice advocate, Sydnee deals with the hottest of hot topics in a cool manner. She stands for something. At times she even fights for something, but not too aggressively, because she knows that many of her readers will not be aggressive personalities. They will tune her out and turn off. So, as SPN educators, we aim for a cool or even warm passion rather than a boiling-hot passion. The latter ends up burning the reader.

Try to take a position on something with strong conviction and with palpable affect in your language. Allow your authorial voice to be clear, distinct, and strong. Resist the conventional academic temptation to be "objective": stoical, qualified, subdued, and distant. It's okay, even desirable, to try to be detached or dispassionate at times, but it's also okay to be fully engaged and excitable—but without being full of rage, self-righteousness, and hostile accusation. It's even okay to be ironic and wistful. Sydnee, one of the co-authors of this book, is a highly effective social justice advocate because she expresses her ideals in a cool, ironic, yet unmistakably committed tone. She is always humble, even when conveying her strongest social justice convictions to others.

Life, as every writer knows, is incongruous, complex, and paradoxical. It can bore us, soothe us, upset us, and piss us off, sometimes all at once. Try always, therefore, to be honest. Say what you mean, and believe what you say. But make it a point to leave room for the *vice versa* that you can always utter after every story that you tell, and every truth that you proclaim, and every sentence that you write. The *vice versa* will keep you humble and down to earth. And it will sustain your reader's interest in what you have to say, because you won't sound like a know-it-all expert.

Here is the Pulitzer Prize-winner Annie Dillard (1990), one of our favorite writers on writing, regarding the need for passion in writing.

> One of the few things I know about writing is this: spend it all, shoot it, play it, lose it, all, right away, every time. Do not hoard what seems good for a later place; give it, give it all, give it now....The impulse to keep to yourself what you have learned is not only shameful, it is destructive. Anything you do not give freely and abundantly and passionately becomes lost to you. You open your safe and find ashes.

Guideline 8: The Best Way to Get Readers to Consider Your Perspective Is to Tell Your Story in an Open-Ended Way

Closely related to Guidelines 6 and 7, Guideline 8 urges you to narrate your story in such a way that it might help your reader to see the world a little differently—not to accept your view of the world, but to accept the fact that others do, indeed, see the world differently from your reader, and this is good. Don't be too interested in securing any kind of agreement or disagreement on your reader's part. Aim instead for a kind of tentative "maybe you've got something there." An even more desirable response on your reader's part might be one that says, "I'd like to read a little more, think a little more, talk a little more, before I can really understand where you're coming from."

Of course, it would be delightful if somebody were to say that the wisdom in your narrative is so compelling that you have pushed your reader to go way beyond the usual taken-for-granteds. The greatest ego-boost, however, would be to hear somebody say something like this: "Your work has been truly transformative! You have changed my life!" But you can't go wrong if you expect nothing more than this from your reader: "You caused me to think a little more deeply. I don't necessarily agree with you, but you captured my interest. Even though you and I are poles apart, I think that I understand your take on the world and on your personal issues. Thank you for sharing."

Oh, that we might all write in the non-possessive spirit of the *Tao Te Ching*. Lao Tzu says: "When you wish to seize something, you must momentarily give it up. This is called 'subtle insight.' The soft and the weak in you will always conquer the hard and stubborn in you; and in others as well" (*Tao Te Ching*, Verse 80, Ma-Wang-Tui Manuscripts).

Write softly and subtly. Be willing to surrender your truth to a better truth, if only for the moment, or maybe even for a longer while. Wisdom begins in all that is gentle and generous in you. In order to convince others of your truth, you need first to overcome your writer's hard and stubborn ego to declare *your truth* as *The Truth*. When and if you write softly and subtly, yet passionately and clearly, you might even change the world. Or in the ironic words of both Lao Tzu and the Buddha: You only get to keep what you are willing to give away. On the other hand, letting go of your story enters the mainstream and, as a result, has the potential of changing the mainstream. Think, for example, of catching a fish and then releasing it. The release feels better than the catch, both for you and the fish, because now each of you has a story to share. It is when writers are most generous with their readers that they end up getting the most satisfying returns.

Guideline 9: Remember That Writing Is Both a Craft and an Art. One without the Other Is Incomplete

Know well what a turnoff a sloppily prepared, carelessly edited manuscript can be, even if the ideas are dazzling. Often, editors of scholarly journals and publishing houses will not even send out slovenly manuscripts for external review—either in hardcopy or via email attachments. Authors end up getting a terse but polite email, or form letter, telling them that their manuscript does not fit the needs of the particular publication or publishing house. More than worrying about getting published, though, do not allow your personal narrative writing to be an excuse for sloppiness. Let your readers know that you take your genre seriously enough to construct it meticulously.

Writing is both a craft and an art. The *craft* of writing calls for grit and determination. It is the initial struggle to get something on paper. It's the down-and-dirty work of trying to translate your half-baked ideas into delectable sentences and paragraphs. It's looking for a way to organize a welter of material into a smoothly flowing, coherent, and engaging narrative. We do not know any writers who feel that every time they sit to write, it is like taking perfect dictation from some Divine Power. Few students we have known are content to write an unrevised manuscript. Actually, for most authors, putting that first draft together is a lot more like having root canal surgery without Novocain than hearing a Divine Power's edit-proof words.

Moreover, please know that you will have at your disposal an infinite number of avoidance strategies when you first sit down to write an SPN. These range from giving in to those sudden yearnings for caffeine and junk food; to working out; to catching up on the latest stock market report; to feeding pets, children, and partners; to reading and sending "very important" emails or checking a Facebook page; to texting that albeit pithy but urgent message; to spending inordinate amounts of time wandering aimlessly about on Google; to playing, and re-playing, that addictive video game; to paying a long-overdue bill; to checking the status of yesterday's laundry still sitting in the washer; to visiting amazon.com in order to locate the one book that will finally get you started on the SPN manuscript you are so assiduously avoiding. All of these diversions go by the name of "procrastination," which means "putting off to the morrow" what you ought to be doing today. All the writers we know have perfected the practice of procrastination.

But sooner or later, if you are serious, you will have completed what Anne Lamott crudely but accurately calls your "shitty first draft." Now you can look forward to engaging in the *art* of writing, which necessarily complements the *craft* of writing. This is the continual polishing and tweaking that you must learn to love to give to your manuscripts. Polish and tweak your "shitty first draft" frequently. Rewrite, revise, resist, and recover. Make music out of your noise. Create cosmos out of your chaos. Clean up what one of our students calls that "first-draft, total brain-dump mess." Declare yourself, once and for always, an unashamed, unabashed artist-tweaker. The *craft* of writing can be sheer drudgery. In Red Barber's words, it is sitting down, cutting open a vein, and bleeding. The *art* of writing can be sheer joy. In our words, it is sitting down and preening.

Guideline 10: Keep Your Language Simple, Clear, and to the Point

Your ideas may not always be scientifically defensible, or even erudite. But if you can keep your language somewhat simple—fresh, honest, personal, and down-to-earth—then it could get you closer to your goal of being eloquent in your writing. Powerful, fluid, graceful, and persuasive language can cover a lot of mistakes. These four adjectives, by the way, cover the first meaning of the word "eloquent" in Webster's New World College Dictionary. We leave it to you to decide how much professional writing you've read in your lifetime reflects these four adjectives.

Margaret Atwood (2002) has said that writers need to answer these three questions before they start any manuscript: "Who are you writing for? Why do you do it? Where does it come from?" According to Atwood, attending to these simple questions will keep your language within reach of all your readers, not just a select few. She goes on to say: "Writing has to do with darkness, and a desire, or perhaps a compulsion, to enter it, and with luck, to illuminate it, and to bring something back out to the light." There is nothing like using simple, clear, direct language as a way to illuminate your own darkness, as well as the darkness of your readers. Atwood, in a sense, is talking about how to frame an SPN. *Framing* a manuscript is every writer's inescapable prerequisite for achieving even minimal direction, focus, organization, and clarity in a book, dissertation, thesis, or essay.

In addition to doing some very careful framing (and this could take some time), work frequently on improving the clarity of your writing. Create a signature writing style that virtually shouts to your reader: clarity, clarity, clarity! Strunk and White (2000) talk about the importance of clarity in this way:

> Muddiness is not merely a disturber of prose; it is also a destroyer of life, of hope: death on the highway caused by a badly worded road sign, heartbreak among lovers caused by a misplaced phrase in a well-intentioned letter, anguish of a traveler expecting to be met at a railroad station and not being met because of a slipshod telegram. Think of the tragedies that are rooted in ambiguity and be clear.

In the interest of clarity, try to rid yourself of your infernal writing "tics." Everyone has them. Your sentences might be too long. You might overuse adverbs or adjectives or passive voice. You might be tempted to show off your amazing vocabulary. But style and flash, no matter how brilliant, can frequently get in the way of your substance.

We are definitely not saying that clear writing means you must pretend to have the vocabulary of a 12-year-old. Although simple language is sometimes the best way to explain the most complex ideas, we do not believe that you have to write down to your readers. Writing down to anyone, no matter what their age, always insults them. Neither are we saying that you can never draw on the specialized language of your discipline to buttress your ideas. Too many "experts" on "creative writing" make it sound as though, if you do not write like Ernest Hemingway, or Dr. Seuss, then you are writing incorrectly, or worse, writing like an "elitist."

We refuse to set up a false dichotomy: simple = always good; complex = always bad. We have found that good writing can be both difficult and clear at the same time, or at different times, even in the same paragraph. Some ideas are just too complicated to grasp in a sentence or two with no word over two syllables, or in a chapter that doesn't require the reader to consult a dictionary at least once or twice. We in the academy need to understand the distinction between technical jargon and an extensive vocabulary.

Good writing means finding the delicate balance that exists between big and small words, informality and formality, long and short sentences, simplicity and complexity, elegance and clarity. A good rule of thumb in writing is this: Does the cogency of your idea drive your use of language, or is it the opposite? If it's only the latter, then you've got things backward. Try to achieve a nice complementarity of style and substance in your use of language. This is the work of a lifetime, of course, but it's nevertheless work well worth doing.

Robert's Personal Attempt to Apply the SPN Guidelines

Much of what I teach as an interdisciplinary scholar and applied philosopher has to do with helping my students to create meaning in their lives (Nash & Murray, 2010). I sometimes think of myself as a "meaning-making mentor." I have written extensively on helping college students to find meaning and purpose. I even teach an undergraduate/graduate course called "Philosophy of Meaning-Making for Educators." And so what follows is a reflective SPN piece on who I am, and what I do, as a "meaning-making mentor." I have tried to include in my essay some of the material that has come up in this chapter in the Guidelines. (Some of what follows appeared in another form in Nash & Murray, 2010.)

Hey Professor....So What Is the Meaning of It All?

Robert J. Nash

Students, no matter how marginalized, disenfranchised, or underrepresented, frequently come to me seeking the larger meaning of their lives. I look at them with bewilderment and helplessness, but more so with empathy and solidarity. I don't even know the meaning of *my* life, except that I was born, I live, love, loathe, and learn, and I will die. I often wonder if there is anything more to my life, or to theirs, than this "eternal recurrence," the Hindu view that time repeats itself cyclically *ad infinitum*. Approximately 100 billion human beings, since the beginning of human time, have lived this repetitive cycle. Nobody escapes it. Few are remembered for long. Will I be remembered even years after my death, let alone decades or centuries? Or will I merely melt into one enormous statistic as billions of others have before me?

An old philosophy professor of mine, steeped in Nietzsche, Schopenhauer, Buddhism, and Hinduism, used to make the following comments over and over again, whenever we were arrogant enough to think we'd come up with a sensational new insight about the meaning of life: "Such as it always was. Such as it always is. And such as it always will be. So what? Now what?" We did not know then that he was restating Schopenhauer: "The true philosophy of history lies in perceiving that, in all the endless changes and motley complexity of events, it is only the self-same unchangeable being which is before us."

Nevertheless, my professor's familiar riposte always brought us up short. Even though it pissed us off, it also forced us to look deeper within ourselves to accept our responsibility to make meaning of our lives, no matter how repetitive and predictable life can be. Some of these 100 billion people, of course, lived life better, some lived it worse. Some died living, some lived dying. Some lived for the next life, some lived for the now. Some lived without a concern for meaning, some found it impossible to live without meaning. The meaning of life's ceaseless ebb and flow is not for me to assert for my students, but only mine to declare for myself. And so I look back at them in response to their question, and ask in my teacherly way: "You tell me. What *does* your life mean? What do you *want* it to mean?"

And this is what they say. *Older adolescents* respond along these lines: "Only I can live my life for myself. Nobody else can tell me who I am and what I must live for. From this moment on, I'm the one who has to make sense of my life. And I've got almost forever to do it, because I'm young and healthy, and I feel immortal. Even though this independence is scary, I'm looking forward to being on my own, without anyone telling me what to do." Seneca's *Praebere se fato* ("choose yourself") is the imperative of this stage of meaning-making.

Young adults (the "quarterlifers") offer this account of their meaning-making: "I have a responsibility to become what I am, because someday I must die. I now understand that my life is not forever. But what is it I can do that is worthwhile? Who should I love? When should I make lifelong commitments? What should I believe? Others are depending on me to fulfill my promise as an adult. Just what are my duties to myself and my duties to others, though, and what should I do when these are in conflict? Is it really possible for me to live a life of personal integrity when every choice I make stands to harm or to help others?" All of these questions can be summed up in the quarterlifers' dominant unspoken question: *Quid hoc vita vult?* ("What does this life mean?").

Middle adults are still in the process of constructing meaning, but now it takes on a sharper, existential edge. It's more tuned in to the limitations of finite existence and bounded choice-making, as well as to what the Greeks called *fortuna* ("chance" or "luck"). No longer is the middle adult a superman or superwoman. Happiness, at best, is a fleeting thing, and the years are as passing seasons. During this cycle of making meaning, middle adults ask: "Is there any enduring meaning in my life? I've done everything I'm supposed to do. I'm in a satisfying relationship, I've worked hard, and I've raised wonderful children. To the outside world, I'm an unmitigated success. But why is it that inside I feel so unsettled, so restless? I've still got half my life to live, if I'm lucky. *Ubi vadeo ab hic?* ("Where do I go from here?").

Older adults tend to express some version of Goethe's assertion, "Age takes hold of us by surprise." Often, when I listen to older adults talk about the meaning of their lives, I am reminded of a Woody Allen line: "I'm not afraid of death. I just don't want to be there when it happens." Older adults' more sober reflections, however, often take this tack: "Life occurred almost when I wasn't looking, and, lo and behold, I'm old. Now what? I've still got so much left to do, but I'm realizing my time is running out. How can I avoid slipping into despair? Do people still love and respect me even though I am not as active a risk-taker as I used to be? What in the world do I have in common with people who are younger, more creative, and vital than I am, including my own children? Do I look too eccentric and settled to them, completely out of touch? What could I possibly give to them?" A comment that older adults sometimes make, each in their own way, is this: *Vitam perdidi, operose nihil agendo?* "Have I wasted my life busily doing nothing?"

I am one of those older adults, and I am more and more becoming a creature of rituals and routines. In the words of Victor Hugo, I am trying to "recover the ground beneath my feet." But I don't want to become a "rock that is massive, haughty, and immobile" in my older age. Instead, I strive for *gelassenheit*, or "letting be." How often do I find myself delivering to students, and to other loved ones, these clichés: "Live and let live. Practice some generosity toward others, especially toward those whose choices, ideas, and lifestyles you dislike. Let go, and let be. Enjoy. In the end, it's all a matter of taste and temperament, anyway."

These bromides are nothing but the outward manifestation of my particular, generative cycle in the process of creating meaning. They are also the outgrowth of my understanding that, developmentally, we're all more alike than not, even though our individual stories are very different. Few of us want our stories "stolen" from us. We want to tell our stories in our own ways and have others tell theirs similarly.

As an educator, I believe that what binds us together is the universality of our questions, and the commonality of our psycho-biological needs. What separates us, though, are the unique, age- and cycle-related stories we fashion in order to deal with our particular cries for meaning. But this separation needn't resign us to a life of isolation and loneliness. And so, at the first class meeting of the semester, I often say to my students, whether they be adolescents, young, middle, or older adults: "Chances are I'm not going to change your mind about anything and vice versa, nor do I really want to. In my opinion, keeping company with you in order to change you is energy misspent. It might even be immoral. At the very least, it's damned presumptuous. Who the hell am I to know what's good for you?

"So let's make a pact with one another—a mutual non-imposition treaty, if you will. Let's assume that you and I are all about discovering and making meanings that will sustain us in the days and years ahead. Let's also agree that your meanings may not work for me and vice versa. Therefore, don't tread on me, and I won't tread on you. Don't foist your successful formula for finding the keys to your existence on me, and I'll promise to return the favor. Meanwhile, whenever it's necessary, let's agree to huddle together within the protective cocoon of our mutual humanity for the comfort and affirmation we need when things go dismally wrong or, for that matter, ecstatically right. You share your meanings with me, and I'll do the same with you. Beyond this, we cannot, indeed, dare not, go."

How I Teach for Meaning: The Short Version

No matter what subject I teach, I always try to evoke the personal stories of my students. The personal stories hold the key to the meaning of academic content for students. Without students' personal stories, subject matter withers and dies immediately after the exams. Worse, students themselves wither and die, little by little, each and every day they sit dazed and quizzical before us in our seminars and lecture halls. Many wonder why they just can't memorize the textbook or the lecture notes, and let it go at that, without having to suffer the 4-to-6-year ordeal of parking their bodies in an impersonal lecture hall, trying to stay awake and look interested.

We tell our stories to prove that we've lived, that we're still alive, and that we intend to live into some unknown future. Without our stories, our lives are without form or content. So too with subject matter. When all the technical trappings are removed, an academic discipline is really a particular group's storied view of the world, and the story changes often. Find the story of the subject matter, and you've located the core of the academic discipline. You've also brought it to life.

Sooner or later, we all must face the "real questions." In Sartre's language, each of us is "condemned to make meaning." There is no escape, no easy way out, no blessed exit from our responsibility to live the authentic life, and to create, and re-create, ourselves with every choice we make each and every day. I raise the meaning questions in my teaching whenever and wherever and every chance I get. I do this because what I have learned from my own meaning-making is that amidst those periods of our worst anguish, only faith and hope remain. And so I teach with hope. I live with faith. My intent is to help students to create stories of meaning that will sustain them through the hard times when they find themselves in Leo Tolstoy's "cold, dark, meaningless place." I am convinced that freedom is always there for the taking. We have the power to make meaning of our anguish as well as our joy. In fact, we can turn one into the other. Viktor Frankl made meaning amidst the daily horrors of the death camp at Auschwitz. Nietzsche said "He who has a 'why' to live can bear almost any 'how.'" My students need to know how to create their "whys" as much as they need to master the "hows."

And so, in the days, months, and years that I have left as a teacher, I resolve to hold my students close but always with arms wide open. I will continue to hear their individual stories based on their real-world differences, but I will also try to find overlaps between their stories and mine; and between their stories and their classmates' stories. I will do everything I can to prepare them well for the flight into a cosmopolitan world that will face each and every one of them. I will also encourage them to make the leap into making meaning on their own. This is what I have learned most of all as a result of teaching for nearly half a century.

6

The Four-Fold Path to Liberation in SPN Writing

Generation, Percolation, Translation, Publication

Before we move to a closer look at the practical SPN questions and tips in the next two chapters, we need first to explain every writer's unavoidable (sometimes agonizing), four phases of producing a manuscript—*generation, percolation, translation*, and *publication*. We always make it a point to remind our students that even when they are not actually *writing*, they are, indeed, *writing*! How so? Because as writers ourselves, we know that these four phases, whether experienced in or out of sequence, are the *sina qua non* for starting, sustaining, and finishing a completed manuscript!

We offer this short chapter to those SPN writers who, at some point in their writing, need a little comforting, encouragement, and inspiration, as well as some reality testing. All the authors we know, including ourselves, have a need to step back at times and put the progression (or regression) of our writing into realistic perspective. We need to know that even when we are not actually writing, in fact we *are* writing. Nothing we intuit, think, feel, or discuss about our writing project is ever wasted. Whenever we are involved in a writing project, it is important for us to remember that our writing will include at least four phases. Being aware of these inevitable writing phases will protect us from those writerly demons of guilt, depression, anxiety, and impatience.

Generation

Whether you are a professional author, faculty member, student, or simply an "author wannabe," you will need a preparation period to generate ideas about the manuscript you want to write. While it is true that sometimes we write *before* we think, and sometimes we write *while* we think, still, most of us will need at least some time to think *before* we write. We think of generation as *pre-search* (Nash & Bradley, 2011).

The *generation* period can take a short or a long time. It can be both unconscious and conscious. But it is always necessary. You will need time to "beget" or "procreate" (from the Latin *generatus*) a manuscript-offspring. Many would-be authors get hung up on the generation stage because they cannot seem to bring an idea or story into being. Either they do not trust their natural abilities to come up with anything worth writing about, or they freeze at the prospect of having to produce an extensive piece of writing.

We always tell our students that the generation period of writing is one of the most important stages for any author—either well-published or never-published. Without the sometimes endless and painful period of generation, you simply cannot produce a manuscript. During this generation process, please be patient with yourself. Sooner or later you will find something worth writing about.

Think about some event in your life that evokes a strong feeling from you. Is there an author, or public figure, who has inspired you in some way during the past few years? What is it you believe with all your heart? What do you yearn for more than anything at this time in your life? What have been some major disappointments and regrets in your life? When, and under what conditions, have you experienced the most success (and the most failures) in your schooling up to this point? If you had the political power to change anything locally, nationally, or internationally, what would it be? When you think of terms like "fairness," "discrimination," "marginalization," or "oppression," do any of these apply to your life or to the lives of people you love as partners, friends, or family members?

Most of our students think of this *generation* phase of writing as an *inspiration* phase. Sometimes it is. But we prefer to think of it also as a *perspiration* phase, because, truth to tell, the generation of ideas and topics is hard work. Sometimes you will sweat. But remember that sweat is good. Sweat is the body's way of cleansing and purifying itself; it regulates body temperature and releases toxins. For example, it cools off the marathon runner's body so that crossing the finish line at the 26.2-mile mark is possible. Similarly, without perspiration, the serious writer—who, after all, is a metaphorical marathoner—implodes ("hits the wall") during the generation period. So "sweat joyfully and productively," we always say to our students.

Percolation

Percolatus, in Latin, means "to strain or to filter." Thus, for a writer to percolate is similar to a coffee drinker waiting for the coffee beans to brew so that the coffee is fit to drink. No percolation, no satisfying cup of "java." If there is no percolation period for the author, then no ideas are able to bubble up and eventually permeate an SPN manuscript. What the author generates by way of topics, ideas, stories, and through-line themes never comes to pass, because the author has never filtered or strained them. They remain only "unbrewed theme beans," as it were. We think of percolation in SPN writing as *pre-search*, *me-search*, and *re-search*.

Percolation (when applied to writing, the term is used by the award-winning poet and writing teacher Bonnie Goldberg, but the interpretation is ours) is the creative pause that follows generation. Now that you have discovered the topic, themes, and ideas you will be writing about, you will need a sustained time to percolate. You can read. You can try out your ideas on others. During the percolation period, you can revisit your topic anytime and anywhere in order to rethink it, to clarify it further, and to build imaginary structures and frameworks to stage it, so to speak. Use this period to re-invigorate yourself. Take some notes from your background reading, and your online and/or library research; jot down some "nuggets" from your creative imaginings; and get into the excitement and adrenaline flow of creating something from scratch as you await the translation phase of producing an SPN manuscript. Goldberg (2002) says that the percolation period offers every writer the gift of "accepting, embracing, and developing" the gifts that are gestating within you. We say: "Give yourself the time to percolate before you translate."

Translation

The time will come, however, when you will need to translate the results of your generation and percolation phases into recorded or written words. The Latin root of the word "translation" is *translatus*, and it means to *transfer* ideas into action, to move from one form to another—or in the specific sense in which we are using the term, to translate what's in the head to actual print. This might be pen-and-paper journal writing. Or, perhaps, you will begin to do some more systematic, reflective thinking about a topic on your desktop computer, laptop, or MacBook. Maybe you will be ready to put together a rough outline or a detailed prospectus for your manuscript. Or, possibly, your particular way of structuring a scholarly paper is to do some free-form writing and see what comes out of your musings. We think of translation as a complex yet seamless combination of pre-search, me-search, research, and we-search being put into some type of print for the first time.

Some of our students begin to do serious writing by first blogging or posting an entry on Facebook that is a bit more thoughtful than usual. A number of our students start the translation process by writing a series of letters to people they like and respect—but, more important, people they can be vulnerable with—in order to get early feedback on a planned personal narrative manuscript. "Close friends" writers support groups are becoming more popular among our SPN students. It is within such groups that authorial risk-taking and literary self-exposure are welcome, and that the feedback is both constructive and productive. Above all, it is humane. Some students take a little time each day to free-write whatever comes into their heads on the topic they want to explore in a more formal writing project. In whatever ways our students enter the translation process, however, sooner or later the move is necessary. *Translation*—the transfer of ideas, information, musings, inspirations, daydreams, and nightdreams to a more concrete writing medium—is the inescapable precondition for *publication*. Or in the language of healing: Publication holds the promise of inner transformation.

Publication

Now the time has come to expose your writing to a public audience. To publish (in Latin, *publicare*) does not necessarily mean to produce a piece of writing for a larger readership via a periodical, journal, magazine, newspaper, book, or blog. Publishing a manuscript means that you have reached the finish line in authoring a scholarly paper, thesis, dissertation, or whatever else might be required for the successful completion of a course or a degree program. Publishing what you write means that you have managed "to go public" with the finished product of all your generation, percolation, and translation. Now the time has arrived for you to put your work "out there"—for a professor or committee to read, for example. It is the time for you to announce, proclaim, divulge, and promulgate your ideas in an open manner. There are risks to doing this, but there are also huge benefits.

The major risk, of course, is that somebody could reject your publication. Critique of an SPN can sting, because the writing is so personal, sometimes even raw. We have heard from our students that a failing or mediocre grade on an SPN paper leaves the worst feeling a fledgling author can ever experience. For an SPN writer to fail in someone else's judgment (whether a professor, agent, editor, or colleague), particularly if that someone is a respected expert on your topic, is to risk never writing again for fear of public rebuke or humiliation. In effect, for an authority figure to pronounce your SPN a failure means that someone has rejected outright the worth of your life stories and the hard-won insights you have gained from them. The authority figure has sent you a message that your life does not signify (or at least the way you write about your life fails to convey the significance of the message you intend to send to others). This can hurt…greatly.

But, on balance, for us as SPN authors and teachers, the benefits of going public with writing outweigh the risks. Our students tell us this every single day. Each in his or her own way echoes Gandhi's words: "Change occurs when deeply felt private experiences are given public legitimacy." Or, as Mary Pipher (2006) says: "When we write a good personal essay, we become aware that our wave of truth is part of the bigger ocean of truth" (p. 190). During those moments in their SPN writing, when our disenfranchised students feel free and proud enough to tell their truth in their own authentic ways, there is no educational experience that is as liberating.

Our students become, in the words of Gandhi, the change they want to see in the world. They move from disenfranchisement to enfranchisement, from underrepresentation to representation, from marginalization to transcendence. For most of our student-scholars, it is the first time they realize that they are as much the teachers as the taught; as much the truth-tellers as the truth-receivers. No longer must their stories exist on the margins. Now their identity epiphanies can have meaning for others. This is why we say that "publication" is "we-search" at its best. It is Liberation with a capital "L." The publication that matters the most is the writing that touches the lives of others in such a way as to unite, rather than to divide, its readers.

Applying the Four-Fold SPN Writing Path to Creating a Professional Life

What follows is an SPN reflection written by one of Robert's former doctoral students. Kyle Dodson, an African American man, believes that the framework of the "four-fold writing path" applies not just to the SPN writing process, but also to navigating a professional life-plan. In many ways the paths are similar. Whether it is writing or creating a professional life, each of us must pass through the cycles of generation, percolation, translation, and publication. Each of us must create our own life-story of liberation.

Kyle Dodson is the Director of Community Service and Civic Engagement programs at Champlain College in Burlington, Vermont. Before joining the Champlain College staff in August of 2008, he founded and spent 4 years as the Principal of the Lee Academy Pilot School in Dorchester, Massachusetts. He was a member of the inaugural cohort of the Boston Principal Fellows Program, a 1-year intensive program to train new leaders for the Boston Public Schools. Before becoming a principal, Kyle spent eight years as a Student Life Administrator at Saint Michael's College in Colchester, Vermont. Prior to his career in education, he was a vice president of mortgage-backed securities trading at PaineWebber, Inc. in New York City. He played 4 years of varsity basketball in college, including being elected captain his senior year. He holds a B.A. in History from Harvard, an M.B.A. in Finance from Columbia, and an Ed.D. from the University of Vermont in Educational Leadership and Policy Studies.

Finding My Leadership "Sweet Spot"

Generation

In this section, I will write briefly about my generation process to make sense of my life. How did I give birth to the self that I yearned to be? I start with this question: What does it mean to be a positive, contributing, African American male in the world, the United States, and, finally, Vermont? That was the question that ultimately led me to embark on the journey toward a doctorate in Educational Leadership in the Fall of 1996. At the time, it was not at all clear to me that I was being driven by this underlying quest to make sense of my own existence. Up to that point in my life, my identity as a smart, charismatic, athletic, and high-achieving individual seemed to be enough of a *raison d'être*.

At the time, I was working at Saint Michael's College (SMC) as an admissions counselor specializing in the recruitment of students of color. It was my entry-level job into the world of higher education, and although I liked the "people" part of the job, I knew that my time there was going to be short-lived. I hadn't yet fully figured out the "game" of academia, but I knew that the sort of responsibility, compensation, and respect that I aspired to would require me to acquire an additional educational credential. And that credential was a doctorate.

Speaking candidly, I knew very little about the process of earning a doctorate. I knew that it took a long time and that, in general, the more prestigious the school, the more clout the degree would hold. Since I was a history major as an undergraduate, that seemed like a logical place to start. And since I got my B.A. from Harvard, and it is a prestigious school, that was where I began. After only a few conversations about the rigor of admission into the Harvard doctoral program in History, combined with the rigors of the actual degree program itself, I was pretty certain that I didn't want to be part of that program or any other History doctoral program. I am not driven by a desire to do research. As an undergraduate I spent all the time I ever want to spend holed up in the stacks of the Widener Memorial

Library, and my intellectual interests are far too varied to develop the sort of narrow and intense focus that a program like Harvard's would require. In addition, my wife and I really like Vermont, and I wasn't terribly keen on relocating.

This exploration and subsequent realization sharply narrowed my options for earning my doctorate. There are only a few doctoral degree-granting institutions in Vermont, and, of these, the University of Vermont (UVM), a "public ivy," is clearly the most prestigious and competitive. Due to the fact that I was working in a college, it was a natural progression for me to land in the admissions office of the UVM Graduate School of Education. After a little bit of research, I learned that UVM had a doctoral program in Educational Leadership and Policy Studies. And after several conversations with folks who had completed the degree and/or folks who were familiar with it, I learned that it was a very flexible degree with a wide variety of potential applications. Pair that with the fact that one can pursue the degree part-time while continuing to work, and I was all set to plunge in.

The initial problem with going after a doctorate in Educational Leadership and Policy Studies was that I had no idea what sort of leadership I was interested in, nor what policies I wanted to study. In terms of the work I was doing at SMC, in addition to my admission office duties I had begun to get heavily involved in multicultural issues on campus and in the community. For all of the people who knew me before I came to Vermont, there was a certain irony in this turn of events. During high school, college, and business school, I didn't spend very much time worrying about identity—mine or anyone else's. As far as I was concerned I was very comfortable with and proud of my African American identity, and I didn't need to join affinity groups or be an activist to solidify that identity. (Over time I learned that my relationship to my Blackness was a little more complicated than I was willing to admit or confront at that time.)

So despite the fact that I didn't fancy myself a multiculturalist, nor did I have aspirations to become professionally involved in issues of diversity and inclusion, I found myself spending lots of time dealing with issues of race and community. And when one looks at the fact that Vermont is the Whitest state in the union, it isn't hard to see how an affable, articulate African American male who has spent time living in an urban context would find himself being looked to as some sort of "expert" on matters of race. Given my lack of internalized professional focus, the degree to which many folks in Vermont were projecting an identity of diversity expert onto me, coupled with the fact that issues of racial and social justice were really heating up on college campuses in the 1990s, it is easy to see how my early doctoral writings and readings veered toward the topic of race.

Percolation

During the percolation period in both my personal and professional lives, I began to think about what was really important to me by way of a vocation. I had started to identify the key questions and themes in my professional work during my generation cycle. It would be during this percolation period that I experienced the "creative pause" necessary to think deeply about social justice themes and challenges that would become a key part of my vocational life. Although I was already 30 years old when I began my doctoral program, and at an age where many adults have already arrived at the person they were meant to become, I feel like some of the most salient aspects of my racial identity fell into place over the time that it took me to complete a dissertation. It seems like a contradiction, but I learned the most about who I am as an African American male right here in Vermont, the Whitest state in the union. For me, that was made possible because of the emotional, intellectual, and spiritual space that Vermont provided to me.

Up until age 27, I lived in New Jersey, Boston, and New York City. All three are densely populated places with well-established Black communities. Those places always felt somewhat stifling to me in terms of racial identity. I felt hemmed in by expectations, stereotypes, and archetypes. It was the 1970s and 1980s, and there seem to have been at least three major sub-communities within the overall African American community. There was the working poor; the working-class Black community that was clustered in and around cities all over the country; and the middle class and upper middle class where the parents, and even grandparents, were college educated. Some even owned second homes in places like Martha's Vineyard. The first group was connected in actual physical and spiritual terms, living next to one another, and they moved in the same social and religious circles. The latter group was connected more by associations such as Jack and Jill of America and Black fraternal and sororal organizations such as Alpha Phi Alpha and Delta Sigma Theta.

And then there was a third, somewhat diffuse group into which my family fell. This group was composed of Black families, who like many White Americans, wanted to move out of the crowded, sometimes dirty, and increasingly crime-ridden streets of urban America into the green-lawned, white-picket-fenced serenity of the suburbs. But unlike the college-educated, middle-class group of Black folks, this amorphous middle group had no reference point, no real models of how to make this transition, and little cultural capital or social network to gird them against the resistance they met. These families were pioneers. They were blazing a new path. Many of these families were the first to integrate their neighborhoods, and they remained the only, or one of very few, Black families in their community. In terms of support network, these families certainly had the connections to family and friends back in the communities they left. But those connections couldn't provide much in the way of a road map for navigating the complicated social and political dynamics of the new community.

The portrait I just painted is incredibly crude and simplistic. But it is more or less what I see looking in my rear-view mirror. I do believe that it is a reasonably accurate, if not complete, account of some of the racial and social dynamics that were playing out within the Black community while I was growing up. This is the world that shaped me. My family moved out of the working-class Black community when I was 7 years old, and from that time in 1973 through 2003 when I moved to Dorchester, Massachusetts, I lived in predominantly White communities. That experience profoundly shaped me and how I see the world. I am an extremely extroverted and social person. Some of my African American peers who had a similar upbringing moved through the mainstream White community in a superficial manner, but their hearts stayed in the Black community, and they sought out those connections and nurtured them.

I, on the other hand, am the sort of person who needs to connect with the people who are in my direct experience, whether that is in Nicaragua; Holland; the French Alps; Kingston, Jamaica; New York City; Dorchester, Massachusetts; or Burlington, Vermont (a few of the places that I have lived in or spent some time). I love my Black heritage, my family, and our history. But I also feel like a citizen of the world, and I have always yearned for a cosmopolite identity that could be this *and* that, rather than this *or* that.

This brings me back to the notion of Vermont as a place where I felt more free to explore the many dimensions of who I am. Growing up in the New York metropolitan region, I felt like the social and political categories that defined Blackness were too prescribed and didn't allow much freedom. But here in Vermont there are so few Black people that I felt like I could go deep inside to understand myself and then try to construct something unique and authentic out of what I discovered.

I used my doctoral work as an opportunity to do this self-exploration in a structured way. My early writings were all about me and trying to understand my journey out of Newark, New Jersey, through the mostly white suburb of West Orange, New Jersey, on to Harvard and Columbia (where I earned an MBA), into New York City and a job in a Wall Street firm, and ultimately to the Green Mountain state and a job in higher education. At the time I thought that perhaps I would discover some insights and understandings that might be put into some sort of framework that could help other college students with their own identity development whether that involved race, gender, sexual orientation or other dimensions of one's personal identity. I was looking for the universal in the particulars of my experience.

Translation

I knew that sooner or later the time would come for me to translate my insights about race and social justice into recorded or written words. I would have to translate what was going on inside my head, and my life, into some kind of systematic, reflective form. In retrospect, I now realize that the generation and percolation years of my dissertation were an intense period of "me-search." That work really kicked into high gear when I discovered Robert Nash. I was a member of the first doctoral cohort to take his Religion and Spirituality in Higher Education course. This was the first course of its kind ever offered in a professional school in the United States. It was "love at first sight." I loved the diversity of our class (about half non-white, ages 18–75, Jews, fundamentalist/evangelical Christians, agnostics, atheists, gays, and on and on). I loved the depth and scope of our conversations, and I loved the way Robert facilitated conversations.

This was somewhere around 1997, and Robert was in the early years of developing the research methodology he would call Scholarly Personal Narrative (SPN). Like many non-dominant students, the opportunity to connect my scholarly interests to the intense search for meaning-making that I was involved in turned out to be just what I needed. I was able to transform my thinking about the doctoral process as being a dry, uninspiring next "hoop" I had to jump through in my long educational journey into a personally fulfilling quest. I was now able to answer some intimately personal questions about the meaning of my life that might have some more universal applications.

But as is often the case, the timing of my discovery of SPN was not the most opportune in terms of where I was in the doctoral program. I entered the program in 1996. By 1999 I had completed my coursework, passed my comprehensive exams, and successfully submitted my original dissertation proposal. This put me in the position to embark on the heavy-lifting portion of the program—writing a dissertation. But, sadly, it also put me on track to end up with the most common degree earned by students who take on the challenge of getting a doctorate—the ABD (all but the dissertation).

Other events in my life were occurring around 1999 and conspiring to make the ABD a more imminent possibility. When I began the doctoral program in 1996, I was relatively new to Burlington, Vermont, recently married, childless, and working in the admissions office of Saint Michael's College (SMC). By 1999, I was well connected in Burlington, serving on several community boards, and working in a new position at SMC as the Director of Multicultural Student Affairs. Also, I had just had my first of three sons. Needless to say, it became more of a challenge to carve out time to work on writing my dissertation.

From 1999 to 2003 I had tried, with Robert Nash as my new dissertation advisor, to achieve substantial progress toward finishing my dissertation. And, although I made some progress, I still hadn't honed my topic down to the compelling and relevant essence that would allow me to push through to the other side. I had not truly found my thematic "sweet spot." Then in 2003 I had another life change that was ironically the thing that almost killed my hopes of earning a doctorate while simultaneously making it possible for me to finish it.

Publication

At this time in my life, I realized that sooner or later I needed to go public with all my learnings about doing diversity and social justice work. Also, I needed to complete the doctoral program. I needed to put my work "out there" for others to hear, read, and support. But before this could happen, there was a key event that occurred in my life. Over the summer of 2003, I left SMC, and my family and I moved into the heart of Dorchester, Massachusetts. We relocated so I could enter the inaugural cohort of the Boston Principal Fellows (BPF) program. BPF was a year-long training program that provided its students with an intensive internship with a successful Boston principal, and coursework for a Masters of Education. These were the prerequisites for administrative licensure in the state of Massachusetts, and a full-time salary.

I spent the 2003–2004 school year completing the BPF training program, and in the fall of 2004 I was hired as the founding principal of the Lee Academy Pilot School (LAPS) in Dorchester, Massachusetts. The Lee Academy had several characteristics that drew me to it. Its plan called for it to start with 2 years of early childhood education for 3- and 4-year-olds and a kindergarten. It would then add a grade level each year until it fully matured into a pre-K to 5th grade school after 5 years. I was so excited about LAPS that my wife and I decided to enroll our own children there.

LAPS set out with the bold ambition of providing a fundamentally different type of educational experience for its community. We would create a constructivist, child-centered curriculum that was play-based. We would build in the social-emotional staffing and supports that all children need, particularly the many vulnerable children whom we would be serving. We would focus intensively on building relationships and engaging our families in a deep and meaningful way. Lastly, we would serve as a laboratory school for progressive educational practices, and we would seek out multiple partnerships and collaborations to share practices and hopefully develop some successful models.

My experience as the principal of LAPS was the most challenging and most rewarding of my life. It brought everything in my life into focus—my family, my upbringing, my education, my racial identity, and my professional background. But it also wreaked havoc on my dissertation work. After a futile effort to attempt to continue my dissertation work during my first year or so in Dorchester, I effectively abandoned my studies and resigned myself to joining the legion of all the other ABDs out there.

After 5 years in Boston, however, I reached a point in my trajectory as a principal. It became clear to me that to continue the work that the school needed was most likely going to put pressure and stress on our family, so much so that we might not be able to make it through. So, after a great deal of soul searching, and with a lot of mixed emotions, I decided I needed to retire from my role as principal of LAPS. In a case of serendipity and maybe even fate, my wife's, and my, search for the next phase in our journey landed us back in Vermont, where, in a certain sense, it all began. I ended up taking a job as the director of the Center for Service and Civic Engagement at Champlain College in Burlington. This move provided a perfect platform for me to reconnect with the community of Burlington and to continue my interests in figuring out how to help neighborhoods—particularly ones like Burlington's Old North End community—to grow in capacity and to become healthy, connected, and self-sustaining.

One day I was walking across the parking lot behind my campus office, and I ran into none other than my dissertation advisor, Dr. Robert Nash. It was wonderful to see him. He has an infectious smile, and I felt like he and I had established a real connection from 1997 to 2003. But, in all honesty, I had been subconsciously avoiding him since I returned, because I was embarrassed and ashamed about letting my doctoral work wither on the vine, as it were. But Robert had a different narrative for me than the one I had resigned myself to. As he is wont to do when he needs to sit down and talk with one of his mentees, Robert suggested we have breakfast and catch up. It turns out that the breakfast meeting was a real turning point in my life.

At that breakfast, Robert gave me hope that I could actually complete my dissertation. He gave me a roadmap of the steps I would need to take and the people that I would need to talk to in order to restart my program. But most importantly, he listened to the story of my experience in Boston. He recognized the deep passion that I had about the work of educating impoverished and disenfranchised students. He saw that I had taken my exploration of who I am as an African American male and my quest to understand my purpose, and connected it to work that fed my heart, mind, and soul. He helped me to realize that I had found my "sweet spot" where vocation, training, temperament, and passion meet. And, most importantly, he helped me to believe that I had something meaningful to say about the challenges and rewards of leadership in urban pre-K–12 public education.

Obviously, the mere process of finding my "sweet spot" didn't make a completed dissertation manuscript suddenly appear. But once I discovered that nexus, the heavy lifting was done. A lot of what had held me back up to that point was the fact that I didn't have a deep internal purpose for finishing my dissertation. I was a bit ashamed to be ABD, but that alone was not getting me to put my "ass to chair." But once I knew *why* I was writing a dissertation, I was more able to concentrate on the *doing* of the dissertation.

The rest of the process was about time-management, self-discipline, and stick-to-it-ness. I am a procrastinator and a verbal processor by nature, so finding my sweet spot didn't do anything magical to change all of that. But with Robert's unwavering support, motivation, and occasional good-natured taunting ("Kyle, there is no shame in being ABD; lots of people never finish their dissertation"), I was able to focus my energies enough to tell my personal story of one man's leadership journey in the world of pre-K–12 public education. Moreover, I was able to weave that story into a scholarly tapestry that will hopefully allow it to say something broad enough to be useful to others. This is what going public means to me.

7

The Writer's Toolbox

Practical Tips and Questions for SPN Writers: Part One

Here and in the following chapter, we return to the ten general guidelines for writing SPNs that we examined at length in Chapter 5. We will use these guidelines for a kind of toolbox scaffolding. We will not repeat these guidelines as much as we will refer back to them to ask some pointed and practical questions, and to offer you some tips along the way to guide you in writing scholarly personal narrative manuscripts. Thus, think of these as our SPN "tips, quips, and questions" chapters, as a writer's box of "tools not rules" (Clark, 2006). We also intend to write directly to those disenfranchised, marginalized students who might be undertaking an SPN writing project for the first time. Therefore, we will be addressing the second-person "you" as well as writing in the first- and third-person voices.

Excerpts from an SPN Writer's Dissertation

We will introduce this section with a series of excerpts from the first few chapters of Dr. Robin Hood's SPN dissertation (yes, this is actually her name). We will refer back frequently to her dissertation in this, and in the following chapter, for concrete examples, within the context of the practical questions raised in the section immediately following this excerpt. Robin, a White woman, self-identifies as marginalized because of her extremely poor, "no-collar," working-class background. She explains how, given the poverty of her lower-class background, and the fact that her two parents never got beyond the 10th grade, she was able to earn three degrees, including a doctorate in leadership and policy studies. The title of her dissertation nicely sums up her story.

Finding Hope and Meaning in Poverty and Personal Tragedy: An Educator's Story

Dr. Robin Hood (literacy expert and director of special education, (Winooski, VT)

Dissertation Excerpts

Several weeks ago I attended a conference on international education. Minfong Ho, an author of children's books, spoke about her writing. What she said was beautiful. I wish that I could describe my writing in such an eloquent way. Minfong spoke about how she came to write when she was a little girl growing up in Thailand. One birthday her mother bought her a diary with a key. In that diary is where she learned to write about things that were very private and close to her. Minfong spoke of writing that is fused together like a patchwork quilt. She fuses the writing of her heart, hands, and head together to revisit the past. Writing for her is the glue that brings together all of the languages she has heard in her family over the years. I see this type of writing as a parallel to SPN writing. The writing of the head is the scholarly piece, the heart is the personal, and the hands tell her story in the narrative form. Who am I as a writer? Do I write with my heart, my head, or my hands? Do I write from my soul? I do not know myself intimately as a writer in the way that Minfong does. But, I will!

One goal in writing this dissertation is that I will discover who I am as a writer, just as Minfong, as I begin this daunting, exhilarating, and enormous task of writing an SPN dissertation. Mary Catherine Bateson, author of Composing a Life, *describes writing as a work in progress. She says, "Not only is it impossible to know what the future holds for them, it is impossible to know what their memories of the past will be when they bring them out again in the future, in some new and changed context."*

What do the memories of the past hold for me? I must bring them out to see. I continue to stop along the way. The aspiration to write is inside of me, but the fear of going too deeply, bringing up things that I have not shared with others, or "airing my dirty laundry," as my mother would say, keeps me quiet. I am trying to enter my world, but the digging is deep. I want to write about who I am, and why I have interacted with others in the way that I do throughout my life. The longing is there, yet it is easier for me to act as a cold observer who quickly moves over the formative years to get to my work with literacy education and comprehensive school reform. Certainly, I can make a few connections. I can talk about why literacy is important, and how learning to read and write is critical in anyone's education. I know that I must write about so much more. Are my fingers being defiant in typing out what my brain is thinking? Or am I just stopping along the way?

As writers, we make ourselves more vulnerable when we tell about the dark, heavy, and dramatic sides of our lives. I am not afraid to do so, and will, when I believe it serves a purpose. However, there are also many light and happy stories that I plan to share as well. I believe that writing both kinds of stories requires skill. Ruth Behar describes being vulnerable as a skill. She says, "Writing vulnerably takes as much skill, nuance, and willingness to follow through on all the ramifications of a complicated idea as does writing invulnerably and distantly." When we make ourselves vulnerable to the reader, the stakes become higher. Behar goes on to describe this vulnerability as risk taking. What if people don't like it? What if they find it uninspiring? I propose that through the context of my writing, not only will I find out who I am as a writer, I will learn more about myself as a person, educator, and researcher. And with that, I can't help but change.

Writing this SPN I assert that I grew up in poverty in a low social economic class. In spite of this, I learned to read and write, and continued my education into graduate school. Many students who grow up in poverty fail at the basic task of literacy acquisition. I am passionate about helping all students acquire literacy skills, especially those students who live in poverty. I believe that all children can learn to read and write at a proficient level. I know all too well these children with low literacy levels. I work with them every day. I believe that it is my job, our job, as educators to meet the critical literacy needs of our students. Where did my source of literacy come from? The expectation that I would learn to read and write came from my parents. My parents' achievement ideology enabled my "self" to rise. Somehow, they assured that opportunity structures existed for my siblings and me, and saw that we took part.

As my parents, they had the power of position and authority in my family. I acknowledge that my parents pushed me to succeed educationally. My father with an eighth grade education, and my mother, having completed only tenth grade, exerted their influence on my siblings and me. We were taught nursery rhymes in our cribs, as well as poetry at a young age. These early learning opportunities encouraged us to engage in reading and writing and to see literacy as a functional and important skill to develop. My drive to succeed at my education grew into a form of cultural capital. Cultural capital is what is valued by a culture. People can have cultural capital that is not valued, or cultural capital that works against them.

I would like educators to gain a better understanding and acceptance of the stu-

dents they work with. *Coming from a low social class was difficult for me. I was poorer than many of the other children I went to school with, and the cultural capital that I brought to school was often different from the middle-class values that other students and my teachers had and valued. Anyon claims that social class structure is defined by one's relationship to capital. How did my parents know to build capital that was valued in their children? In school I often experienced a mismatch of mental models between what I thought school should look like, and what my teachers thought I should be like; I also felt a mismatch between the values and beliefs from my habitus (home) and school. Our habitus encompasses culture, economics, and family life. I see a similar mismatch in schools today.*

As an educator, I observe resilient children, who come to school despite poverty, loss, abuse, or other tragic experiences and continue to function in some way. These children bring their own cultural capital. Do teachers ask to see it? Do they value it? Do they even know it is there? Why am I making these points? I want educators to gain a better understanding of their students, all students, our students. All students, especially those who are poor, should be provided with every opportunity to be successful in school. Every child should be able to gain access and find an entry point. We, as educators, need to know how to let them in.

Central Themes

The themes for this SPN dissertation come from inside my personal experiences with poverty, cultural capital, and social class. I will also discuss the effect of tragedy on my life at an early age and how this experience has remained with me throughout my life. How is it that my poor, uneducated parents instilled a powerful achievement ideology in my siblings and me? I will explore the concept of poverty and its relationship to this achievement ideology. Cultural capital is a powerful concept that I will also unpack. We can spend it; it is worth something!

Social class is often used as an indicator of success or lack of success in school. When I speak about social class, I will also refer to the concepts of social reproduction theory. MacLeod (1995) describes social reproduction and its impact in the United States. "Social reproduction theory identifies the barriers to social mobility, barriers that constrain without completely blocking lower, and working, class individuals' efforts to break into the upper reaches of the class structure." I think about the power of position, authority, patriarchy, hierarchy of a system or program. The higher the social class, the more power one has.

Another concept that I will explore is human agency. This term emerged out of reproduction theory and means that we are not objects to have things "done to." We have the power to change things. Coupled with the concept of empowerment, I will describe how I have used my human agency to help others and myself. Without human agency, my prospects of change would be limited. Agency means action; human agency is what we do as people. For example, I used my human agency in order to create a position for myself as a reading specialist at the middle school where I work. In addition, I used my human agency to write a comprehensive school reform grant, which also created a position for me as a literacy consultant.

Who Am I as an Author?

I am a mother, wife, sister, friend, teacher, and colleague. I am also a doctoral student. In each role, I have strived to be the best that I can be, not to compete with others, but to challenge my own self. My parents, who both cared greatly for me and my brothers and sisters, instilled this work ethic in me. Although I struggled as a child, I did not have to struggle in the way my parents did. However, I did experience contradictions, tension, and conflicts throughout my own education, adult life, and teaching profession. MacLeod believes that class-based differences decrease in importance as one climbs the educational ladder. I felt, and continue to feel, a class distinction. Although I am now in the middle class, my lower-class roots will always be with me. I did not give up my personal identity when I moved to a higher social class. I have worked in public education for almost twenty-five years and observe first-hand the challenges that poverty brings to families, children, and schools.

In his book, Savage Inequalities, *liberty and equity are the core of the framework Jonathan Kozol uses to describe the conditions in many of America's schools. Kozol raises the issue that equal opportunity does not ensure equal outcomes. To build his case of inequality in education, Kozol describes both urban and suburban schools. He describes two systems, one for the well off, and one for the poor. He describes urban schools that are broken beyond repair; schools where raw sewage backs up into bathrooms and kitchens on a daily basis; staffing shortages and few supplies are commonplace. The dropout rate is high. These schools are severely segregated by both race and class.*

The wealthier, White suburban schools feature beautiful buildings with manicured lawns. They not only have the best facilities, but the best teachers as well. Teacher salaries are seven to ten thousand more dollars than the urban schools. Students have multiple options for courses, sports, arts, and music. I agree with Kozol's belief that poverty can cause educational problems. Students who live in poverty often begin school at risk. I see this in my job each day. The urban students he refers to not only begin kindergarten several years behind, but are the product of poor prenatal care. These children have parents who are unaware of how to nurture healthy development. They are in a cycle of poverty.

I see this cycle of poverty in Winooski, Vermont, where I teach. Although the degree of the problem is not as severe, some Winooski homes certainly mirror the homes of the urban children that Kozol describes. The difference in my school is that we have the resources to attract qualified teachers, purchase up-to-date textbooks, and offer adequate class size. However, even with all these resources, many of our poor students stay poor. The children that I teach look to their parents as role models, and many of our parents do not have a good education or work ethic. I am frustrated by this, and I work to be a role model to these children in hopes that they can break the cycle of poverty that so many of them have grown up in.

I believe that all parents want the best for their children. We have parental support from many of our working-class parents. Parents want more for their children, yet many of them cannot afford the tax increase that would allow this. Some years it can take as many as four budget votes for a level-funded budget to pass. Many people are working just to pay for the basics—rent, clothing, and food. I have first-hand experience in working with students who are beginning school already behind. Although we try to close the gap of disparity among schools, it remains that many of our children are from destructive families and impoverished homes. I believe that I can help these children, and have helped many, through my work in literacy.

What Will Be the Takeaways for My Readers?

Can caring occur in institutional settings? Absolutely! What is the responsibility of educators to care? What is the ultimate form of success? Is it high test scores? Is it social mobility? What is the impact I hope to make? I hope that educators who read this will look at their students using a different lens. I want them to put their own values and beliefs aside for a moment, to see what makes their students tick. What do they know about their students? What do their students bring to the table of learning? What can they learn from their students that will enrich their own lives? What must they teach their students? Why, in the end, will any of it really matter to those students who have been marginalized and disenfranchised throughout their previous schooling? These are the questions that I want to ask of every single educator who reads this dissertation, because these are the questions that demand responses.

Practical Questions and Tips

In this chapter and in the following one, we will present a series of bulleted lists of starter questions in order to offer helpful tips to fledgling SPN writers. All of these SPN writing questions and tips have been field-tested with students over many years. You probably won't find all of them equally helpful, but we are confident that at least some of them will speak to your writerly needs. We will make it a point to refer back to several of Robin Hood's dissertation excerpts for concrete examples whenever we think appropriate.

Guideline 1: How Do I Create Guiding Themes and Catchy Literary Hooks?

Ask yourself these SPN starter questions: Why do you want to write a Scholarly Personal Narrative manuscript in the first place, as opposed to other research approaches? Why do you want to do such intensive self-probing? Why are you willing to take on a kind of writing that puts the focus on the "I" and uses the "they" (the "experts") mainly as secondary backup? Because SPN is in the early stages of its evolution, are you willing to accept the task of making up many of your own SPN writing rules and inventing some of your own writing tools as you go along? Robin Hood explains at the beginning of her dissertation excerpt why she felt that SPN was the best way for her to write about literacy education in the public schools. She needed to tell her own personal school story in order to draw out the larger story of illiteracy, poverty, and educational neglect in public schooling.

Here are some *theme-centered questions* to ask yourself as you begin thinking about writing an SPN. These types of "theme questions," asked in order to extract a particular point of view about life from the would-be writer, are potentially infinite in number.

- What's important to you in your life at this time? What message do you think that your life sends to others? What pivotal lessons have you learned from living your life in the last few years? What simple advice would you give people who are starting out in a profession, marriage, parenthood, student political activism group, and so on?
- What gives your life meaning? What gets you up in the morning, day after day, year after year, decade after decade? What convictions do you care about so passionately that you would be willing to go public with them on the front page of your state's daily newspaper? If you were a book, what would be your central theme(s), and what would be the book's title and subtitle? What special memories about yourself would you want to leave to your loved ones in an oral or written history?
- How would you like to be remembered in a eulogy delivered at your funeral? What have you done to change anything in your life, either privately or publicly, small or big? Who do you love, and why? Who do you hate, and why? Who do you fear, and why? Who is your friend, and why? Who is your enemy, and why?

Robin Hood establishes the main themes of her dissertation early in her process: She writes:

The themes for this SPN dissertation come from inside of my personal experiences with poverty, cultural capital, and social class. I will also discuss the effect of tragedy on my life at an early age and how this experience has remained with me throughout my life. How is it that my poor, uneducated parents instilled a powerful achievement ideology in my siblings and me? I will explore the concept of poverty and its relationship to this achievement ideology. Cultural capital is a powerful concept that I will also unpack. We can spend it; it is worth something! In this dissertation I will write about educational institutions' responses to cultural capital. How does an institution such as the University of Vermont use and respond to culture capital? I will describe my experiences upon applying to the doctoral program. How do schools use cultural capital to confirm a student's status? Cultural capital confers status on a position.

Here are some questions to ask yourself about *hooks* in your writing: Does your title (hook) catch the attention of readers? What have been a few titles of articles, books, films, reality television shows, songs, and so forth that have "hooked" you enough at the outset to get, and keep, you reading, listening, or watching? What do you think makes for a catchy title? Does your manuscript introduction lay out your intentions in language that is both accessible and seductive? Have you made your readers curious enough to have them at least begin reading your manuscript?

Have you thought about some creative ways to explain the major themes in your writing? How, for example, can you draw portraits of your characters and describe particular situations in such a way as to hook your readers? How can you create real-life dialogue between the protagonists and antagonists in your life-story that sustains the attention of your readers? Are you telling a personal story that has a clear through-line with a beginning, middle, and end—a start, a climax, and a denouement—that is both absorbing and guaranteed to sustain your readers' attention right up to the last page? What are a few stories you have read that have hooked you in this way? What made them work? How can you use these authors' techniques and still write your manuscript in your own unique style, voice, and language?

Robin Hood uses the dramatic hook of personal self-disclosure (what she calls her "memories of the past") of her own first-hand experience with poverty in order to raise the larger *thematic* social questions of literacy education, inequality, and the need for school reform. Perhaps her most engaging hook, however, is her title—*Finding Hope and Meaning in Poverty and Personal Tragedy: An Educator's Story*. Readers know up front that this dissertation will not devolve exclusively into an extensive literature review of poverty, illiteracy, and the work of a Paulo Freire or Pierre Bordieu; or a dispassionate, third-person, theoretical examination of the nature of poverty; or a manuscript full of important technical terms that some writers are content to let swim in the poststructural ether. These are well-worn, poststructural terms such as "habitus," "cultural capital," "social constructionism," "social class structures," or "social reproduction theory." When she uses these terms, every single one of them is buttressed, and illustrated, by Robin's direct experience as a child of poverty and as a professional literacy educator.

Guideline 2: How Do I Universalize My Particulars?

It has been said that each of our moments contains eternities, if only we are willing to look for them. Similarly, each of our ordinaries has the potential to give birth to our extraordinaries. So, too, there is universality in our particulars and particulars in our universality. We live our day-to-day lives in our particulars. But, in the end—if we are willing to admit it—they add up to universal truths that overlap with other lives, no matter how different and unique these lives might be. When push comes to shove, and when all our differences look like they might irrevocably separate us from one another, something amazing sometimes happens—usually during, or after, an unprecedented crisis in our families, neighborhoods, states, countries, or world (for example, the 9/11/01 Twin Towers tragedy). We come to realize that all too frequently the best we can do as human beings is to huddle together (embrace one another) against the darkness (ignorance, oppression, injustice, failure, disappointment, finitude, cruelty, to name a few).

Why? Because despite our individual and cultural differences, we are all human beings—fallible, searching for meaning, and looking for ways to make deep connections with others. In the exploration of our individual profundity (our depths), there are times when we need to "bend low" in order to examine the vastness of our human experience. It is in "bending low" that we find connection with others who are doing the same. As Nietzsche said: "If you stare into the abyss long enough, pretty soon the abyss stares back at you." You see, we need one another because we all must face, and deal with, the momentary and ordinary day-to-day problems of living that often transcend race, social class, sexual orientation, religious difference, and so on. For example, while few of us will ever face extreme poverty, all of us are bound to face a poverty of the spirit at some time in our lives. We need to find what binds us together even when we are threatening to tear one another apart.

What are some of the particulars and ordinaries that you live in each and every day, week, month, and year of your life? What do they all add up to…if anything? Is there any larger meaning to your life? How, exactly, are your particulars also your universals, and your universals also your particulars? Just how does your ordinariness become extraordinary? If it doesn't ever seem to happen, how can you help to make it happen? How, if at all, do you try to live your life larger, rather than smaller, than it seems to be?

Is there any deeper meaning in your writing that your readers might be able to identify with? What in your life might have universal relevance for others? For example, what in your life allows you to connect with your family members, your neighbors, your classmates and teachers, your larger community, your nation, and the world? Or are you so unique that not a single reader could ever identify with your particular hopes, causes, dreams, fears, successes, or trials and tribulations?

Robin Hood is especially adept at universalizing her particulars, as well as particularizing her universals. Here is a fine example of how an SPN author can make the leap from her own experience to the impact that this experience can have on others: *As an educator, I observe resilient children, who come to school despite poverty, loss, abuse, or other tragic experiences and continue to function in some way. These children bring their own cultural capital. Do teachers ask to see it? Do they value it? Do they even know it is there? Why am I making these points? I want educators to gain a better understanding of their students, all students, our students. All students, especially those who are poor, should be provided with every opportunity to be successful in school. Every child should be able to gain access and find an entry point. We, as educators, need to know how to let them in. As I have pointed out earlier, I was one of those students. The lessons I have learned from my own poverty-stricken, social class background have made me a far more effective literacy educator than I might have been.*

Guideline 3: How Do I Draw Out Lessons from My Personal Stories?

While this guideline is closely related to the previous one, ask yourself a different series of questions—ones that might have more of a political (not ideological) bent. Although your personal story is unique, what do you think might be some life-lessons for others to learn, whether political, apolitical, or trans-political? Possible lessons for others might address such particular audiences as friends, partners, or colleagues. Or it might include larger groups of an educational, social, cultural, religious, or political nature, to name just a few possible "others."

This is why it is crucial for you to identify a particular audience for your SPN writing. Are you writing for your professors only? Are you writing on behalf of a particular marginalized group? Are you writing to anyone who has suffered injustice in any way? Are you writing to specific types of individuals with whom you empathize because of a common bond that you might share?

What in your personal stories might you draw on to analyze a larger practice or principle that you consider an injustice, a stereotype, a self-deception, a dangerous belief, or a misconception? How does the story from your own life-experience illuminate the larger practice or principle? How can you extrapolate from your own personal life to the lives of readers you may never have met? How can you reach across the printed page (or the monitor) to speak to the "strangers in your midst"?

How do you think that your readers will become wiser about their own life-narratives as a result of reading your unique narrative? How clearly can you suggest possible parallels between your story and theirs? In reading your personal stories in all of their glorious particularities, will your audiences be able to see any of their own particularities in a more glorious way? Is there some greater, or even lesser, social meaning in your SPN that might be relevant to your readers' situations, no matter their particular backgrounds? We call this type of author-reader-transfer writing "We-search."

Or are you writing to specific individuals rather than to members of one social group or another? Is your SPN more psychological or philosophical than it is social or political? For example, are you deliberately writing about an issue in your life more from a personal perspective than from a social one? Is it possible for you to separate the personal from the political or the political from the personal? If yes, explain to your readers why this is doable. If no, explain to your readers why it isn't.

One of the most effective strategies that an SPN writer can employ to draw out more general lessons for readers is to identify clearly the intended audience. Robin Hood has an entire section describing those she is writing to: children of poverty and the literacy educators who teach them every single day. She first tells her own stories of poverty. And then she shows the larger implications. Here are her words:

Can caring occur in institutional settings? Absolutely! It did for me. What is the responsibility of educators to care? What is the ultimate form of success? Is it high test scores? Is it social mobility? What is the impact I hope to make? I hope that educators who read this will look at their students by using a different lens. I want them to put their own values and beliefs aside for a moment, to see what makes their students tick. The best teachers in my own life did exactly this. What do they know about their students? What do their students bring to the table of learning? What can they learn from their students that will enrich their own lives? What must they teach their students?

Guideline 4: How Do I Effectively Use Relevant Research and Scholarship?

Let's be clear at the outset: Research and scholarship form an essential part of the core of good SPN writing. While they might not comprise the whole core of this type of writing (personal storytelling, artistic forms of expression, and real-world, we-search implications are also necessary), research, when done well, can produce many benefits. One of the most important benefits is the credibility and legitimacy such traditional approaches give to a new medium like SPN writing. SPN writers need to be scholars as well as storytellers. It is important to remember, however, that the SPN writer's story is always the primary source of scholarship. All else is supplementary—important to be sure—but directly dependent upon the writer's personal vantage point. This SPN point is a non-negotiable.

During your pre-search for a topic to write about, have you made sure to consult whatever literature might be available on the topic? This can be as simple as doing a Google Scholar search, visiting your college library, contacting scholars at your university who know something about your subject, or sending out requests for information and readings via email, Facebook, or other social media. Remember that re-search literally means "searching over and over again for information." There are many places to find this.

Have you made sure that your general proclamations and propositions regarding marginalization, social justice, and/or disenfranchisement, or whatever topics you might be writing about, are both defensible and sustainable? Are you able to refer to a variety of scholarly sources for backup in addition to your own personal experiences in your writing?

The most effective use of the formal research and scholarship in SPN writing is when it enlarges, deepens, and enriches the points you wish to make. Do you know what others have said about your topic from a variety of disciplinary perspectives? If not, begin a sustained period of pre-search for the research that will undergird your writing.

Robin Hood uses her store of background knowledge effectively. At the end of the excerpt we quote below, she re-identifies key themes she will be looking at in her narrative dissertation, as well as the key literature she will be drawing upon. She writes:

I will draw from a variety of scholarly literature sources. First, I want to look at the influence of family on aspirations for both school and work. How did my parents teach me to be a caring and compassionate person? This happened in spite of a major family tragedy. My parents had little support in dealing with tragedy at the time. I plan to research more about the types of support that bereaved parents and siblings need. Second, I would like to read more about the conserving role of schools. Bowles and Gintis state that schools play the role of serving the economic order. Meehan helps us to understand inequity in schools. I will reflect upon my work in public education and my own understanding of equity in schools. I plan to research resistance theory. In high school, I resisted being part of groups. I wasn't going to play the game. Either I could not, or I was unwilling to penetrate the dominant ideology of the school. I wouldn't buy in. In terms of identity, I did not have to "belong" to a group. This leads me to want to learn more about the social norms of schools. There is work by Dreeben that I would like to research in this area.

I am also interested in learning more about social constructivism: How does one go about constructing meaning within our classes at school? How do our students construct meaning? Do we encourage them to ask, "Whose knowledge is this anyway? Who said this?" Does the learner transform, or is education nothing more than the transmission of knowledge? How do I construct meaning from my experiences in education?

Additionally, I wish to research teaching pedagogy, both visible (strong classification and framing with low social classes) and invisible. I will also write about the present state of education. What opportunities do we offer for students within the structure of capitalism? How can we move toward a more "just system"? What contributes to school failure? School success? What is my paradigm or set of beliefs that I stand upon? How has my paradigm shifted? What are my overarching and interconnecting assumptions about the nature of reality?

Guideline 5: How Can I Avoid Reference Overload?

First, notwithstanding anything we have said about the necessity of scholarship and research, it is important to understand in SPN writing that "me-search" and "we-search" are also credible forms of research. So, too, are the more traditional forms of research that include APA citations, references, bibliographies, empirical and theoretical studies, footnotes, endnotes, and laboratory investigations. The point is not which forms of scholarship are inferior or superior. Rather, we believe that all of us, whether teacher of student, possess a vast store of background knowledge (both formal and informal), and we need to know when, and when not, to use it. Our first rule of order in SPN research is to use scholarship effectively by using it judiciously. It should be neither avoided nor overused. Reference overload in an SPN manuscript is truly the "killer of the SPN writer's dream." Why? It subordinates, even exterminates, the voice of the SPN writer. It also confirms an old truth in academia: Your voice is less valid, less informed, and less interesting than the "experts."

Do you think of yourself as a unidisciplinary, bidisciplinary, multidisciplinary, or interdisciplinary thinker and writer? When you write an SPN, will you draw primarily from one discipline, two disciplines, or from several disciplines that may or may not overlap? This is an important procedural question to decide, because the response will determine what role you want formal scholarship to play in your SPN, how much of it you will use, and what types.

Do you know how to use scholarship and research to further illuminate and explain your themes and ideas? Or do you use references to show off? In SPN writing, research—to make an Aristotelian distinction—is necessary but not sufficient. It should never stand alone, nor ever call attention to itself. Displaying your erudition to readers is not the best reason for writing an SPN manuscript.

How are you trying to achieve balance among the scholarship, personal reflections, and the narratives you are telling? Are you thinking of SPN as a "trinity" or, better still, a "unity"? How can you keep in check the always-tempting academic tendency to overquote, overcite, overquantify and overqualify, and overtheorize? While it is true that background studies and research can strengthen the points you are trying to make, it is also true that too much reliance on formal research can draw attention away from the personal insights you want to inspire in your readers. It is the me-search and the we-search that form the essential core of SPN writing. The research is there to support, enlarge, deepen, and enrich the personal search. Me-search, we-search, and research need one another. All of these form the necessary connective tissue of SPN writing. All should be complementary and equally respected.

Remember that there is nothing sacrosanct about "data." The term does not describe an "objective reality," as so many social scientists think it does. Every fact, figure, and piece of "evidence" needs to be chosen, processed, interpreted, and evaluated by an observer. And, for SPN writers, there is no such thing as an "immaculate data-perception or data-reception." Observers and authors make inferences. They draw conclusions. They decide which data are worthy of being collected, stored, and processed. And all of this, whether we like it or not, is determined, at least in part, by the perspectives, value systems, assumptions, biases, beliefs, and emotional predispositions of the author/scholar/researcher.

The Latin word *datum* means "that which is given [to consciousness]." Fortunately (or unfortunately, depending on your point of view), no individual's consciousness is free of preconceptions or subjective preferences. We see and study what we believe. So here is a basic, philosophical question for you to ask yourself: Is there anything in my writing that I consider to be "objective"—that I can honestly say is not affected by what I need, believe, feel, love, hate, or fear? Everything that we have written so far in this book is a function of our authorial subjectivity as well as our scholarly "objectivity"—everything, even this statement, as well as every statement after this, and every statement after that, *ad infinitum*. As Robert often says: "It's subjectivity all the way down."

How will you respond to a professor, a colleague, a fellow student, or members of a formal committee who are bound to raise the inevitable and omnipresent question: Why haven't you included more research, background theory, and hard data in your manuscript? Isn't SPN writing "soft" rather than "hard," "easy" rather than "rigorous"? We have learned that the best tactic in dealing with the SPN naysayers is to be patient, explain clearly and simply what SPN scholarship is all about, compare and contrast it to other types of like-minded, narrative scholarship that we discussed in Chapter 4, and, above all, know how it differs from, and overlaps with, the more classical quantitative and qualitative types of research. Explain all of this with a slight smile on your face, in a respectful, but not timid, tone of voice, and with a pride and confidence that you, too, are a scholar.

Robin Hood's dissertation is full of footnotes, endnotes, parenthetical references, and an extensive bibliography. She is truly a "scholar" in the traditional sense of the word. But for us, the words that best speak to her determination to become a balanced SPN writer are these:

I will use SPN to draw out my story and to give voice to my ideas and experiences. SPN allows me to "play" with scholarship in order to construct meaning and to deliver my ideas to readers in a way that is personal—using my voice. Anne Lamott speaks of voice. It is my voice that you will hear in this dissertation. I will not use another methodology that might suppress or "disappear" my hard-won writing voice. Or as Lamott says, I will not "dress up in someone else's clothes." We all find our voice in different ways. SPN is my way! I've lived a lifetime trying to find and express it.

8

The Writer's Toolbox

*Practical Tips and Questions for
SPN Writers: Part Two*

In this chapter we continue to offer practical writing tips, pose personal questions to our readers, and share whatever knowledge we have accumulated through the years from our students about writing scholarly personal narrative manuscripts. We will follow the structure of the previous chapter, beginning with Guideline 6, in building our "writer's toolbox."

Guideline 6: How Do I Tell a Good Story?

Here are a few questions to ask yourself as you construct your SPN story:

Is your story a way of conveying some truth that you know is important, something that you have learned about equality, life, love, or vocation, for example, that you would like to share with others?

Does your story serve to exemplify and explain your central themes? Why exactly are you telling your story? Is the story an attraction or a distraction for your readers? Stories are engines that keep the train on track. Are there any potential train wrecks in your narrative?

To whom are you telling your story?

What will keep your story from becoming just another form of exhibitionism or a passing, confessional trifle, entertaining but forgettable?

When you describe a particular character or a group, what have you done to make them come to life on the printed page? Do they evoke emotions? Are they worthy of the reader's emulation and fascination, or consternation and frustration? Are your characters one-dimensional or multi-dimensional?

Are you able to start, sustain, and finish a complete story line, so that readers will stay the course until the narrative is complete? Do you have a plot line to hold everything together? Do you describe the conflicts in your story in such a way as to keep your readers in suspense? Do you "show" more in your story than you "tell"? Do you save your "telling" until the main story has unwound? Or do you both "show" and "tell" as you go?

Have you created a clear climax to your narrative? At what point in your SPN have you decided to resolve the narrative tension that you've created, at least in the early going? If you "tell it all too early," then readers have no reason to continue. If you "tell it all too late," then you run the risk of readers' becoming impatient and pulling out prematurely.

Robin Hood tells engaging personal stories throughout her dissertation. Here is one example of how a few short paragraphs can captivate the attention of her readers:

How did I respond to the pain of my brother's death? Even before he died? How did I respond to the pain of watching my parents struggle? I became a "take-charge" person. I liked to take charge, and that's what I did. I was a take-charge person, and I still am. I don't sit around and wring my hands. My mother always felt like she had no control over things. She was a hand wringer. Sometimes I couldn't stand it. Now, I would do anything to have her back. I never realized how strong she was until I watched her in her last year of life, and stood by her as she died. I did not get my strength from my father alone. I realize now that both of my parents had great strength.

I was so devastated when my son became ill with a rare blood disease that almost killed him; I just wanted to curl up and forget about everything. My father said, "Get up out of that god-damned bed—that little boy needs you." This was much like how he told my sister Mary, "Get your ass back up to college" when she tried to quit. He was a remarkable role model of not giving up. At times I rejected my mother's model; it seemed so weak. Although my dad was just a lowly little laundry man, he still had strength, goals, and drive. I learned from him that I could not control situations, but I could control how I reacted to them.

I always worried about mental illness. I thought because my mother had a nervous breakdown, that it meant I was going to be depressed. The stigma was not as bad for me as it was for my older sisters when they were growing up. At times I was ashamed. Home was often unpredictable. There were many times that my mother threatened to take a "powder out." This meant suicide.

I stayed teaching in Winooski, Vermont, one of the poorest communities in the state, for almost a quarter of a century, because many of the children I teach don't have resilience. What are the kernels of truth in my experience for humanity? Why am I bothering? I am bothering to tell this story because it shows the flexibility and the perseverance of the human spirit. It demonstrates the resiliency of the human spirit. I was tossed about by much tragedy and heartache throughout my childhood. Many days in my life were hard. I lost my little brother. I had a mother who suffered from mental illness. I lived in poverty. I watched my poor father work and work, and still not get ahead, and then die.

At the time of my little brother's death, I was getting ready for the whole teenage transition. This can be a terrible time for anyone. For a long time after his death, there was a pall (funeral cloth) over my home. My father couldn't talk about my brother's death, and my mother needed to. It put a strain on their marriage. I was grieving, and could tell no one how I felt. In spite of it all, I went to school and worked hard each day. I found a way to survive and thrive at the same time. If I could do this, so can the children and families I work with each and every day as a literacy educator.

Guideline 7: How Can I Write with Cool, Rather Than with Red-Hot, Passion?

Humility, not pride, wins over readers. The Greeks had a name for an overweening pride—they called it *hubris*. For them (and for generations of writers afterward), it was *hubris* that always brought down the protagonist in their stories. (Read Shakespeare, for example; without the concept of *hubris*, there would be no Shakespearean tragedies or even comedies.) So, too, gifted essayists, who have strong convictions and a social message to deliver, know from experience that authorial hubris is the "tragic flaw" that turns off readers. Dogmatism, certainty, and over-zealousness on behalf of the goal of social justice, for example, are too often the products of a non-negotiable, red-hot passion for a particular cause or conviction. No reader wants to be belittled, scolded, or bullied. No reader wants to be indoctrinated. No reader wants to be overwhelmed with authorial self-righteousness and doctrinal certainty. The trick for SPN authors is to learn how to exhibit a "cool," or even a "warm," passion about a special theme or topic in their writing without "burning up" their readers. The best way to do this is to tell your personal story, and then back it up with others' stories. And stay out of the bully pulpit!

Try for some deliberate understatement in your writing. Experiment with stating a strong belief you have about something with a question mark at the end of your sentence instead of an exclamation point. When it comes to asserting a strong conviction, have you ever tried writing an understatement about it? Is there some way to find a middle-ground statement between over- and understatements that doesn't compromise the intensity of what you believe with all your heart? When Robert thinks he is coming on too strong (and he often does), he visualizes ending each of his sentences with a question mark or ellipses, even though the printed page might show a period. In fact, someday he might actually be willing to end all his sentences with a *vice versa*, because, as an "out" postmodernist, he realizes that there is never a "final word" on any truth…including this "no-final-word" truth that he has just asserted.

Remember, however, that at the right time, passion can be good. Be clear with yourself what form your passion will take. Again, balance is preferable. Do you want to express pain or pleasure in your writing, or perhaps a mixture of both? Again, expressing too much pain in a personal story tends to win more pity than sympathy or empathy, and too much pleasure tends to soothe rather than motivate readers to take action. Ask yourself this question: How can I be dispassionate (calm) in my approach without losing my sense of passionate urgency? Can I still express a strong, hot commitment to a belief or cause while striving to be humble and cool? Or is this a contradiction in terms?

Sydnee changes hearts and minds on the topic of social justice without making people feel guilty or defensive. She displays the qualities of irony and empathy to get them thinking. In her writing she is balanced, and her tone is reasonable and open-ended. She tells personal stories as a way that gains the trust of her audiences. Vulnerability is her key, because she believes that vulnerability begets vulnerability. In Sydnee's words, "In order to understand what I truly believe in, sometimes I have to unlock the shame in my own personal narrative. This allows me not just to be in control of my own vulnerability and to overcome it, but to connect with others' shame-narratives." After all, no matter how privileged or underprivileged any of us might seem to be, we are all "wounded" in some way. The Latin word *vulnus* means wound. Who among us goes through life without a single wound that leaves us bleeding…either metaphorically or literally? Ask yourself this question as you write: Am I crafting personal stories that reveal my own vulnerability and humanity as a way to connect with my readers? Or am I only crafting what comes across to readers as invulnerable rants in the form of absolute commandments and omniscient lectures?

In the closing section of her dissertation, Robin Hood's writing shows both passion and humility, as well as vulnerability and strength. Here is what she writes about the strength of the human spirit to rise about the poverty of a child's upbringing.

Growing up in poverty can be an opportunity to prosper. My siblings and I are examples of prosperity. It does not have to be a death sentence, which leaves a person with-

out hope. My mother's mantra, "Hold your head high, you are as good as anyone else," is one that I use today with my own children and the children I teach. This type of emotional energy from my parents helped me to get though each day. Freire would say my parents perceived "the reality of oppression not as a closed world from which there is no exit, but as a limiting situation which they can transform." Although both of my parents are no longer living, I feel their protective arms around me. I hear them whisper, "You are as good as anyone else." I continue to feel their love.

Although poverty has the ability to identify, track, and destroy a person, life does not have to be this way. My parents accepted poverty proudly and rose above it. This is what human achievement is all about. We may have experienced material poverty, but we never experienced poverty of the spirit. Our poverty strengthened our spirit. My family did not use it as an alibi. We were what I call "a different kind of poor." We didn't let it beat the shit out of us; we didn't see ourselves as victims. My parents gave us the gift of human agency. We were not objects to have things "done to." No, we had the power to change things. Without this human agency, I believe that the prospect of change would have been limited for my siblings and me.

Guideline 8: How Can I Tell My Story in an Open-Ended Way?

We believe that open-ended storytelling invites readers to reflect on their own stories in a more self-forgiving, self-affirming way. Why? Because they learn that no story is, *ipso facto*, superior to theirs. No truth is "truer" in principle than any other. Each and every story contains its own kernel of truth, its own intrinsic, often hard-won, wisdom. The major purpose of telling a story is to invite the reader into your life in a more personal way than most formal academic writing does. The best SPN storytelling is open-ended in the sense that it never claims the Absolute Truth, or becomes the Ultimate Authority, for the lessons it intends to convey. "Conversion" is not the goal of SPN storytelling. Rather, the objective is "connection" and "generativity." This is achieved by extending an open invitation to the reader to be part of a relationship in order to learn something beneficial about how to live a life of meaning and purpose. And so the central question is this: Am I encouraging connection, dialogue, and mutual understanding? Sydnee often says: "Am I taking a step back in order to let others step forward?"

Don't preach or screech in your writing. These are the strategies that over-exuberant activists, political ideologues of one persuasion or another, and absolutist religious believers choose in order to change people's minds and behaviors. Try instead to ask yourself these short questions: Why exactly do I need to convert someone to my way of thinking? Why can't I be content with just getting people to hear my story? What do Lao Tzu's words mean to me when he says: "When you wish to seize something, you must momentarily give it up. The soft and the weak in you will always conquer the hard and stubborn in you, and in others as well." Or, in Sydnee's words, "I am more comfortable asking questions even if this means that I look weak. Why? Questions are an invitation for others to join me in my struggle to find a sustainable truth."

Try writing very "softly" about something that you take very seriously. Again, Lao Tzu believes that wisdom begins in all that is "gentle and generous" in you. Can you make your stories gentle and generous without losing your strong sense of conviction and purpose? Have you ever read something that inspired you—not because it screeched or preached, or *called you out*, but because it *called to you* gently through the softness and generosity of its words?

What do Lao Tzu and the Buddha mean when they say that "you only get to keep what you are willing to give away"? What exactly is it that you are willing to "give away" in your SPN writing?

In the following excerpt from the final pages of her dissertation, Robin Hood tells a "soft" and "generous" story of "caring." She "gives herself away" in the Zen sense by becoming vulnerable and self-disclosing. But she gets something back: She is able to inspire others about the virtue of caring in her work with students because she draws upon an actual incident in her own life (involving Robert) to make her point. And she does this non-didactically and open-endedly.

My work in education has been gratifying. For twenty-one years I worked as a classroom teacher. Together, I worked with my students developing a learning environment that was engaging. Together, we set goals and high expectations for ourselves; we all worked as a team to meet our goals. I was also a storyteller. Almost every story you have read in this dissertation has somehow made its way into my classroom. My love for my students and desire to create a safe place where learning can occur has always been the utmost priority. I cared deeply for my students and their families. I believe that caring is a part of the prescription for success in education.

In her book The Challenge to Care in Schools, *Nel Noddings opens her first chapter with the following: "To care and be cared for are fundamental human needs." She goes on to say, "We also need to care, but not all of us learn to care for other human beings." Some people genuinely care for others. My parents cared deeply for my siblings and me. Mrs. Giffin, my kindergarten teacher, cared so much about her students that she renovated her chicken coop into a kindergarten. Sister Roberta cared so much that she made homemade bread for our Little Red Hen play. I cared for Richard Sicely, my* student on the school bus who was being bullied, by sharing my seat, so he had a place to sit each day. My colleagues showed caring for me when they brought me a breakfast bar each day, and sat with me while I ate; they were trying to support a friend who developed an eating disorder. These are all examples that illustrate the notion of care that I remember. This is the caring that I believe we must model to our students.

While writing this dissertation I experienced this caring I describe from my professor, Dr. Robert Nash. After sitting at my laptop for hours and writing very little, I experienced what I thought was writer's block. Feeling scared, I sent Robert a desperate email telling him I needed help. We met in the late afternoon in the middle of a Vermont snowstorm. We drove through snowy, slippery roads to meet at a local restaurant. While waiting at the window of the restaurant, I heard his familiar happy whistling, my heart skipping a beat, as I knew that help was on the way. Robert walked into the restaurant with his usual smile, kicking the sticky snow off his feet. We sat together at a table by the window. Robert sat across from me and listened intently to my every word, my every worry. I cried. He continued to listen. That alone made me feel so cared for.

Later in our conversation, Robert helped me to scaffold my dissertation and to identify concepts that I would later translate into assertions. He suggested I type these themes in 29-point bold font and place them around my desk. When I cried, he told me that everyone who writes a dissertation gets scared. He suggested that perhaps I was worried about being "best enough," when really I needed to focus my writing on being "good enough."(He quoted from Kant on the difference between best and good in living the moral life.) He suggested I read Anne Lamott's chapter on perfectionism. Robert stayed with me until almost five o'clock. His act of caring transformed me. Later in the evening, I wrote Robert the following:

Hello Robert,

I feel so fortunate and happy to have you as my advisor. You exemplify the caring Nel Noddings describes in her book. After leaving you today I drove home on the snowy roads feeling so much better. I have a sense of peace now. It is 7:53 and I just finished reviewing my notes from our discussions, typing up my themes in bold font, and typing the steps of scaffolding for my dissertation. Now, they are all taped up on the wall in front of me! I also got the picture out of me in front of my house when I was a little girl. I have shown it to you before. The deer are hanging on the front porch, and I am standing with my little brother, Frankie, and my dad. My brother-in-law Ronnie is on the front porch. Sadly, I am the only person in the picture who is still alive. But, my little brother's smile is worth a thousand words, and probably one of only a few pictures there are of us together. The next thing I am going to do is read Anne Lamott's chapter on perfectionism. Then, I will start the last chapter of my dissertation. Thank you again. I now look forward to going into a weekend of writing. I'll stay in touch.

Robin

Robert knows me as a person. I am not only his advisee. He takes time for all of his students. When I thanked him for meeting with me on that snowy day, and for selflessly giving me his time, he told me that is what he does. Robert has accepted Nel Noddings's challenge to care in the academy.

In my present job, I am a reading specialist and literacy consultant. I continue to be passionate about helping students to take that next step. My work as a literacy consultant places me in the context of school reform and standards. My responsibility is to provide professional development to teachers to help them construct their teaching methodology. Ultimately, the goal is to improve student learning. You may ask, "Is this work which increases the academic rigor for students and raises expectations in conflict with the caring you describe?" My answer is no. I believe we can do both. We can both care for our students and have high academic expectations. We must!

Guideline 9: How Can I Be Both a Craftsperson and an Artist in My Writing?

To *craft* a manuscript takes the same skills and mindset that it takes a manual craftsperson (e.g., a mechanic, a carpenter, an electrician, a builder, etc.) to put anything together. The best craftsperson is someone who is skilled, painstaking, and technically dexterous. To *create* a manuscript, though, is to move from the *craft* of constructing it to the *artistry* of refining, polishing, detailing—and yes, even beautifying and stylizing it. All SPN writers need to be both craftspersons and artists in order to have the most impact on their readers.

As a writer, what is more tedious, or odious, for you—to get the first draft written or to get the second draft polished, edited, and ready to go? Whatever your response, we want to remind you that an unedited, unpolished, untweaked manuscript is an unreadable—yes, even lazy—manuscript. On the other hand, without that "shitty first draft" (the phrase is Anne Lamott's) that some of our students have called "a free-write mess" or a "total word-vomit," there can be no manuscript in the first place to tweak. In other words, without the craft there can be no artistry. First and second drafts are close, "kissing" cousins. So, too, are third and fourth drafts. Re-drafting more times than this should signal to you, the writer, that perhaps you are in a state of denial, delay, or even what Robert calls "perfectionism-freeze." There is always a time when you must overcome your fears, or in Roy Clark's much starker words, "murder your darlings" (that is, stop holding on to your cherished avoidance behaviors).

Make a list of all your particular "writerly avoidance strategies" that we mentioned in an earlier chapter. Which ones are truly necessary for you in order to find your authorial mojo, and which ones can you skip because they prevent, or stall, your mojo? Is it possible for you to use a few of your favorite "avoidance strategies" to reward yourself at certain intervals for keeping to your writing schedule and/or for producing something (maybe a great paragraph, page, or chapter) that you are really proud of? One of Robert's rewards is to check his email at 2-hour intervals (he doesn't do Facebook), or to go online once in the morning and once in the afternoon to read the latest Boston pro-team-sports gossip on his favorite websites. Robert also rewards himself with a chunk of chocolate at the end of a very satisfying writing session that makes him feel like a Pulitzer Prize-winning author (fortunately, these sessions rarely occur, so the chocolate treats do not pose a serious weight problem). One of Sydnee's pet avoidance strategies is to Google each and every question that comes up when she is writing. Another strategy for Sydnee is to go quotation hunting, sometimes for hours on end.

What do you suppose one of our student writers means when she calls herself a "prose poet"? Or another student who refers to herself as a "word-picture artist"? Or still another who calls himself a "musical-phrase maker"? Identify something that you've written in the past few years that you think reflects both the craft and art present in good writing. What would be a brief phrase you would use to describe yourself as a writer? Sydnee calls herself an "economically whole-hearted writer with an ironic bent." Robert refers to himself as a "distributor of maxims and etymologies." How would you want your readers to describe you as a writer?

At one point during the writing of a recent book, Robert actually felt like he performed both as a careful craftsperson and a creative artist. The following section, *Seven Real Profiles in Courage*, was the result of an entire day of constructing "shitty first drafts" and "creative tweakings." In this particular book chapter, Robert was trying to make a distinction between what he calls "Upper-Case Courage" and "lower-case courage" that goes beyond simple dictionary definitions and ethereal philosophical abstractions. It was in his third draft that he got the idea of using illustrative examples of what most people would not ordinarily think of as an Upper-Case "Courage." He decided to draw several portraits of actual students with "lower-case courage" who have attended his classes during the last several years. While he is not fully satisfied with the results, Robert is pleased with the "art and craft" of what follows.

Seven Real Profiles in Courage

Robert J. Nash

I want to introduce you to seven students, the types who find their ways to my personal narrative writing seminars as well as to all the other courses I teach each year. These seminars include graduate students who are employed, helping professionals, as well as those who are full-time undergraduates. There are also a number of graduate students in training who will eventually pursue positions in a variety of human service professions.

First, meet Joan, a middle-aged special educator, who is battling a rapidly metastasizing stomach cancer. Her long-term prognosis is not good, but she refuses to crawl into her bed and feel sorry for herself, after meeting daily with her oncologist for the energy-sapping chemotherapy and radiation treatments she must undergo. Instead, she goes to school every day to work with special-needs children, enthusiastically teaches, attends evening classes at the university, and is in the process of writing a book about her life as an educator and union organizer.

At times, Joan arrives in my seminar pale and shaken. Her eyes are bloodshot, and her wig is disheveled. She wears her perpetual stomach nausea on her face. She can be eerily quiet. Occasionally, during the term, she'll get up and leave in the middle of the class, and we won't see her again for a few weeks. But she always returns, sometimes, in an act of defiance, without her wig, and with a big sigh of relief that she has once more met the chemotherapy beast and overcome it. Now she can write her story for yet one more day.

Over here is Marilyn, a student in a graduate program in public administration. Marilyn is an evangelical Christian, a person who believes with all her heart and soul that Jesus Christ is the answer to the most unsettling questions about the meaning of life, including why bad things always seem to happen to good people. Regarding the latter, Marilyn's mom suffers from a long-standing, crushing depression, and during her worst times, she secludes herself from everyone who loves her, including Marilyn. She locks herself in her bedroom for hours at a time, mumbling incoherently, often crying, until she is ready to emerge to try to live her life anew one more time. Marilyn has never felt so helpless during these up-and-down cycles. She turns to the Scriptures to find the solace and strength she needs to endure, and she is convinced that the answers are there.

At her "public ivy" university, Marilyn is a fish swimming in strange waters in her graduate program, because most of her peers are secular, skeptical, and politically progressive. Many in her seminar cohort are also religious cynics who present themselves as spiritual agnostics, but who are actually wounded ex-believers, angry and often bitter. Because Marilyn is an out-of-the-closet evangelical Christian, she rarely misses an opportunity to witness—to talk openly in a seminar about her religious beliefs and the comfort and wisdom they bring her. She works very hard not to be haughty, judgmental, or proselytizing, though, because she knows that many of her peers disdain her conservative Christian principles. She often feels alone and isolated, like her mom in a way, in a very secular, liberal, university environment.

Over there is Kathy, a diabetic since her teen years, and whose diabetes has progressively worsened over the decades. She literally lives from one blood sugar test to the next, hoping that she won't go into insulin shock and coma. She also lives constantly with the overriding fear that she might very well die an early death from diabetes complications the way that her mother did at age 40. Kathy herself has just celebrated her 40th birthday, and the bitter irony is not lost on her. Her mother's physical condition deteriorated at a relatively young age to the point where she had to undergo amputations, blindness, and a host of other degenerative disorders, before death mercifully took her.

Kathy has not let the nightmare of this insidious illness slow her down, however. She plunges ahead and has become a highly successful local and national educational leader. She is currently working on a doctoral dissertation, maintaining a satisfying marriage, working full time as an administrator in a state department of education, and purposely engaging in a huge number of special philia relationships with people throughout her small state. It seems that Kathy has become everyone's friend and safety net. Because she has suffered both physically and mentally by learning how to cope with her diabetes, she makes a compassionate sounding board for her fellow professionals. Like the rest of us, they often need a little encouragement to hold up under the stresses of their busy lives.

Just now, over there, sitting down at his usual spot in the seminar circle is Fred, an undergraduate, who must work 48 hours a week as a tech in the local hospital emergency room to make ends meet. His parents and siblings live in a trailer park in the poorest community in his small, rural state. This is a community with the highest incidences of unemployment, domestic and drug abuse, and alcoholism in the state. Fred receives very little financial aid from the university, and what he does get goes exclusively to defray high tuition costs.

Fred earns little more than a bare subsistence wage by working all night in a hospital crisis center. He has seen patients in all kinds of terrible disrepair, due to catastrophic accidents, and he has held several automobile crash victims in his arms while they died. There are times when he is so tired after working a grueling night shift that he can barely keep his eyes open during class; but he does. Fred wants an education more than anything, and he never fails to show up for class wearing his hospital scrubs along with a broad, enthusiastic smile.

Oh, sitting over there is Bruce, an Asian American, first-generation undergraduate college student who always feels out of place in an academic setting. While in high school, Bruce was diagnosed with a "learning disorder," and he carried this burdensome label with him throughout his high school years. Bruce thinks of himself as "stupid," compared to his "brilliant," "preppie" buddies. He cringes whenever he reads course syllabi that expect him to participate actively in seminars. He tries to avoid these types of learning environments, but, as an English major, it's almost impossible to spend an entire undergraduate experience sitting anonymously in a lecture hall.

Bruce fears that whenever he starts talking in a seminar he will expose himself, once and for all, for the academic fraud that he thinks he is. He seriously considers taking my course as an Independent Study, because he suffers from something he calls "presentation jitters." For the present time, though, Bruce is determined to remain in the seminar as a full-fledged member of the class. He resolves to speak up, if not in the large group, at least in the small group sessions, and at least once during each meeting. Most of all, though, he forces himself each session to read sections of his personal narrative writing to the group.

That African American woman getting herself settled in her seat is Shelly. The small child with her is her daughter, Niki, 7 years old, and nicely behaved while sitting next to her mom during a 3-hour seminar every week. Shelly is a single mom and caretaker, a full-time graduate student, who also holds a permanent leadership position in residential life at the university. Shelly has been on her own since her middle teens. She refused to heed the well-meaning advice of her friends, and parents, to have an abortion when she was pregnant with Niki. As a result, everyone near and dear to her abandoned her because they thought she was being "selfish" and "foolish," and would have to go on the "public dole" called welfare.

So Shelly went to live for a year in a homeless shelter at the tender age of 16. She gave birth as a young teenager, went on to successfully complete high school and college, and is now in her final semester of a very prestigious master's degree program in higher education administration. She has already been accepted at a well-respected doctoral program in another state. As a recent winner of the very competitive Gates Millennial Fellowship, her dreams of becoming a college professor are starting to take shape.

Matthew, a first-generation Chicano student, rushing into class a little late, the young man with a determined but sleepy look on his face, is a very talented varsity athlete. He is also a brilliant student, a political science major, carrying a 3.8 academic average into his senior year. As a two-sport, elite athlete at the university, Matthew spends all his free time studying and practicing. He wants to attend law school. He also wants to become an all-American hockey player, the university's most acclaimed varsity sport.

Matthew once said in class that he averages 3 hours of sleep a night, and that he regularly pulls all-nighters in order to "ace" his exams. So far, he has withstood the terrible temptations that many workaholics and over-achievers in academics and sports face—to over-caffeinate and over-medicate his constant state of fatigue. He once fell asleep halfway through class on a late afternoon, and only his own loud snoring woke him up. He then spent many weeks apologizing to all of us for this misbegotten slumber and promised that it would never happen again. It didn't.

Before the semester ends, students like these, whatever their ages or stages, will have exemplified the meaning of courage as I think of it. Every person who comes into my seminars is waging a personal battle, and most enter the fray with exemplary courage. Most manage to stand up to their fears, stare them down, and work hard to overcome them. Some will show their courage in their sheer tenacity to persevere despite all the odds. Some find a hope, religious or philosophical, to hold onto in order to deal with their present suffering, so that they can avoid falling into despair. Some choose, by a determined act of will, to remain joyful about their prospects, even when life appears to be bleak and even hopeless. Some, because of their day-to-day struggles to endure the hardships imposed on them by events over which they have no control, become more generous and merciful toward others.

But, as in every single case that I mention above, my students manage to bear up under life's sturm und drang without losing heart. They do this by living their ordinary lives in an extraordinary way. Few, if any, of them ever call undue attention to themselves—either to their sacrifices, or to their well-deserved victories. Instead they construct themselves as valorous human beings via a daily display of "lower-case courage." It is unlikely that any of these students will ever be idealized in the national, or even local, media. All of the people I have just described have been students in my seminars on personal narrative writing over the last few years. I will never forget a single one. Each and every one of them, for me, is a genuine profile in courage, even though not a single one of them would qualify to be included in John F. Kennedy's book Profiles in Courage. What a shame!

(A version of this essay appeared in Nash & Murray, 2010.)

Guideline 10: How Can I Write Simply without Oversimplifying?

Simple writing is the golden ticket to accessible writing, but particularly to SPN writing. When we use the adjective "simple" in connection with writing, we mean easy to understand, unembellished, clear and direct, basic, focused, and, above all, succinct and storied writing. Simple writing is absent either guile or deceit. Also, telling simple, understandable stories helps writers get to the point. Stories clarify the meaning of key ideas by serving as down-to-earth, engaging, real-life illustrations of ideas.

"Simple" SPN writers ask understandable questions. They do not try to bowl over the reader with erudite displays of genius, sophistication, and ultra-complexity. They resolutely avoid the use of deadening technical jargon. This is the way, unfortunately, that too many academic writers go about their work. Ralph Keyes calls this kind of writing "baffle-gab" writing. Robert calls it "tenure-track writing." Complexity in writing has a place, to be sure, but over-complexity is sometimes a way for authors to show off their academic pedigree, to trumpet how many authors and studies they have read (or conducted), and to qualify (and quantify) every single assertion until readers are left to ask in despair, "Why am I reading this piece, anyway? What is the point?"

Be honest—how many of you can't wait to leave class, or your office, in order to rush to the library to read the latest copy of your discipline's scholarly journal, or to immerse yourself in reading the next textbook assignment, particularly if you do not need to? Better still, pretend you are on your deathbed. Can you picture yourself screaming out just before you "pass" that your one major regret in life is that you didn't read enough scholarly journals or books in your field? More to the point, how many of you would want one last chance to read your favorite, or least favorite, professor's most-recent, well-documented, highly specialized article before you die?

So the question remains: How can you write with simplicity without falling prey to over-simplification? We are firm in declaring that clarity should never be equated with being simplistic or unscholarly. Neither should powerful, fluid, graceful, and persuasive writing be seen as unworthy of the academy. In fact, ironic, humorous, unreferenced writing can often be the most profound writing of all. After reading hundreds of thousands of so-called "scholarly" research papers written by both students and colleagues over a 45-year professorial career, Robert is willing to go on record with this academically sacrilegious proposition: The most eloquent writing is the writing that is the least specialized and data-based as well as the most marginalized (in the sense of "pushing the margins" or "crossing the borders"), inventive, and risk-taking.

Every writer has irritating writing "tics." Do you know what some of yours are? Perhaps your sentences are too long. Do you tend to overuse qualifiers? adverbs? dashes or colons? Do you go into comma coma? Do you look first for the polysyllabic (this word is one of those), technical word in order to establish your academic "cred"? Are you a name-dropper? One of Robert's most bothersome writing tics is to overdo etymological analysis. He loves word-roots. In fact, he is at times obsessed with them. He is prone to commit what he calls the "etymological fallacy": Find the Latin or Greek root of a word and—lo and behold—you have exhausted the total meaning of a word. There is really nothing more to say about it. This is just plain silly, of course, because words are continually evolving. Robert also tends to construct painfully long sentences that are full of compound, complex clauses—sometimes featuring literary allusions—with an endless array of adjectival, prepositional phrases, series after series, dashes and ellipses...which in the end amount to nothing more than Shakespeare's "tale told by an idiot, full of sound and fury, signifying nothing." (We have intentionally put on full display many of Robert's irritating tics in this last sentence.)

When you are writing, stop every now and then and try to re-write a particularly long sentence. How can you break up the sentence into a series of separate, bite-size chunks? Also, check out the technical terms you are using. Are these absolutely necessary? Why are you using them? Do they actually help the *reader* to understand the points you are making? Or do they mostly help *you, the writer*, to get the "A" in the assignment, the committee's approval for your thesis or dissertation, or an article accepted for publication? Be honest.

Having said all of the above about clear writing, however, we must also establish the proposition that every effective SPN manuscript contains both simple and complex sentences, ideas, themes, and questions. As we pointed out in the previous chapter, the key is to keep simplicity and complexity in balance. Jargon, however, doesn't do it. Neither does excessive technical terminology that is guaranteed primarily to mystify readers by keeping them outside the club of "experts." Overuse of technical disciplinary terms is just another way to marginalize students and outsiders. Have you struck the delicate balance in your writing between specialization and generalization? Are you writing to just one audience or several?

Do you know the work of Roy Peter Clark, one of the best contemporary writers on the nuts and bolts of effective writing? If not, order his two latest books immediately, and consult them at least twice a week both before and after writing— *Writing Tools: 50 Essential Strategies for Every Writer* (2006), and *The Glamour of Grammar: A Guide to the Magic and Mystery of Practical English* (2010). Moreover, if you are courageous enough, recommend these two books to your writers support group, teachers, academic advisors, editors, committee members, and whoever else has the power to make or break your writing.

For good measure, add two other nuts-and-bolts approaches to writing: Val Dumond, *Grammar for Grownups: A Guide to Grammar and Usage for Everyone Who Has To Put Words on Paper Effectively* (1993), and June Casagrande, *It Was the Best of Sentences, It Was the Worst of Sentences: A Writer's Guide To Crafting Killer Sentences* (2010). If the makers and breakers of your scholarly future reject your recommendations, tell them that Robert and Sydnee sent you. And then be ready to deal with the fallout. But keep in mind that academicians—more than anyone—could really benefit from the insights of these nuts-and-bolts experts who have no interest in mystifying or dazzling readers with their intellectual superiority. Instead, they are more concerned about "trimming the fat" that "weighs down" so much specialized, scholarly writing.

If all else fails, however, try Gerald Graff and Cathy Birkenstein, *"They Say/I Say": The Moves That Matter in Academic Writing* (2006). Graff is the former president of the Modern Language Association (a prestigious academic honor, indeed), and his main objective is to "demystify academic writing" by pointing out that every "they say" in a scholarly manuscript also needs an "I say," and vice versa. He adds: "…academic writers across most disciplines now tend to make liberal use of 'I,' 'we,' and their variants." Graff must have heard about SPN writing. If he hasn't, please text or email him immediately.

9

Four Authors Who Have Lived on the Margins— and Written about It on Their Own SPN Terms

Part One

Introduction

Here and in the following chapter we feature a series of personal reflections by eight authors discussing how and why they decided to choose an SPN methodology for writing their final degree projects. They talk in very frank terms about their own personal experiences with the upsides and the downsides of doing SPN writing. All of these writers, former graduate students of Robert's, have since gone on to earn graduate degrees in Interdisciplinary Studies, Leadership and Policy Studies, or Higher Education and Student Affairs Administration. All of these authors made the decision to write their theses and dissertations using an SPN approach, many for the very first time.

Moreover, all of these SPN authors self-identify as being "marginalized, under-represented, and/or disenfranchised," at least at some time in their lives. All are multi-identitied persons of color. They represent a diversity of social classes, sexual orientations, genders, ethnicities, internationalities, and religious backgrounds. All have overcome much in order to go on to success in higher education and in the workplace. All have had first-hand experience with "liberating their own voices" by telling their stories and believing with all their hearts and minds that these "stories matter." As readers, you will find their meaning-making journeys to be inspiring, hopeful, and intensely engaging. Of equal importance, you will see that the challenges in their life-narratives are accessible and universalizable. You will see pieces of yourselves in the stories that our authors have written about the transformative power of SPN.

Even though each of our authors is so very different, what each has in common, not only with the others—but with all of you as readers—is that at some level they are striving to achieve the following in their lives: self-validation, authenticity, liberation, self-empowerment, resistance, resilience, and reconstruction. These are themes that are both universal and inescapable, because they are the common stuff of life. Who among us has not experienced, at least once in our lives, what Joseph Campbell describes when he says: "As you go the way of life, you will see a chasm. Jump. It is not as wide as you think." All of our authors have made the decision to confront their particular "chasms"; some have gone even further and made the "jump." As authors of this book, it is our hope that you, too, will find the courage to "jump" across your "chasm." We want you to jump into SPN writing in such a way that you are able to "become yourself."

Here are the poetic words of the octogenarian May Sarton on the same topic: "Now I become myself. It's taken time, many years and places. I have been dissolved and shaken. I have worn other people's faces." Some of our SPN students confront their chasms by jumping, and some by retreating, and some just by standing there and looking over the edge. Some spend less time looking behind and before them and a great deal of time looking at what lies within them. Some, though, look mainly to the past, or stay with the present, in order to gain self-understanding. And some experience their more dramatic life transitions as an opportunity to take the call.

Others, however, refuse to take the call to change. They prefer instead to concentrate on the terrible aftermath of their crises as a way to tell their stories of failure and redemption. Whatever their differences in theme, approach, focus, and hook, however, our marginalized students who write SPNs of transition and self-empowerment, of authenticity and resistance, of liberation and resilience, are striving to come to terms with what Jung calls "archetypal" developmental themes. They are all asking similar questions about the meaning of their lives: how to negotiate change and how to become empowered in the midst of it.

We will include four short reflections about SPN in this chapter, and four in the next chapter. At the beginning of each reflection, we will include a brief personal bio of the writer. The writers have written their own bios, either in the first- or third-person voice. Also, please note that we have made minimal substantive changes to their manuscripts. (Each of the following authors has given Robert and Sydnee, and Peter Lang Publishing, Inc., full permission to publish their SPN reflections.)

Two SPN Reflections by Senior Higher Education Administrators

Essay #1 by Alvin Sturdivant

Alvin Sturdivant *is the Assistant Vice President for Student Development at Seattle University. In this role he serves as a member of the senior leadership team and provides visionary and administrative leadership for a number of key departments toward fostering student success and an integrated learning experience. Dr. Sturdivant is also an adjunct faculty member in the Liberal Studies Program, where he teaches a course focused on deconstructing hate in the United States and abroad. Prior to joining Seattle University, Dr. Sturdivant was the Director of Housing and Residence Life at Saint Louis University in St. Louis, Missouri. Prior to joining the Division of Student Development at Saint Louis University he served as the Associate Director of Residential Life at the University of Vermont, where he was also an adjunct faculty member in the Higher Education and Student Affairs Administration program and an instructor at the Community College of Vermont.*

Dr. Sturdivant received his Doctor of Education degree in Educational Leadership and Policy Studies with an emphasis in Higher Education Administration from the University of Vermont. He earned his master's degree in Education and bachelor's degree in Psychology at North Carolina State University. His scholarly and professional interests include examining the effects of oppression and discriminatory practices in college communities, exploring the experiences of students of color in higher education, examining campus climate in the context of bias-related acts and behaviors, and exploring the experiences of African American men in higher education. Dr. Sturdivant takes great pride in working one-on-one with students of color and gives considerable attention to serving as an advocate, role model, mentor, and confidant. His work was inspired early in his college years by his own mentors and reflects the commitment shown to him by them. His greatest joy comes from the development of authentic relationships with students and providing them with the opportunity to be their most authentic selves on their respective campuses.

Journeying Toward Truth and Authenticity: Amplifying Marginalized Voices through Scholarly Personal Narrative

In 2006, noted actor and Harvard Law School graduate Hill Harper published *Letters to a Young Brother: Manifest Your Destiny.* I found his writing to be thought provoking, insightful, and beneficial. I was inspired to use my voice in a similar fashion after completing a Scholarly Personal Narrative (SPN) course as part of my doctoral studies at the University of Vermont. Feeling overwhelmed by an abundance of questions that seemed unanswerable, I set off on a search for direction, definition, and destiny in the academy through the use of SPN. Accordingly, I departed from the more "traditional" structure that had guided my writing throughout my educational journey. I was interested in advancing young Black male scholars, college administrators, faculty, and staff in a Scholarly Personal Narrative representing my experiences as an African American male in the academy.

As I began the process of writing an SPN dissertation, I was often drawn back to the merits of my writing and the contribution I would be making to higher education. I reflected often on the research and scholarship paradigm as I understood it and struggled extensively with my choice but journeyed ahead with my dissertation. Despite my hesitation and significant internal conflict, I recognized the value in exposing hidden truths through the use of narrative. As had been the case with other forms of research and scholarship, SPN was about making a unique contribution to your discipline, answering questions, provoking thought, advancing learning and the pursuit of cognitive truth. SPN was about creating and contributing to intellectual discourse. Reliving, retelling, and amplifying my narrative served as a mechanism for raising awareness about my largely unrecognized voice in the academy.

Through SPN I discovered my voice, answered some of the more difficult questions associated with my research and experiences, and transformed my thinking in the process. I am forever changed, and I expect that those who read this essay and my dissertation will be changed as well, because I not-so-willingly stepped outside the traditional research paradigm and explored intimately my own narrative situated within the context of scholarship. In order to fully understand how SPN helped me in recovering my authentic voice, it is important to know more about who I am and the process I engaged in.

Who Am I?

> After the Egyptian and the Indian, the Greek and the Roman, the Teuton and the Mongolian, the Negro is a sort of seventh son, born with a veil, and gifted with second-sight in this American world,—a world which yields him no true self-consciousness, but only lets him see himself through the revelation of the other world. It is a peculiar sensation, this double-consciousness, this sense of always looking at one's self through the eyes of others, of measuring one's soul by the tape of a world that looks on in amused contempt and pity.
> —W.E.B. Du Bois, 1903

For my entire life, I have felt like a caged bird, longing to spread my wings and fly free and clear from those who have owned my mind, body, and spirit. I have never known true freedom, as I have spent my life imprisoned by my own Black skin. Even as I grew more educated, gained more social and cultural capital, and achieved higher levels of status, my reality has remained the same. I am an ancestral descendant of African kings and queens, physicists and mathematicians, architects and educators, and leaders of great vision. I am also unapologetically the son of African American parents: a fifteen-year-old mother and a nineteen-year-old father. I am the product of a poverty-stricken youth, shaped by exploitation, marginalization, and powerlessness. Despite popular belief, I am neither endangered nor obsolete. I am not an actor, athlete, musician, drug dealer, hustler, or pimp, though my interactions with the larger White majority would often have you believe otherwise. I am of blue-collar roots working toward white-collar dreams. I am the mouthpiece of a generation of African American men who have been abandoned and silenced in both mainstream society and the academy. My life largely represents determination, perseverance, compassion, hope, and the fire of life absent in so many of us. My life represents for me and many others the possibilities, the potential that exists in all of us, and the benefit of holding on to your dreams—the benefit of living dangerously and dreaming with your eyes open.

Malcolm X (1965) once asked, "Why am I as I am? To understand that of any person, his whole life, from birth must be reviewed. All of our experiences fuse into our personality. Everything that ever happened to me is an ingredient." This quotation foreshadows the journey that I am about to embark upon. Both scholarly and personal, it represents my quest for direction and definition; to expose the conflict and tension I experience as an African American man on an intellectual journey. My SPN dissertation focuses on the cultural, racial, economic, and political dynamics of higher education, and provides a perspective on the educational socialization process for an African American male from a low-income, working-class background, so as to provide strategies for serving the needs of African American males from working-class backgrounds at predominantly White institutions. It explores the intersection and realities of being an African American man in a United States educational system that denigrated my very existence, invalidated my cultural heritage at every opportunity, and lacked the resources to support the achievement of African American male students like me.

Further, my dissertation explores family relationships, teacher and peer abuse, religion, and cultural and ethnic heritage. It is about a boy who was almost moved to violence, even murderous rage, but who rather sought solace and support from his family as a means to cope with bullying at the hands of teachers and students alike. It is the story of a boy, a man of great strength and compassion in the face of humiliation, frustration, struggle, and eventually triumph. It traces the trials of a child in severe crisis, who despite the lack of popularity associated with achieving in school carved his own path at the direction of his paternal grandmother, who was his primary caregiver. It is a confrontation of cultural and educational inequalities, an attempt to unleash the genius that exists in children, but is often overshadowed by an educational system that holds no respect for what African American boys bring into the classroom.

My dissertation was largely intended to answer the following questions: (1) How have the political, social, economic, and racial dynamics of higher education influenced my development of identity and sense of self? (2) How has history influenced the development of a narrative of exclusion and disillusionment? (3) What factors contributed to my ability to overcome the numerous obstacles encountered on my educational journey? (4) How can my experiences be universalized to empower Black men and deconstruct institutional racism? (5) How can my narrative influence the academy toward change and less exclusivity? (6) How can the rewriting of my narrative serve to transform and inspire a new consciousness? These questions are profoundly personal and yet scholarly. Each contributes to the development of a new understanding of African American men in the academy.

W.E.B. Du Bois (1903) posited: "One ever feels his two-ness,—an American, a Negro; two souls, two thoughts, two unreconciled strivings; two warring ideals in one dark body whose dogged strength alone keeps it from being torn asunder." Here lies the true dilemma. How can a man who straddles two worlds find purpose, self, direction and destiny, when both worlds tug and pull in opposite directions? While I live a middle-class, highly educated life, I am reminded each time I return to my home community in North Carolina that I originate from blue-collar roots. Each time I engage my mother at the convenience store where she is a clerk, or have my groceries bagged by a high school classmate, or sleep on the couch in a home that is hardly big enough for all of us, or visit a family member in prison, I am reminded of the more shameful, humiliating, and defining part of my narrative. This is who I am or who I pretend to be because my true self is not welcomed or valued in higher education. It was in search of this answer that I engaged in this journey of self-discovery; exploring the intersections of my identity, and discovering my place as an African American man in the academy. It was truly a journey toward authentic self-discovery.

Through my dissertation I explored several major themes that were essential in my experiences and the authoring of my narrative. These themes included (1) History of Exclusion, (2) Black Male Identity, (3) Race and Racism, (4) Class, (5)

Family, (6) Education and Professional Leadership. Within each theme, I explored my experiences from a broader perspective, bringing in demographic information, statistics, research, and other writings to illuminate my own narrative. Because of the paucity of research on the experiences of Black men, I drew on the scholarship of Black male biographies, historical works, and literature to extend and universalize my own experience.

I then expanded on the methodology, Scholarly Personal Narrative, and explored why this methodology fits appropriately with both the purpose and the subject of my dissertation. I specifically explored the ideas of writing as liberation, finding voice and the contribution of nontraditional methodologies to the academy. I will share a bit more about that in a moment. I then situated Scholarly Personal Narrative in the larger context of personal narrative that provided voice and outlets to my Black male predecessors. I concluded by providing strategies for both African American males and administrators at predominantly White institutions based on my experiences in the academy. For African American males, it speaks to the struggles faced daily and provides instruction on how to find their place in academia. For faculty, staff, and administrators, it focuses on crafting individually designed plans for meeting the needs of the African American male scholar. It also provides strategies for incorporating what have been invisible narratives into the fabric of the institution. I chose to divide my dissertation into these discrete sections for the purpose of showing the breadth and depth of my narrative identity.

SPN as a Tool for Discovering Direction, Definition, and Destiny

My dissertation was the culmination of many years of a lifelong journey. I hardly expected as a child that I would even go to college, let alone complete a Doctor of Education. Eighteen years ago when I entered North Carolina State University as an undergraduate, I dreamed of one day achieving a doctorate, but never truly believed it possible. My modest beginnings and family history of poverty and substance abuse predicted a different outcome. Being born to teenage parents in a drug-ridden and crime-infested community suggested that I should be living a different life than my middle-class reality. But here I sit, 5 years past what has been one of the more remarkable feats of my young existence.

My narrative, I expect, will open the eyes of many to the inequalities in the American school system, the impact of a capitalist society on education, and the relationship among race, culture, and opportunity structure. It is an account of how social inequality is reproduced from generation to generation. It paints a new, more realistic American dream that denies the adage that any child can grow up to be

President. My narrative illuminates and brings light to the rags-to-riches myth, the bootstrap mentality, and the marginalized and oppressive state of the low-income, working-class poor. Disappointment has been a major force in my narrative. As I make my way up the "Ivory Tower," I am reminded that the dominant narrative is not one like my own, but rather is one of White superiority. My dissertation is an attempt at disrupting the mainstream expectations, an attempt at rewriting the dominant narrative. It is an attempt at giving life and voice to the oppressed.

The Value of Scholarly Personal Narrative

My Scholarly Personal Narrative dissertation represents despair and pain, but also hope and power. It goes some distance toward refuting the notions of Black inferiority. By opening my life for others to view, I hoped to create a genuine and authentic understanding of the individual nature of the Black experience; to disrupt the dominant narrative and weave the Black experience with the experience of other racial groups. I granted others through my dissertation the privilege of seeing my true self and hearing my most authentic voice. I learned from my paternal grandmother and guardian that true voice can only be discovered and exposed when one engages in truth telling and reflection. In higher education, I often felt like a silent participant: invisible, voiceless, and almost impalpable. I rarely felt comfortable expressing myself, largely because I had been taught that any expression of identity and self would be considered both soft and radical in the academy. Despite much experience and personally relevant topics, I found scholarly research and writing to be laborious and boring, rote and mechanical.

In order to understand my place in history, society, and higher education, I had to undertake my own curriculum. This curriculum was largely personal narrative and autobiographical. I chose Scholarly Personal Narrative because it is the only methodology that allowed me to build on the voices of previous narratives and autobiographies and, of course, journal articles and statistics, to frame and contextualize my own story. I drew on the empirical literature to inform the broader issues while examining the broader narratives of noted Black male authors from Du Bois to Obama in order to investigate these issues more deeply through the use of Scholarly Personal Narrative methodology. From this, I then universalized my story to Black men making their way through the academy, whom I supported, reached out to, educated, mentored, and taught.

I could very easily have written about well-ordered theories, but each paled in comparison to my own memories and narrative. The greatest contribution that I could make to higher education was in exposing the truth in my own narrative; to remove the blinders of those who saw only the present and not the cumulative history that engaged each time I did. I lived much of my life in regret, being embarrassed about who I was and where I came from, attempting to rewrite my narrative. Barack Obama (1995) explained in his autobiography: "I spent most of my life trying to rewrite these stories, plugging up holes in the narrative, accommodating unwelcome details, projecting individual choices against the blind sweep of history, all in the hope of extracting some granite slab of truth upon which my unborn children can firmly stand" (p. xvi).

Scholarly Personal Narrative as a methodology is about finding voice and liberation. It is about deliverance and freedom. Scholarly Personal Narrative is about transformation, consciousness, and definition. It is about understanding the subjective experiences of individuals from their own lens. Scholarly Personal Narrative is about constructing an understanding of the past, present, and future. It is the place for secrets and hidden voices to be exposed. It is about providing intellectually discursive space for the pursuit of new meaning and understanding. Scholarly Personal Narrative is about redefining scholarship. It is about redefining expectations. It is about rewriting the words of the oppressor in the words of the oppressed. Scholarly Personal Narrative is about broadening the scope. It is about abandoning the status quo and moving to a greater and more inclusive understanding. It is about making the invisible visible and giving the voiceless voice. Scholarly Personal Narrative is about reframing experiences, renaming reality, and retelling the truth.

Scholarly Personal Narrative can be the doorway to a new understanding of Black and other marginalized experiences in higher education. Scholarly Personal Narrative represents the resurrection and restructuring of life-story methodology, biographic interviewing, discursive and hermeneutic analysis, autoethnography, and oral traditions. It is a journey of the self, an analytical and personal account of one's own story. It is an opportunity to explain differences from an insider's perspective. Scholarly Personal Narrative is a systematic inquiry into self, an examination of self in relation to power structures. It is about finding personal voice and rewriting marginalized narratives. Narratives and storytelling exist in the African American community and other traditionally marginalized communities through the telling and passing down of oral histories. For African Americans, narrative writing serves the role of ameliorating marginalization and oppression endured since slavery. There is richness in the narratives of African American men told in our own words. bell hooks (1989) suggested:

> Autobiographical writing was a way for me to evoke the particular experiences of growing up southern and black in segregated communities. It was a way to recapture the richness of southern black culture. The need to remember and hold to the legacy of that experience and what it taught me has been all the more important since I have since lived in pre-

dominantly white communities and taught at predominantly white colleges. Black southern folk experience was the foundation of the life around me when I was a child; that experience no longer exists in many places where it was once all of the life we knew. Capitalism,
upward mobility, assimilation of other values have all led to rapid disintegration of black
folk experience or in some cases the gradual wearing away of that experience (p. 158).

My Scholarly Personal Narrative dissertation represents the sound of my voice,
the significance of my life experiences, self-revelation, the abstract and the concrete,
hope, and meaning. It is about passion, anger, fear, and love. It is about rewriting,
redefining, retelling, restructuring, and renaming the experiences of African
American men. Scholarly Personal Narrative is about emotion and vulnerability,
mattering and marginalization, and truth. Above all else, it represents my search
as an African American male for direction, definition, and destiny in the academy
and the search of so many others whose voices have been left at the margins of the
academy.

Finding Voice

So what? Why should the world care about poor Black men and other marginalized voices? Why should the world care about me? What significance does my narrative hold for higher education? What contribution can a narrative of poverty, racial
marginalization, and Black male inferiority make to the academy? How can the
retelling of memories, incidents, encounters, and experiences inform the experiences
of Black male students in college and the work of faculty, staff, and administrators
who are a part of their daily lives? Unquestionably, changes in the United States
resulting from *Brown v. Board of Education* and other landmark developments of
the Civil Rights Movement have made it possible for Black men and other marginalized populations to participate freely and fully in all walks of American life,
including higher education. However, the narratives of many marginalized populations remain misunderstood, invisible, and at the margins of the academy.

I offer this scholarly personal narrative reflection as a testimony to the state of
emergency and urgency among Black men, as evidence of the ravaging nature of
our experiences. It is about dried-up dreams, hidden truths, and survival. I am no
expert or high authority on the experiences of all Black men, people of color, or
others who have experienced marginalization, but I am a living witness to the catastrophic damage caused by the exclusion of Black men like me in society. I have,
over the course of my life, studied the roots and systemic ways that the outside forces
of White America have continued to subjugate, terrorize, and decimate Black
men. I have also reviewed the attempts on the part of Black men and the supposed

attempt on the part of White America to rectify this situation and have come to one resounding conclusion.

The answers to our problems, the road map out of this maze of self-hate, deprivation, indifference, and defeat can be found only in our collective effort to move Black men and our marginalized counterparts from the margins to the mainstream of society. We must experience a uniting of our efforts as students, faculty, and administrators. We each have a role and purpose in encouraging the development of marginalized populations. Only in shedding the layers of lies of the weakness and inferiority of Black men and marginalized populations in general can the wounds be healed.

In the years leading up to the completion of my dissertation, I experienced the benefit of numerous relationships and experiences that impacted my growth and development as a student and a professional. With each relationship and experience, I learned lessons that have influenced my shift from the margins of society to the walls of academia. It was through these lessons that I gained the courage to share these reflections with the hope that it will inform practice, teaching, and the development of authentic relationships based on trust, understanding, and respect. I also share these reflections with the knowledge that there is no one way to meet the needs of poor Black men or other marginalized populations. We all have unique voices that deserve to be heard and are deserving of the opportunity to bring our fully authentic selves into life's laboratory.

Conclusion

My situation is unique, as all individual lives and stories are unique. And yet, my story can inform the experiences of African American men and other traditionally marginalized persons pursuing higher education. For many reasons I was able to earn a bachelor's and move forward to a graduate degree. Some of these reasons were due to individual characteristics that my grandmother instilled in me. Some of them are organizational, like the African American Symposium that welcomed me to NC State. Others are from chance encounters or deliberate outreach from others, such as from the Director of African-American Student Affairs at NC State. At times sheer luck, as when a chance observance of my behavior landed me a Resident Advisor position, played its part in my being able to engage fully in the campus experience. The grace of God influenced all of my decisions, chance encounters, and opportunities. Yes, along the way, I experienced racism. I experienced this racism from professors, from classmates, and from the many other ways that institutional racism influences the experiences of a Black man in college. I cannot tell you how all these reasons and experiences worked together or which were more important than others in bringing me through my undergraduate and graduate experiences successfully. I can tell you that they did. I can also tell you that I am very grateful that they did, and as appreciation for the outcome, I have embraced the chance to support other African American male students through the process.

While I hope that members of the academy find my narrative valuable, my intended audience has primarily been my fellow Black scholars who, as indicated by my close friend and colleague Jacob Diaz (2002), find themselves in unfamiliar territory, oblivious to their cultural histories and narratives. I hope they find this motivating in the most crucial moments of their professional journeys. I want to create an academic environment where marginalized narratives can exist in symbiotic relation to dominant discourse. Only then will my goal be achieved.

Essay #2 by Leslye Kornegay

Leslye Kornegay *is a life-long learner. She is a recent graduate of the College of Education and Social Service Doctoral program at the University of Vermont. She holds a Master of Administration from Central Michigan University and a Bachelor of Science in Business Administration from Mount Olive College. Dr. Kornegay's doctoral dissertation, Leading to Change the World: One African American Woman's Journey into Positions of Leadership in Predominantly White Institutions (PWIs), focused on her unique experiences as an African American woman leading in PWIs. Dr. Kornegay used SPN research methodology to share her personal and professional experiences as a student and leader. Dr. Kornegay's research introduced to the literature the use of "confidence circles" as a resource for African American women in PWIs to sustain their leadership.*

Dr. Kornegay's research provided several recommendations for PWIs around diversity and inclusion and multicultural competency for students, faculty, and staff. Dr. Kornegay is currently the Director of the University of Vermont's (UVM) Custodial Services Department, one of the largest diverse organizations on the UVM campus. She brings 30 years of leadership, and executive leadership, experience in the areas of facilities management, custodial services, hospitality, and conference services. Dr. Kornegay serves as Chair of the Division's Diversity Committee, providing leadership for major divisional diversity initiatives including the division's ongoing diversity professional development series, and multicultural competencies assessment process. She also serves on the President's Commission on Racial Diversity at the University of Vermont and is the Chair of the PCRD racial diversity subcommittee. She is a member of the adjunct faculty at a local institution of higher education and has presented numerous presentations and workshops in her area of expertise. Dr. Kornegay was awarded the Susan Hasazi ALANA Award for Outstanding Academic Achievement in Doctoral Education from the College of Education and Social Services at the University of Vermont. Dr. Kornegay is a member of the international honor society Pi Gamma Mu.

The Reflections and Best Practices of One African American Woman's SPN Doctoral Writing Experience in the Academy

As a recent doctoral graduate of the College of Education at the University of Vermont, and a former student of Dr. Robert J. Nash, I fully embraced the Scholarly Personal Narrative (SPN) writing style in my doctoral work. As an African American woman, I believe a recipe for successful student writing should include the following key ingredients: power or validation to express the marginalized voice + the student experience = successful student writing (MV + SE = SSW). How and why students like myself have embraced this style of writing to conduct their research has as many reasons as there are SPN writers. Like most non-related additions to a family, the research community has been slow to embrace its red-haired sibling, SPN writing. Nevertheless, SPN writing has, over the years, developed a following within the student community and more recently the academic community at the University of Vermont (Kornegay, 2012).

Why SPN Was Right for Me

I selected SPN as my dissertation research design because I believed it was the best way for me to share my unique experiences as an African American woman in executive leadership roles, as well as a doctoral student in a Predominately White Institution (Kornegay, 2012). It was not until I was exposed to the SPN writing style that I was able to truly include my marginalized voice in my research (Kornegay, 2012). SPN writing gave me a license, if you will, to tell my story in my own voice using a writing style that did not require dressing up my paper for the peer-reviewed process commonly required in qualitative and quantitative research papers and using American Psychological Association formatting (Kornegay, 2012). While other research methodologies obviously have their value in the research field, I believe the best way for me to unleash my marginalized voice is through SPN writing.

My professional and student experiences could not be told without including my personal narrative. I believe that by sharing my voice, I will help to expand SPN methodology writing into another area in the scholarship by using my role as an executive officer who has led support service organizations in PWIs. While there are a number of support service departments within most campus communities, I think one that impacts every area on campus, but often works behind the scenes, is the Housekeeping Department. Until you walk in my shoes, or come into my world and hear my experiences as a woman, African American, and executive, it's hard to imagine the complexities of leading an organization very similar to the structure of a mid-size *Fortune* 500 company.

My organization provides service through human capital with all of the complexities that come with working with many employees who represent marginalized populations. This population is comprised of entry-level employees and is often one of the largest departments on campus. Some of the employees are adult students like myself; however, the majority of employees who work in the profession of housekeeping, whether it is in higher education or any other sector, are representatives of some of the most marginalized populations in their communities. This is true of the Housekeeping Department at the University of Vermont. As a nontraditional first-generation college student, having the option to include my personal narrative in my writing was critical to successfully completing my studies. I believe this is another reason why the social groups that have traditionally not had a voice in the literature have embraced SPN writing.

If something inside you is real, we will probably find it interesting, and it will probably be universal, at least at some level. So you must risk placing real emotion at the center of your work. Write straight into the emotional center of things. Write toward vulnerability. Don't worry about appearing sentimental of soft. Worry about being unavailable; worry about being absent or fraudulent. Risk being unliked. Tell the truth, as you understand it. If you're a writer, you have a moral obligation to do this. And it is a revolutionary act—truth is always subversive.

I strongly believe that when you write the truth from the heart, your audience will likely be able to find something universal in your writing. Write with emotion, and don't hold anything back. Be real, write with integrity, and don't worry about being liked. As long as you like yourself, and can look yourself in the mirror, write on. Chances are my perception of unpacking some aspect in my life is not going to be the same as someone else's. An example of this is the restoration of childhood from my lens. I know my experiences were different than what my mother or other adult members of my family might recall from their adult lens, so I needed to tell my story the way I remembered it. My perspective on my story has shaped the person who I have become today. SPN has freed me to tell my story and to keep my audience at the front and center of my research.

Why Should We Want Our Stories to Matter?

So what does this mean for marginalized students who want their stories to matter? There is a personal story here, of course. As a child my favorite pastime was stories. I can recall eagerly awaiting story time from my elders, but these were not just any stories, they were stories about my ancestors and my heritage. I was born during a time when my history was not written in the history books. It was passed down from generation to generation through story—oral history. While some of my ancestors' history followed a similar path to Alex Haley's book *Roots* (1976), the first exposure to my history was passed down from my elders, which was passed down to them from their elders. Therefore, stories are how I learned to connect to my heritage. As I grew up, the value in personal stories that I had been taught as a child was not in the history books. What I learned in school during those early formative years was the dominant groups' version of history. SPN writing enabled me to go back to my roots and to recapture what was missing in my writing as well as to embrace my womanism worldview.

I did not decide right away that SPN writing was for me. Early in my doctoral program, I decided to conduct a qualitative research study. It was not until 18 months into preparing my dissertation proposal that I realized I needed to change my research direction. It was during this time that I began the pre-search stage of SPN writing without realizing it. By the time I reached out to my new advisor, Dr. Robert Nash, about my research goals (putting myself in the center of my research—the *me-search* stage), writing the proposal came very easy for me. I was finally able to bridge my research with something that excited me. I had heard from former students who had successfully completed their doctorates that if you want to be successful with your dissertation, make sure you choose a topic you are passionate about and select the RIGHT methodology. My professional experiences kept bringing me back to a desire to include my narrative in my doctoral research. SPN enabled me to bridge the social, political, historical context of my leadership journey through my personal, professional, and student stories.

All of this was possible through my narratives and letters. Epistolary Scholarly Personal Narrative (ESPN) letter writing (Nash & Bradley, 2011) helped me to universalize my experience even more with the scholarship and women like myself. I wrote a number of letters in my dissertation that I used to help bring closure to my chapters and to bridge (transition and connect) them along the way. The letter from my "Father to Myself" was healing and therapeutic. I was actually able to write the words that I believed my father would have said to me if he had still been living. While the letter was powerful in itself, when I actually read the letter out loud to myself, I was moved to tears. I am convinced that somehow my father had reached me from his resting place and was finally able to say to me in death what he wasn't able to say in life. I felt a sense of peace and closure with this experience. This is the beauty of SPN writing. My experience in the SPN course, coupled with listening to my peers' stories, affirmed for me that this writing methodology gives voice to students like myself.

In the SPN writing course, we were encouraged to share parts of our work as the course progressed and to get constructive feedback from our peers. The value I found was not only in the feedback they gave me, but also in listening to their stories and how I was able to contribute ideas and suggestions for them that helped them with their writing projects. There were visiting scholars who shared their SPN research with the class as well as their advice on how to start, sustain, and finish a successful writing project. I found all of these experiences invaluable. The exposure to this writing style unleashed a flood of writing experiences that only grew during the length of the course. There is a sense of community and support that transpires when you embrace SPN writing. I cannot put my finger on WHAT it is, because it is many different things. The sense of community for me took the form of new friendships, exposure to a new way of thinking, and something that had been missing in my student experience, a feeling that someone really cared about my research goals and me. SPN is not just a way of writing; it fosters a culture of community, and it helped me to articulate a research term that came out of my dissertation, the use of "confidence circles."

Recommendations for Successful SPN Writing

Embracing the SPN writing style forced me to change how I approached my writing. I realized that I had created stumbling blocks for myself, which actually hindered my ability to write. For example, until I embraced SPN writing, I never wrote in a group or with a partner. I never wrote outside my home. I had created barriers to my own progress. I found, during this experience, that my willingness to change made a significant difference in my overall approach to writing. Prior to this change, I could never see an end to my dissertation journey or how I was going to get there. I just knew it was not an option to fail. Combined with the commitment to meet a writing partner 4 days a week in the library 4 to 5 hours a night, my writing took off. Once I committed to doing an SPN and removed the barriers that were keeping me from it, my timeline to complete my dissertation unfolded, and I was marching to receive my degree within one year.

Through my dissertation research I was able to make recommendations to PWIs about the value that SPN writing brings to the scholarship when voices of marginalized groups are included in the literature. Only then can true social change begin to take place. Additionally, as shared in my dissertation, I believe SPN writing would benefit formal mentoring and sponsoring programs for non-traditional students and professionals. The student mentees would be able to share their experiences with their mentors in their own voices. This would provide another vehicle for mentors/sponsors to be able to provide support to students. SPN writing reaches the masses who do not aspire to be researchers, but who strive for meaning-making in their daily lives.

In summary, I would like to offer the following tips that grew out of my SPN dissertation as proven best practices for anyone who aspires to be an SPN writer:

1. Have faith that your story has value
2. Find a writing partner
3. Find a safe physical space to do your writing
4. Schedule time to meet with your writing partner
5. Write, then edit, then write, then edit . . .
6. End your writing sessions with a clear starting point to set up your next writing session
7. Let your scholarship complement your writing...not the other way around
8. Be creative and open to what you learn about yourself along the way
9. Have FUN! Contrary to so much student opinion, scholarly writing does not have to be a "dreaded drag." SPN writing is actually something to look forward to. Imagine!
10. Know that SPN is therapeutic. Be prepared for personal transformation.

Two SPN Reflections by International Students: "Neither Here nor There!"

Essay #3 by Jennifer Jang (Chang Wen-Hsin)

Jennifer Jang *is a multilingual (Chinese, Japanese, English) global citizen—resilient, intuitive, and passionate scholar, philosopher, and educator. She has served as a higher education administrator at the University of Vermont, and Loyola University in Chicago, Illinois. Her multiple identities are composites of her highly mobile Cosmopolite lifestyle, transitioning from countries and cultures in her childhood. Her experience as an Asian international woman, and a first-generation working-class college student, has grounded her passion in holistic wellness, financial management, life coaching, and intercultural education. Her research interests include quarterlife meaning-making, moral conversation, scholarly personal narrative writing, and social justice advocacy dialogue. Jennifer has been a featured speaker throughout the country on a number of topics related to her scholarly interests. She has also published some of her SPN work. As a reflective practitioner and life-long learner, Jennifer strives to contribute thought-pro-*

voking and inspiring perspectives in her personal and professional interactions, while supporting and bringing out the best in others.

Neither Here nor There

Have you ever felt like you are completely alone and left out, do not belong anywhere, or stuck in between worlds? This status of limbo is a strong emotion, and a harsh reality, for many in this fast-paced age of globalization, where we are more connected via electronics than we have ever been before—but, ironically, we also feel the most disconnected. There are increasing numbers of people who are raised in multiple cultures and countries. This contributes to an overwhelming sense of confusion and isolation. When raised in an either-or world, these global citizens take on parts of each culture but cannot fully identity with one. As a result, they live and experience existing "neither here nor there."

How Does SPN Connect Globally?

> The real voyage of discovery is not in seeking new places, but in seeing with new eyes.
> —MARCEL PROUST

We all have our own particular style of processing and relating to experience. Some of us are thinkers, storytellers, actors, musicians, and so on. SPN is one writing style among the many avenues to interpret and communicate thoughts, ideas, and emotions. While SPN writing is versatile, it illustrates the power and connectivity of storytelling. It demonstrates the evolutionary survival need to share narratives; thus, it is certainly more widely practiced than formal "research," and it is consistent throughout the worlds of cultural difference. Storytelling and sharing narratives serve the evolutionary purposes of solidarity, inclusion, and validation. Thus, narratives confer survival benefits on persons and cultures.

To narrativize is to paint mental pictures in the minds of people, and this boosts community building, enriches related experiences, and stimulates a sense of bonding and solidarity. Sharing narratives promotes inclusivity as it transports memories. It can be a combination of the visual, audio, and kinesthetic; therefore, it can provide room for different learning styles in the classroom, work, and interpersonal settings. Storytelling creates a shared intellectual and emotional experience that enhances humor and laughter. This, in turn, affirms and validates a sense of belonging. SPN connects us globally across cultures and generations.

Uniquely Me—Universally We

> We are already one and we imagine we are not. And what we have to recover is
> our original unity. Whatever we have to be is what we are.
> —THOMAS MERTON

The beauty and glory of SPN writing is that there is a universalizable piece that connects to the human core of each and every one of us. Despite your heritage, background, upbringing, current status, or lifestyle, there are fundamental values and emotions of what it means to be human that connect us all. For example, the challenges and experiences of being a Cosmopolite can be universal and applicable to anyone who grew up in a cross-cultural context. Foster youths may share the sense of insecurity and a lack of belonging. Youth who identify as LGBTQ may feel like they are "the only ones" growing up. Similarly, bi/multi-racial individuals who drift and never feel able to find that solid identity and foundation might feel, as do many Cosmopolites, neither here nor there. Some who straddle socio-economic classes are torn by feeling as if they have to choose between their lower, working-class backgrounds and their present professional status. So, too, there are transfer students who feel alienated from their peers; there are the growing groups of immigrants in the Western world who feel cut off from their families; and there are individuals with disabilities, and underrepresented racial populations within the United States who are alienated, estranged, and lonely.

Universalizability is one of my major objectives in this piece of writing. I hope themes of straddling cultures, afraid to be vulnerable, wanting to belong, finding balance, empowering self and others, challenges of isolation, and desire to be validated will become resonant for you as I write this piece. It is my hope that you are able to make connections to your own life narrative, and allow them to help you explore your own feelings of being "neither here nor there."

The What, Why, How to Who I Am as a Cosmopolite

> A successful woman is one who can build and lay a firm foundation with the
> bricks others have thrown at her.
> —DAVID BRINKLEY

It seemed only a few years ago that a father made a quick announcement of his decision to move the whole family from Taipei, Taiwan, to Saipan, Commonwealth of Northern Mariana Islands (CNMI). In less than a month, in a state of devastation and shock, a 10-year-old girl was ripped away from the only life she had ever known. Everything that she called home vanished. Without knowing a single letter of the English alphabet, she was thrown into an English-speaking environment 2 months later. My name is Jennifer Jang, and I was that girl. With one airplane ride, my whole world had died.

Eight years later, as a 4.0 high school graduate, having triumphed over being teased, harassed, and bullied in school for my language deficiency in the first several years in Saipan, I was on another flight. This one was a bit longer, leading me eight thousand miles away from home in Saipan to Wyoming, USA, where I embarked on the journey of undergraduate studies. My time in Wyoming, Colorado, Vermont, and Illinois since then has been a great learning experience. I grew and expanded in multiple dimensions, gained in intellectual value, and deepened in emotional net worth. I became a better version of myself through the polishing and refinement of surviving alone on the continent, struggling through multiple identity development, strategizing toward financial liberation, and striving for fulfillment from the inside out. As the above quote eloquently illustrates, I built a stronger foundation with the bricks others and life throw at me.

From a distance, my childhood may seem glamorous to some. It has not, however, been without its trials and turbulences. This highly mobile lifestyle comes with unsolicited baggage and a complicated maze of emotional instability, insecurity, and a sense of rootlessness, just as when a tree is transplanted too often, its roots can never grow deep. I struggle with a mixed sense of identity, interrupted development in my childhood, and the nuances of navigating certain relationships in each culture. Compared with other mono-culture peers, I must alternate between various cultures and incorporate an array of values and standards from each. These challenges get at the root of who I am, and can be so overwhelming that they seem to cancel out the benefits of my unique life-journey. It took me more than 12 years to come to terms with what I am—a Cosmopolite.

As my most salient identity, the Greek roots of the word "Cosmopolite" are *kosmo* and *polites*, which mean citizen of the world. I live in a neither/nor world, a culture that is neither my parents' nor my own. Having spent a significant part of my developmental years outside of my parents' culture, I am a composite of all the cultures I have lived in (Taiwan, Saipan, Japan, and several states in the United States); but no single one fully encompasses all of who I am. I have built relationships with all of the cultures, but I do not have full ownership of any. This leads to a range of marginalized identity experiences in this culture and country.

Living on the Edge: Labeled as the "Other"

> Difficulties are opportunities to better things; they are stepping-stones to greater experience.
> —BRIAN ADAMS

Marginalization happens in all societies, pushing the people outside the norm-group to live on the edge. When on the edge of society, one continues to receive implicit and explicit messages of insignificance, insufficiency, and indifference. Often excluded from meaningful participation in the heart of society, marginalization takes people to the periphery, often seen as questionable and with minimal quality. Subtle messages of difference and separateness from the others prevent the marginalized group from feeling normal, accepted, or valid. Marginalization increases the level of an already dismal existence of self-doubting disconnection. These are just a few ways I have been pushed to the margins, based on these multiple identities of mine, which took many years to transform into "stepping-stones to greater experiences," as the Brian Adams quote indicates.

The feelings of disapproval and disconnection are present even when I return to my passport country. When I am in Taiwan, I am too American and international. When I am in the United States, I am too Asian and foreign. The message is that I am never enough. Usually retelling stories from a childhood evokes resonance and reassurance from others about your experience. However, sharing my life narratives is usually not a grounding experience of affirmation or validation, as others usually cannot relate. It is a painful process that reminds me that I do not belong.

Due to my life journey, I have developed a distinctively different worldview—perspective, resilience, way of thinking, and way of taking in information—that sets me apart from most of my peers. In a conventional society where it is more acceptable to conform to the norm, I am the natural outcast. In almost all situations in my life, I have been considered the alien, foreigner—on the edge, not belonging, estranged, nontraditional, and odd. I am always the "other."

Disempowered and Disillusioned: A Woman without a Country

> Sometimes adversity is what you need to face in order to become successful.
> —ZIG ZIGLAR

On top of experiencing being foreign back in my birth country, Saipan, for 8 years, and dwelling on this continent as an "alien" (termed by the U.S. government) by myself for 7 additional years, my journey as the "other" has become even more wearing. I did not have a community where I felt truly understood, felt a sense of solidarity, and accepted as the whole human being that I am. As an international Asian woman simultaneously belonging everywhere and nowhere, I feel boxed in, minimized, and stifled in the United States. This is a very disempowering thought to realize as I began my 20th year as the "marginalized other." I am becoming like a rubber band that, when stretched long enough, loses its elasticity. Technically a non-U.S. citizen, I experience immigration visa challenges, and I run into other legal structures, laws, and regulations that most others never have to think about.

Even when I think that I can at least return to my home if I can no longer stay in the States, my transient lifestyle presents another challenge. My parents have also lived outside of their passport country for the last 15 years, in Saipan, CNMI. Hence, without a valid U.S. visa, I cannot return to where my nuclear family is, which I consider "home," especially since the U.S. government recently took over the CNMI government. These are just a few issues that I am obliged to carry with me everywhere I go, even though I do not constantly articulate this to the world. These are invisible, yet suffocatingly heavy identity stipulations. With no solid ground to build a firm foundation and consistency, it is hard to solidify peace of heart and mind. How do I keep myself motivated when I feel the light to my spirit is dim and broken? In short, I am a woman without a country. Neither here nor there.

Re-Evaluating My Worth: Nine Ways SPN Re-Illuminated My Fading Light

> SPN writing can take many forms. While it is personal, it is also social. While it is practical, it is also theoretical. While it is reflective, it is also public. While it is local, it is also political. While it narrates, it also proposes. While it is self-revealing, it also evokes self-examination from readers. Whatever its unique shape and style of communicating to readers, an SPN's central purpose is to make an impact on both writer and reader, on both the individual and the community.
> —ROBERT J. NASH

My experience with SPN writing has confirmed for me how important it is to include both my personal narrative, and my scholarship, into my learning and research. SPN has clarified, validated, and grounded me into a more illuminated, and illuminating, human being. It has inspired, enhanced, and liberated me to become who I want to be. Gleaning value from all the adversities, challenges, difficulties, and bricks of life, I want to share with you nine ways in which SPN helped me recover and express my authentic, hitherto marginalized scholar's voice.

These insights continue to deepen my own awareness and appreciation for SPN. I also include guiding maxims, which are short sayings that condense wisdom into a few "ingenious, kinetic lines" (Nash & Murray, 2010, p. 179) at the beginning of each insight, because I find that these concisely capture the ideas I propose and expand in the following sections. They are open-ended, convey rich meaning, and stimulate "fresh interpretations" (2010, p. 179). I hope these inspirational maxims will help you draw parallels to your own journey to recover and express your authentic, marginalized scholar's voice.

Gain Clarity

> There is only one journey: going inside yourself.
> —RAINER MARIA RILKE

The beginning process of SPN writing is almost like journaling for me. I pour my thoughts, feelings, observations, and needs onto the page, whether electronic or paper. Writing things out for me is taking action on figuring out the complexities of my life instead of just staring at it, wishing it would simply figure itself out. SPN leads me on a path to my core, to take a deep look at myself on the inside. When we process via writing versus talking, our thoughts flow ten times slower. Hence, I gain more clarity, awareness, and sharpness on the things I am pondering. I can successfully untangle the ball of yarn that has been knotted for a while. I write into clarity as SPN takes me on a journey inside myself to make sense of myself.

Practice Courage

> Everything we want is on the other side of fear.
> —FARRAH GRAY

On my journey to clarity, I have often stumbled into life and writing potholes, no matter how strong and tough I may seem to the world. I was unaware of how I fell into the fear-of-failure pothole, but I was certainly hyper-conscious of how lousy it felt to be stuck in it. I sank in and felt small and unworthy, insignificant and far from valuable. I procrastinated to turn away from facing my fears. SPN allowed me to write at my own comfort level of vulnerability, as it is as personal as I make it. SPN allowed me to face my fears and worries, examine my anxiety, and investigate my insecurities. I practiced being courageous for myself through SPN.

Heal the Pain

> To forgive is to set a prisoner free and discover that the prisoner was you.
> —LEWIS B. SMEDES

Through gaining clarity of self and practicing courage to face my fears, I realized there is a lot of hurt to be healed in my life. SPN provided a venue for me to process internally and externally in order to make sense of my experiences. SPN helped me to accept the imperfection of being human, forgive myself and others in my heart, and release myself from years of imprisonment in guilt, shame, and self-blame. SPN gave me a platform to heal and find peace within myself.

Ground Me Authentically

> Be yourself, everyone else is already taken.
> —OSCAR WILDE

As I gain clarity, practice courage, and heal the pain on my self-discovery journey, I am more able to express who I am. SPN allows me to use my language in my own way, take pride in how I choose to walk in the world each day, and allow my voice to inspire, rejuvenate, and transform others. SPN requires me to do more self-examination, analysis, probing, exploration, editing, reviewing, because it is so personal. SPN reminds me that it is better to write for myself and have no public, than to write for the public and have no self. SPN allows me to embrace true authorship of all my learning, writing, and teaching, so that I can redefine my life and make meaning from my experience. SPN grounds me authentically because I am allowed to bring my whole raw and transparent self into the picture. I found my way back to myself through SPN.

Empower Vulnerability

> And as we let our own light shine, we unconsciously give other people permission to do the same.
> —NELSON MANDELA

Discovering who I am authentically through SPN is powerful. It empowered me to unveil my vulnerable life-narrative. I can put all of myself on the table, not covered up—completely honest, genuine, and open, while still protecting the confidentiality of all those individuals who have impacted my life. SPN is not a competition. It is about me overcoming my personal fears of writing, of life, and of whatever may be holding me back. As we are liberated from our own fear, our presence automatically liberates others. SPN sets up a venue for me to share vulnerably with others; and in turn, we are able to build trust and bind community together…in a spirit of mutual vulnerability and mutual strength.

Validate My Being

> A woman cannot be comfortable without her own approval.
> —MARK TWAIN

Although I may be empowered to share who I am authentically, I still experience self-doubt. I wonder whether I am "too this" or "too that" or simply not good enough. With SPN, however, I learned that every single person's lived experience and stories are so valued because it is *our* life narrative. Nobody can ever take it away from us. Nobody has the right to disenfranchise us. We are the experts in our own life because no one else knows it better than we do. SPN reminded me that I do not write simply because I want to say something. Instead, I write because I have got something to say. Instead of living in denial, SPN allowed me to give the Cosmopolite Asian woman's experience my approval. Thus, I validate my own being.

Strengthen Faith

> However long the night, the dawn will break.
> —AFRICAN PROVERB

> Change the way you look at things, and the things you look at will change.
> —WAYNE DYER

Dealing peacefully with my own self-doubt is not enough sometimes, particularly when outside factors and roadblocks challenge my focus, try to break me down, attempt to corrupt my values, and contaminate my beliefs. SPN reminds me to keep on believing, because everyone who got to where they are had to begin with where they were. I need to believe in the process of re-creation, in myself, in the possibilities, in the potentials. I need to continue to invest in myself, increase my intellectual and groundedness capital, and secure my richness from the inside out. I will remain hopeful and continue to take one day at a time no matter how turbulent it may feel or seem in this moment. When I shifted the paradigm from outside to inside, external circumstances no longer seemed as scary or daunting. Writing into a different perspective by changing the way I look at things, SPN strengthened my faith in the knowledge that no matter how long the night, the dawn will break.

Balance the Core

> Half of our mistakes in life arise from feeling when we ought to think, and thinking when we ought to feel.
> —JOHN CHURTON COLLINS

To be grounded, empowered, validated, and strengthened is inspiring yet dangerously powerful if not managed in harmony. SPN helps me to balance these qualities at my core. With SPN, I compose with my heart soul mind and spirit. As a strong Feeler in the Myers Brigg Type Indicator Assessment (Tieger & Barron-Tieger, 2001), my thoughts flow constantly like a river. I write to allow my free-flowing ruminations to take form, connect to one another, and make sense outside of my mind. SPN provides me with the avenue to balance appropriately the utilization of my thinking and feeling in my scholarship. With SPN, I am able to write straight into the emotional center of things without losing myself in the process. I engage all of my senses beyond the conventional five, and also my sense of balance at the core.

Liberate the Self

> Most of the shadows in this life are caused by us standing in our own sunshine.
> —RALPH WALDO EMERSON

Through gaining clarity, practicing courage, healing the pain on a self-discovery journey, and feeling grounded, empowered, validated, and strengthened as a person, I am now at an all-time-high level of self-awareness and height of self-acceptance. Because I stood in my own sunshine in the past, I silenced my authentic self and tossed my voice away. When I realized how important it was to get my voice back, I did not know where to look. SPN helped me find my voice. Or to be more exact, SPN showed me that I do not need to find my voice. I have always had my voice. I just simply need to get out of the way of my own sunshine, free myself from being in the shadow, and give myself permission to use my voice.

Illuminate Forward: Re-Light Your Voice

> A candle loses nothing by lighting another candle.
> —JAMES KELLER

SPN writing allows me as a quarterlifer to make meaning in the process of my writing, to shine light onto an invisible, marginalized, international population in my writing, and to empower others as well as myself. It is through SPN that I was able to express my authentic, hitherto marginalized, scholar's voice. Delving deeper into the universalizable areas of human connection through SPN has helped me tremendously in gaining self-awareness, enhancing personal connections, and enriching professional relationship dynamics. My faith is strong that everything happens for a reason. My optimism is contagious, and I am confident that it influences those around me. My courage is so resilient that it bounces back from the hardest trials. I will trust and trust again even when others prove me otherwise, because my life deserves more than a small setback can block.

My life skills as a Cosmopolite and expert navigator of life's turbulence reminds me to remain hopeful and, loving, and stay true to my beliefs through it all. I just need to believe in my talents and skills, remember the existence of my core values, and continue accelerating forward. I need to believe that the sun will rise, and that tomorrow will be a better day. I must remember that everything will fall into place and be where it was meant to be.

As a way to illuminate and share the light, I compose not just for myself, but also for those who cannot write for themselves; I share my perspective for those who are not allowed to voice theirs. I share my narrative so that I may shine light onto an invisible population that does not have the same access. The greatest good we can do for others is not just to share our riches with them, but to help them to reveal theirs. And when you have an opportunity to inspire others to look for their passion, believe in their potential, and know that they truly matter, then why wouldn't you want to illuminate forward?

SPN has allowed me to gain clarity and rediscover myself, practice being courageous so that I can heal my soul, liberate myself with balance and validation, and empower myself and others to have faith and to inspire. You do not have to be great to start, but you have to start to be great. I hope these personal and practical SPN writing implications of gaining clarity, practicing courage, healing the pain on a self-discovery journey, and of groundedness, empowerment, validation, and strength will propel you to begin recovering and expressing your authentic scholar's voice.

Essay #4 by Modou Ndione

*My name is **Modou Ndione**. I was born and raised in Senegal. There, after completing a degree in literature and philosophy, I taught African literature at the middle school level and philosophy at the high school level for 7 years. I now live in the United States, where I taught elementary and middle school French. Currently I am working as an instructor at ALMC, a school specializing in the education of autistic children. As an international member of the community, I can say with certainty that the problems we encounter contribute to stifle our voices. As our difficulties to adapt to a different culture remain, for the most part, unexpressed, the solitude we live in becomes weighted. The academic and social institutions, designed to satisfy the dominant White majority, are poorly suited to our needs. In an artificially formalized system that negates the validity of personal stories and leaves the minorities stranded, SPN gives us a sense of power about our own lives.*

Recovering My Voice through SPN as a Senegalese Living in the United States

I was born and raised in Senegal, the western-most part of the African continent along the Atlantic Ocean, at the crossroads of major sea and air routes. I am from a family of six (four boys and two sisters). We grew up in a rural community, going to French and Koranic school during the school year, and farming during the rainy season. My mother, Khady Diop, and my father, Cheikh Ndione, grew up during colonial rule. Unlike my father, my mother only went to Koranic school. She is a very spiritual, sweet, loving, and kind person. She stayed at home and took care of everything. My father was a social worker for the government for 35 years. He went from village to village to help people get education about disease prevention. He also helped create and support local and sustainable economic activities.

In Senegal hospitality, *Teranga* is no vain word. It is one of the intrinsic virtues of the country. Senegalese are warm and welcoming; the pleasure of giving and receiving is real. Whether for a stranger, a close relative, or a friend who comes unexpectedly from anywhere, hospitality remains a moral duty. Oral tradition is a dominant trait of Senegalese society as well. The stories that are told provide moral lessons that facilitate and strengthen relationships within the community. Behind the simple narratives resides a deep philosophical and metaphysical meditation on man and life.

For centuries, millions of people throughout West Africa were hunted, tortured, and sold like common goods in the triangle trade. Many left Senegal through the "Door of No Return" on Gorée Island for America and the Caribbean. After slavery came the era of colonization. In the 19th century, European empires in decline, needing more resources to revive their economies, occupied, subjected, and assimilated new territories. From 1895 to 1960, France held Senegal under the claims of a civilizing mission that resulted in the disintegration and impoverishment of the societal structure.

During and after colonization, very little room was made for the teaching of the history of my own culture. Neocolonial school curriculums put the main focus on teaching French culture, reinforcing, at the same time, the domination. As a result, my culture was considered to be a vulgar thing, barely a fragment of French culture. However, the Senegalese have preserved much of their history in oral tradition. I grew up learning, through tales and legends, the true history of my country, the harmony in which they lived before Europeans set foot on their land. Certainly, discovering the painful past of my ancestors is not the most pleasant thing, but it did help me understand that my own alienation is inseparable from their alienation.

Neither Here nor There

I came to the United States at age 32, carrying most of my luggage in the heart and the mind. The universe into which I was born and raised, with its myths, legends, and tales, the uniqueness of its cultural and religious beliefs, shaped and gave soul to the person that I am, my worldviews, my values, and meanings of life. It is in that universe that I was nourished to believe *Nit Nitteye Garabam*, a Wolof proverb that means *The Remedy for Man, is Man.* For me, this means everything that exists has a soul, and for that reason every being deserves to be treated with respect and dignity. I learned that if we want to access God, we need to celebrate the divine in nature and in humans.

I remember stepping out of the plane at John F. Kennedy International Airport in New York City, going through multiple immigration gates and interrogations, and entering a whole different world in which I was welcomed as an "alien resident." This label caused me to think about my new identity. The word *alien* implying more than being a foreigner, I could consider that I am not even from Africa, from Senegal. In fact, I may not even be from earth. I could not conceptualize this first overwhelming feeling of being a stranger to others in a world that appeared also strange to me. Past the first moments of curiosity and amazement, I realized my new identity, as an alien living in a community of human beings, makes me question my humanity and keeps me at a distance from others, while reminding me constantly that, even though I live with others, I am not and will never be one of them.

I never paid much attention to my racial identity until I started living in the United States, where people are classified according to their race, social status, religion, and so on. Often, when I fill out job applications, or an official document, I am asked to specify the categories to which I belong. I am mostly confronted with the inaccuracy of my racial categorization and the absence of valid criteria to define my true identity. I must check a box, and the only ones that come close are either Black or African American. But not all Blacks share the same cultural traits. Certainly, we share evident biological characteristics, yet a Black Senegalese man is culturally distinct from a Black man born and raised in the southern United States. I am nowhere to be found in those socially constructed boxes in which I am forced to fit, leaving me with no option to simply say I am human.

During my first year working as a French teacher in an elementary school in Vermont, a third-grade student approached me with this question:

"Why is your skin so dark?" asked the student with an innocent tone of inquiry.

After a minute of thought, I replied with a question: "Can you count the number of fish in that aquarium?"

"Yes," she said quizzically. 'One, two, three, four......eleven."

I asked, "Can you name all of the colors of the fish?"

Again she looked at me with confusion, "blue, yellow, black, grey, white, orange, red...*etc.*," she stated.

Finally, I asked, "Do you call all of them fish, even if they are different colors?"

"Yes," she answered brightly, "of course they are all fish!"

"Just like the fish, humans have different colors too!" I told her.

Satisfied with my answer, she went on her way.

I was not surprised by the question; I have heard similar ones from children before and since, with the same naivety. However, it took me a moment to think of a short and clear answer that could help the child understand without giving a long scientific or anthropological speculation to explain why my skin is dark. I wanted her to understand that humans have natural differences that characterize them. We have different colors of skin, but we are all human; differences and similarities are a fact of nature.

There have been many questions from students such as:

"You come from Africa?"

I answer, "Yes."

"Do you live in trees?"

"No."

"Are you Muslim?"

"Yes."

"But Muslims are terrorists; they bomb planes and kill people!"

I truly appreciate that the children felt safe enough to ask questions about my race, culture, and religion. Yet, each time I answer a question I am brought back to the reality of my differences in this culture. I often wonder what those who don't ask, those with preconceived prejudices, are thinking about my identities. To what extent am I free to talk about my identities to others and myself?

Freeing My Voice

> Decide that you want it more than you are afraid of it.
> —BILL COSBY

During our first meeting of the Scholarly Personal Narrative (SPN) course, a classmate confided in me about her fears of writing in a such style: "I think SPN writing would be particularly difficult because it puts the focus on the 'me,' and I have been taught not to talk about myself, in that sense I have been always told 'no.'" Little did she know, her case was similar to mine, and many others. As stated by Robert, "The denial of the value of the self's stories in an academic setting is born in the command all of us heard in school at some point: never use the 'I' in formal writing...[because] the 'I' is incapable of discovering and dispensing wisdom . . ." (Nash, 2004, p. 54)

Perhaps it is universal that social and institutionalized education teaches us mostly that the "self is hateful" (Pascal, 1942, part 1, art. 9, p. 23); therefore it is to be silenced. This reinforces, at a personal level, the fear of disclosing oneself to the self or to an audience. However normal, natural, and instinctual this fear may seem, it can reach such proportions that one chooses to wallow in the false comfort of remaining hidden to oneself and others, to stay silent—neither heard, read, nor seen. Questions such as: Who am I to believe my story deserves to be known? Are my stories meaningful enough to share? Who would want to hear the voice of an African, Black, Muslim man when I know that each of these identities holds a different meaning in my new cultural environment?

Since I was a child, I had a great fascination for water and, at the same time, a great fear of drowning. Every night I accompanied my big brother to the beach, I could see and feel the pleasure he had jumping into the water and swimming with grace for long periods of time. Meanwhile, I stood on the shore torn between desire and fear. One day I asked: "Could you show me how to swim?" "Of course!" he replied with surprise. After endless hours of trying and failing, I started swimming alone, venturing farther and farther away from the shore. One of my first joys was to swim to calm waters beyond the waves, where I could finally lay on my back like I was on my bed, contemplating the blue sky above me, and listening to the gentle sound of water against my eardrums. I discovered a kind of exaltation that I had never known before.

This experience often comes to me when I'm about to engage in new learning—especially, when I know I have the desire to learn something which I believe will give me great pleasure; something that will help me extend myself and relate to others and the world around me. In this case, I had the fear and desire to learn how to do SPN writing. I have always had a passion for writing, yet the serene, accepting atmosphere of Robert's course allowed me, for the first time, to produce personal writings, highlighting my own reflections on topics I feel hold a singular importance.

The more I think about the nature of my original fear of writing in an SPN format, the less hold it has on me. Deep down, a voice tells me: This is an opportunity that has been given to you to bring alive your visions. A Wolof proverb says, "Don't miss out on the chance to dance, if God claps for you." SPN writing has given me the chance to dance with words that are mine, with the voice that is mine. It has offered me the chance to say what I hold most dearly in the heart and mind. I do not want, in any way, to miss out on this chance. By accepting "the challenge to share myself, make meaning of my experiences, and then present them in such a way they are clear and have values for others" (Nash, 2011), I consequently find myself journeying to the revelation of my soul, of my meanings, of my dreams, my hopes, my uncertainties, my role as an educator, and advocate for intercultural and inter-religious dialogue.

Some of the doubts and the fears come back at times when I let my guard down and/or when I am running out of inspiration. This is normal. Doubts and fears arise each time I sit in front of a blank page or face a difficult situation. But I know they can no longer hold me back from writing my own words, conveying meanings wrapped in my own authentic voice, that invariably appear as personal and collective, clear and ambiguous, intrepid and timid, giving and forgiving, passionate and compassionate.

From an early age I was fascinated with words, the same way I have always been fascinated with water. In response to one of my personal writings, Robert wrote, "We live our lives in words; the more words we have, the more life we live." I believe words are like water; they flow as oceans and rivers do, impermanent, fluid, and smooth, sometimes rough and troubled. My love of words originated from the stories that I heard as a child. These are stories that continue to ring in my head, after so many years. Why? Because they were stories told with love and meaning, stories in which words become life and life becomes vivid and powerful words. SPN writing creates the same safe, welcoming place favorable to the flourishing of thoughts, words, and meanings.

SPN as a Means to Transcend Being Neither Here nor There

> The black African writer, it is he who can gather his spiritual nourishment from the roots of his people.
> —THOMAS MELONE (1962)

I have lived 8 years in a culture that is not mine. I know now, from experience, what that means! Despite my predisposition to live in a new society, regardless of the level of integration I could attain, I realize, at times, that I do not belong here. It is as if there is an invisible wall between the others and me, and each time I get close enough to jump over it, it moves away. Regardless of the place where we live, the most basic need for each human is the need to belong. What does it mean for me to belong to a new culture? It means that I have to step out of my primary cultural universe and adopt new attitudes, new ways of thinking, speaking, and doing things, new ways of acting and reacting to the people, the environment, and to the events. My survival in this culture depends upon how well I can balance acquiring new values and maintaining the old. So far, by remaining open and curious, and without worries about what I look like to others, I have been able to experience on numerous occasions what some have called "the warmth of true connection."

At other times, I have experienced moments of disorientation and dislocation during which I am abruptly reminded that I AM a stranger, foreigner, an alien, a naturalized citizen. My life story in the United States as an African…Black…Muslim has the relevance of the *Ambiguous Adventure* (1988). This classic autobiographical novel by Cheikh Amidou Kane takes place in a Senegalese postcolonial context and depicts the story of a young man who went from a traditional, Islamic society to Paris in order to study philosophy. Arriving in Paris with a heart full of curiosity, and a mind full of questions, Samba Diallo at first experienced excitement, wonder, and joy. But soon he started to realize that he is at the margin of a society in which his spiritual aspirations are at odds with the proclaimed materialism. To his anguish of being different is added the existential anguish of simply being neither here nor there. As Samba puts it, "I have become the two" (Kane, 1988, p. 135).

I have also unintentionally become the two at the risk of being neither one. Sometimes, when I go back home to Senegal, yearning to find the home I left behind, I am faced with the reality of change. The ordinary life I had there has vanished; friends and family have changed. I find myself readapting to old and new cultural norms. I have become a foreigner even when visiting home, realizing that the culture I once considered as fully mine is slipping away from me, like sand through my fingers. As a result, I am living in a third dimension, a third world in which I can view myself as a Cosmopolite, one who is always engaged in the process of negotiating values and meanings, recreating my self according to the places I live.

Coming to the United States post-9/11, I could not fully estimate the impact the interrelated issues of racial, religious, and cultural identity would have on how I view myself. I know how great my unease is every time I come across stereotypes about Africa and Islam in a workplace and in the community. Expressing this unease through SPN allows me to free myself from negative feelings. It furnishes me with the ability to step back, thus gleaning new perspectives on who I am, and my place in the world. Furthermore, I have gained the power not to let my self be subjugated by the issues of my identities. I now have the power, thanks to SPN, to reinterpret them, and to understand them while investing myself in new paradigms that foster my personal moral, philosophical, and spiritual growth.

My Story Matters, Your Story Matters

> Writing can help us see why our stories matter, and why we feel a sense of urgency to tell them.
> —MARY PIPHER (2006, p. 43)

Like Samba Diallo, I, too, know that the feelings of inadequacy and isolation, left alone, could lead to complete disarray. It is through SPN writing that I finally understand the roots of my pain and how to remedy them, because the act of writing itself can be therapeutic if one is willing to accept the vulnerability. Through SPN, I am more aware of the motives behind my writings and the importance of my story. I am writing to gain a deeper understanding of my existence, the existence of others, and that of the current state of our world. The more I write my story, the more I rise to the consciousness of its meaning in the sense that, once it is put on paper, it becomes intelligible. It allows for personal reflections, thus inviting me, in turn, to put a new lens on who I am and my role in the world. The question "Who am I?" is inseparable from the question "What was the true identity of the culture that I inherited before it came into contact with Western culture?"

My story as an African, Black, Muslim man journeying and questing for a more tolerant world, counts! It resonates with others, since, in the words of Kane (1988, p. 44), it is positioned into the narrative of a culture that has been "checked, divided, classified, labeled, conscripted, administrated." The same scenario is relevant to our current world. There is the shameful persistence of racism and xenophobia; the constant decline of civil liberties; the soulless isolationism in which we have been confined in so many cultures for so long; the new and subtle forms of slavery, and imperialism; the insidious multiplication of wars waged in the name of promoting some absolute truth—all of which are put in parallel with the increasing number of individuals persecuted, arrested, tortured, and killed because of their religious, cultural or political beliefs. All of this is the tragic evidence of a shared failure, the characteristics of a disturbingly intolerant world, morally blind, drifting each day far and far away from civilization to barbarity. As an African, Black, Muslim writing "…to inspire a kinder, fairer, more beautiful world" (Pipher, 2006, p. 14), my voice is a residual compilation of the voices of my ancestors, those whose identities and voices have been stolen or lost, voices of those who have been uprooted from their land. It is a voice also of hope and reconciliation.

Each one of us has a story, a unique story that, when examined meticulously, holds a universal wisdom, a light that can serve as a guide to navigate throughout the complexities of our existence. By giving me permission to write my story, to stand up to share it or to hear the stories of others, SPN has shown me that despite our differences, we can all relate to universal themes. We are human first, and the other is the mirror in which we have to look to see the self. Finally, I am able to explore, expand, and deepen the main questions I have about identity, religion, culture, imperialism, peace and tolerance, without fear in a safe atmosphere. Delightedly, I find myself swimming in an ocean of thoughts and words, discovering the many facets of life that SPN writing can uncover.

10

Four Additional Authors Who Have Lived on the Margins—and Written about It on Their Own SPN Terms

Part Two

Two SPN Reflections on Authenticity, Resilience, and Liberation

Essay #5 by Khristian Kemp-DeLisser

Khristian Kemp-DeLisser is a writer, learner, and educator working as the Coordinator of Student Retention & Assessment at the African, Latino, Asian & Native American Student Center (ALANA) at the University of Vermont. His duties include counseling and advocating for students of color and students of bi/multiracial backgrounds. He is also a doctoral candidate investigating the educational experience of lesbian, gay, bisexual, and transgender college students of color. His dissertation involves blending SPN about his own experience as a queer student of color with a separate phenomenological study of undergraduates. The two approaches will add to his theory of a queer person of color's perspective on campus life and climate. He spends his spare time writing poetry, walking his dog through the woods, and running. He has run four marathons and is training for his fifth this fall. Running keeps him healthy, fit, and provides lots of time to contemplate how social justice manifests his lifestyle and choices.

Body and Mind: The Power of Narrative

Scholarly Personal Narrative is about being connected with one's body and mind. Those who practice social justice must be able to employ unconventional tools and methods that are connected to real-world lives in order to raise awareness and interrupt oppressive narratives. We must create new knowledge that recognizes the contributions of all individuals and groups to our community. The experiences that bring me to these conclusions are deeply personal ones but just the kind to share through SPN. SPN allows me to connect to the voice inside me and cast a narrative that binds me inextricably to the experience of being human.

Good Times

I do not come from a family of talkers. My mother raised my brother and me by herself. She was the oldest of six girls who, I imagine, she helped her parents raise. She learned from her own mother about quiet acceptance of responsibility. Their silence wasn't about resignation or defeat, just a muted acknowledgment that talking takes energy that can be better used making money or feeding babies. I also suspect she had an intuitive sense that a whole lot of chatter never got her anywhere. She grew up poor and Black in Charter Oak Terrace, one of the largest—and most infamous—projects of Hartford, Connecticut.

Although she was in her 20s during the Black Civil Rights Era, my mother has never talked about feeling any particular sense of empowerment or activism. The woman I've always known has believed in long days and hard work. This is the kind of work that is practical and physical and puts food on the dinner table but requires little to be said. My mother was like Florida Evans on the 1970s TV show *Good Times*. In one episode she quieted her son when he started talking about racism as the family sat down for a meal, by saying simply, "This ain't no time to be Black."

There was a brief time when our family went to see a therapist. I was too young to remember what exactly we talked about, but one memory lingers of my mother saying in passing that she felt relieved to have the opportunity to talk to someone outside of the family. For me, the message was loud and clear: Being Black meant many things, and one of them was that we didn't talk about such things like racism or oppression. Furthermore, the family was not the place to go to talk about emotionally sensitive or personal issues.

This isn't about my mother's raising me to be emotionally stunted. It's about the ways in which my individual family demonstrates larger narratives I internalized about my personal and social identities. Narratives often rob us of our individual power. One narrative the academy perpetuates is that knowledge must be abstracted and theoretical in order to be valid. It seems at times that intellectuals and researchers in our society compete to produce the most esoteric and impenetrable arguments and writing styles. I frequently feel as though the academy only values writing that requires an advanced degree and a thesaurus to comprehend. SPN levels the playing field by acknowledging that "only the homemade theories we create out of our shared lives really help us to make sense of everything that we are" The close examination of our own lives can generate profound lessons.

Black people's stories need to be heard. We have been talking for hundreds of years and discrimination still persists; racial disparities continue to widen. There are many Black people for whom there has literally never been any space to talk; to audibly hear our own voices and thoughts and have them affirmed and acknowledged. It's what Langston Hughes talked about when he wondered out loud, what happens to a dream deferred? What happens to millions of Americans whose voices—whose very existence—has been stifled? What would it mean if we found our voice? How do we know the value of emotional intelligence and intuition?

SPN and Voice

> Working on SPN's, I have witnessed the often small, still voices of personal history and lived experience become powerful affirmations of self, with recognition that self-exploration and conscious awareness of being connected to our own lived experiences can have life lessons for us all.
> —JUDY COHEN (2005)

When I was 10 years old, there was a small still voice inside of me, but I did not know or listen. I didn't feel there was anything of value inside me except for what I could steal. So I slipped into stores and swiped candy and gum, maybe some batteries for my Nintendo Gameboy. I developed something of a knack for stealing and, before long, friends from around the block would know to follow when they saw me headed to the corner store because they could share in the spoils.

At the same time I was a voracious reader. I read multiple books at a time. On a few occasions, I even reached my borrowing limit at the local library and just stole a book I wanted to take out. And I was a writer. Several teachers had shown interest in the descriptive and imaginative short stories I produced whenever class assignments involved a writing prompt. One of them began to tutor me on creative writing, and one day she pointed out that my writing was reminiscent of a writer named David Eddings. I immediately recognized the name because several of his books were sitting on my bed at home. I still remember her saying the best writers borrow literary techniques, language, even plot devices from their favorite authors. I looked at her, my brown eyes wide with disbelief and awe. It was dawning on me that my particular aptitude for shoplifting also extended to taking passages, words, and themes from my reading and incorporating them into my writing. Call it what you will: homage, borrowing, building on, appropriating....In my eyes, I was a thief, and a damn good one.

In time, the day came when my illicit activities became more than the socially excusable "boys will be boys" kind. Candy and batteries from the store down the street became money from wallets from locker rooms, and eventually credit card numbers on the Internet. By that point I was 19 and had slipped into a self-destructive spiral. And like so many others in spirals, I was careless, and I got caught, arrested. I only spent one long night in jail waiting for my arraignment the next day. But one night was all I needed. Of all of my thoughts that night, the one I still cannot shake is that I was a statistic, a stereotype. We all know the classic tropes or narratives about Black men. Educated, well-spoken Black men are the exception, never the rule. Gay and bisexual Black men are less than the exception; they are non-existent, either not discussed or relegated to shadows and mysterious rumors of brothers on the "downlow." Generally the dominant caricature is dangerous and lazy on the one hand, and athletically or physically talented on the other. Overly concerned with instant gratification to feed an appetite for everything from food to sex, to money. More to the point, *your* money.

Black men are thugs and criminals, less likely to be found in a classroom than a prison. I have contended with these familiar narratives my whole life; they are in the ether. I frequently fought against the narratives, but there were times when they seemed inevitable. And as much as I had always believed I was different, they were all there with me in the county jail holding-cell that night. They were all sitting next to me on the cold stainless steel bench, the air around us reeking of a foul mixture of body odor, disinfectant, and regret. If I were to imagine a different destiny, I would first need to decide who it was I wanted to be. I would need to accept responsibility for the actions that had landed me in this predicament and resolve to change. I needed to begin a new story that would bring me a new fate.

The Stories We Tell

> I am the only one who can tell the story of my life and say what it means.
> —DOROTHY ALLISON (1995)

What is a writer to do when he has been taught to steal written words but self-taught to steal items of value in the real world? I write my real-life story using words and ideas I have amassed during my lifetime. In fact, I write and rewrite my life story until I can cast a narrative so broad in scope that it can fit both the ravenous book nerd who filled notebooks with fantastic stories and the thief who stole pretty much whatever he could fill his hands with when he needed an ego boost. I can construct a narrative with a trajectory narrow enough to show redemption and sustain my faith in myself, and my ability to stand before my community and say, "yes, I am worthy of your trust" and have them believe me. That narrative is made possible through Scholarly Personal Narrative.

SPN provides a vehicle for people to find their voice. Helping people find their voice is more than just letting them tell a story. It's more than waxing poetic or idle navel-gazing. Finding one's voice means both speaking and listening. It involves hearing the sounds that emerge from one's lips and also feeling the power that drives those sounds. It means feeling as though one has something meaningful and positive to contribute to the community or society. Injustice exists when people are measured against norms or concepts that have nothing to do with them as individuals with unique talents and characteristics. Social justice offers counter-narratives that allow people to see themselves as multifaceted and multidimensional. In the end, it is our complexity that makes us human, our diversity that unites us. Impartiality and objectivity be damned! SPN connects to that shared humanity. The deeply personal aspect of SPN offers a way to unearth the "bones of our common human endeavor."

In the same way that our social culture is infused with narratives about us, each individual's SPN offers the opportunity to embed references and allusions to new or different norms and stories. SPN writers recast stories using knowledge that is familiar, accessible, and authentic to their reality. Finally, SPN scholarship embraces wisdom and knowledge in the world around us that recognizes no disciplinary, academic, or cultural boundaries.

In my experience, the biggest barrier to students who wish to use SPN as a methodology is that it is not scientific. They cannot quiet that nagging voice inside them that constantly whispers, "your ideas and judgments are not sound unless measured through the scientific method." To them I say, "Whose scientific method?" The same science that calls the validity or rigor of SPN into question was used as a tool to enslave or disenfranchise people of color. It's the same science that continues to fuel outdated beliefs that gays and lesbians can be "cured" of their deviant desires. Any methodology that denies my personhood has no validity or rigor.

SPN: A Methodology of Personhood

The stories I have shared, learning about silence from my mother, and the inevitable consequences of my self-destructive behavior, illustrate how conceptual phenomena can have physical manifestations. In our family we met tangible needs before we met emotional ones. I learned to steal physical items for psychological purposes. The stories I weave through SPN allow me to see the connection between the outside world I inhabit and the inner world in which I live, in a way that other forms of writing, particularly academic, do not allow. SPN avoids academic jargon that inherently builds distance between the reader and writer and, instead, embraces everyday vernacular and description that build intimacy and immediacy (Nash, 2004). It allows a certain level of writer's license to access a greater truth. For example, although exact dialogue may be hard to recall, it can be used to establish a tone, rhythm, and emotion of a memory. Memories can read like scenes, in which details such as sensations, body contact, or proximity convey context and meaning.

Anderson (2001) extolled the virtues of "embodied writing," a style of connecting language and text to the body and sensual experience. Anderson offered embodied writing as a format for psychologists and other social scientists to employ for its therapeutic purposes. It shares many principles with SPN. Particularly, in SPN and embodied writing, the "readers' perceptual, visceral, sensorimotor, kinesthetic, and imaginal senses are invited to come alive to the words and images as though the experience were their own" (p. 84).

Like Nash (2004), Anderson (2001) believed researchers too frequently produce texts that are flat and uninteresting and fail to inspire her. If the texts were "fully present and alive, I would find myself responsive and engaged, not distanced and bored. But too often I feel disembodied as though the report has little to do with me or things precious in my life" (p. 84). She added, "disembodied writing" only "perpetuates the object-subject bifurcation between the world of our bodies and the world we inhabit" (p. 84).

SPN, at its best, is embodied writing. Nash (2004) described SPN as providing the reader "delicious aha! moments of self and social insight" (p. 24). His use of the word "delicious" is telling because of the visceral enjoyment it evokes. SPN frequently comes from the gut—the tactile and sensual experience of the world. It is inviting and accessible, creating a participatory experience in which meaning is lifted, even co-created. A strong narrative carried and moved along by rich, uninhibited writing is as enjoyable as it is informative. Nash and Bradley (2011) wrote that SPN not only has rigor but vigor, which "connotes a personal intensity or strength that calls for a writing style that is risk-taking, out of the ordinary, forceful, full of energy" (p. 82). Finally, Banks (2003) underscored the relationship between social justice and descriptive writing: "When we ignore the 'embodied' in discourse, we miss the ways in which liberation is always both social and individual, a truly symbiotic relationship" (p. 27).

Narratives are controlled and perpetuated by institutions in our society such as the media, culture, colleges, and universities. Those narratives have the potential to subsume the voice of individuals who are a part of marginalized communities and embody difference. They treat individuals as members of a categorical stereotype and rob them of their agency, their humanity, their bodies. Liberation begins when those individuals look inward and begin to articulate the power that lies within their own narratives. That power pulsates strong as a heartbeat and permeates their writing with sensuality and reality. SPN, like social justice, is about forgiveness and meaning-making. Both promote healing for individuals who are wounded, whether by their own self-destructive behavior or by caustic narratives perpetuated by the society in which they live.

Essay #6 by Stacey A. Miller

Stacey A. Miller *currently serves as the Director of Residential Life at the University of Vermont, and is a managing partner for the consulting firm The Consortium for Inclusion & Equity, LLC. She has over 20 years of professional experience in student affairs and higher education as both an administrator and instructor. She began her professional career at Stony Brook University, New York, where she also earned her Bachelor of Arts in Social Sciences, and Master of Arts in Liberal Studies. She received her doctorate in the Educational Leadership and Policy Studies program at the University of Vermont. In addition to her administrative post, Dr. Miller has served as a lecturer for two graduate-level courses in the Higher Education and Student Affairs Administration (HESA) program, and the Master of Interdisciplinary Studies program.*

A Fat Girl's Journey to Find Authenticity and Liberation: The Weight of Scholarly Personal Narrative

> Because by the time you are a social worker for ten years, what you realize is that connection is why we're here, it is what gives purpose and meaning to our lives. This is what it's all about. It doesn't matter whether you talk to people who work in social justice and mental health, and abuse and neglect. What we know is that connection, the ability to feel connected is neurobiologically...that's how we're wired, its why we're here.
> —BRENÉ BROWN (2010)

In the United States of America, being fat is practically a crime, and almost everyone I know is either guilty of weight-larcenies, misdemeanors, or felonies. Friends whose weight is considered normal or average have been tricked into thinking they are fat, or are constantly concerned about becoming fat, counting calories like certified public accounts. Overweight friends, albeit 15, 20, 30, or even more than 50 pounds, trade weight-loss tips like brokers on the New York Stock Exchange. My own battle with the bulge has been futile at best—losing, gaining, and losing again, only to gain the weight back, sometimes double what was lost. For people who have the courage to openly identify as fat or overweight, the struggle to lose weight is constant, frustrating, and at times overwhelming, and societal standards make it easy for us to blame ourselves for the physical condition of our bodies and the struggles we face as larger-sized people.

However, "the overweight and obesity problem in our nation and world is complex. Contributing factors range from individual behaviors and environment to genetic factors; but [make no mistake] none are in isolation from the other" (Miller, 2009, i). On my own personal journey to lose weight and become (seemingly) healthier, I was led down a path to explore the nature of "weightism," and the social constructs behind body image and physical beauty as central to my dissertation. My primary challenge was finding a research methodology that would not just allow me to present statistics and facts, but give voice to the social phenomenon of weight, because weight in itself means nothing without the context of the human condition. This is the primary reason why I decided "that the only true way for me to do [my dissertation was] through the research methodology of Scholarly Personal Narrative (SPN). Like many other forms of qualitative inquiry or interpretivist research, SPN is a qualitative methodology where the researcher serves as the primary subject of study" (p. 5).

Is SPN Narcissistic?

No doubt, some believe SPN to be an inappropriate form of research, because research is supposed to be neutral and objective. Others would say that adding the "me" in research is just plain narcissistic. But I believe in many ways it is the complete opposite of narcissism, because its sole purpose is to make significant and meaningful connections with its reader, connections that are often unmatched by traditional scholarship. The reason why many of us (humans) even bother to pick up a book, an article, much less a piece of research—mostly unconsciously—is to find human connection. How does the information I am about to read shed an ounce of clarity or meaning on my life? SPN is research through connection, as it joins scholarship, honestly articulated personal experiences, and narrative together—which, when done well, is a gift that ties an invisible bow between the writer and reader. SPN brings voice to both the spoken and unspoken universalizable truths and experiences many of us share.

In trying to truly understand the methodology of SPN, Robert Nash's words still resonate for me, as if he had whispered them directly into my ear: "Your life has meaning, both for you and for others. Your own life tells a story (or a series of stories) that, when narrated well, can deliver to your readers those delicious aha! moments of self and social insight that are all too rare in more conventional forms of research"

(Nash, 2004, p. x). This is what often drives scholars to this type of writing.

Before contemplating an SPN, I thought long and hard about using other forms of qualitative methodology or even taking a mixed-methods approach to my research. I agonized about whether or not I would be taken seriously as a scholar if I chose to write an SPN, or if I even had the ability or skill-set needed to write in this way. While others constantly question the integrity of SPN, I had already seen colleagues and friends struggle with the complexity of this methodology. Academics who choose to write in the scholarly personal narrative format know what they are up against from the start. We sit in our chairs, at our desks, just like all other traditional quantitative and qualitative dissertation writers, often starring into space, screaming to the divine for a shred of writing compassion. We pray to our writing muse for help and guidance only to find that she is on a 2- or 3-hour lunch break. You hear her whispering, "I'll be back in a couple of hours to give you some much-needed inspiration," which always seems to happen right before it is time for you to go pick up the kids from school or cook dinner.

Couple this with the fact that we do not have the aid of thousands upon thousands of other dissertations (qualitative and quantitative) with standard formats to guide us through our process—chapter one, introduction; chapter two, methodology; chapter three, research and data collection; chapter four, findings; and chapter five, conclusion—SPN is both curse and blessing. It provides each and every writer the freedom to use their authentic voice to create an original piece of work, with the added pressure of making it respectable and legitimate academic scholarship.

The Challenge of Blending Me-Search and Research

We struggle through the challenge of blending research with compelling and passionate personal narrative, and anyone who has ever written an SPN would be a liar if they did not admit to suffering from a research inferiority complex. We SPNers walk not with the proverbial chip on our shoulder, but with a two-by-four piece of lumber. But, as a Black Woman, living with an inferiority complex is nothing new to me. I live in a world of contradiction, a world that outwardly emulates many of my innate human qualities and characteristics. The world admires the way I talk, dress, my attitude and fearlessness, but, in the next breath, it minimizes my voice, my beauty, and stereotypes the slightest expression of my emotion as "hostile Black Woman syndrome." I also imagine that I am just one of hundreds of thousands of U.S.-born African Americans who struggled through the K–12 educational factory, never having had a teacher who looked like me or led me in the classroom, never learning my history in a truly positive or affirming way; and only watching the "gifted and talented" encouraged to share their intellect in meaningful ways.

It was not until my doctoral program, 36 years into my life, that I truly began to be affirmed both intellectually and academically. My doctoral professors and cohort members looked to me for answers and respected my questions; they wanted to hear my voice and my perspective. And, while I cannot say this is indicative of every doctoral experience, it was of mine. My doctoral cohort's affirmation helped fuel my learning. The long-awaited intellectual rebirth I experienced in graduate school inspired me daily and motivated me on days when I did not want to go to class, and through my many attempts to quit the program.

Becoming visible helped me to acknowledge that my voice, my stories, and my life experiences had meaning, not just for me, but also for others. This is why after the internal struggle, the internal agony, I came to the conclusion that the only way for me to write my dissertation, the only way that I would be able to honor my rebirth and both express and reclaim my voice, was through SPN. For me, it was the most authentic way to complete what was a glorious revival of my intellect.

Having survived four decades of my life, and being inspired by Brené Brown, who has so eloquently articulated the importance of connection—which I have embraced as a human truth—I understand that in order to have connection with others, one must be both vulnerable and authentic in one's approach to life. SPN forces both of these qualities. If you truly want to make a connection with a reader, just tell the truth, *your* truth, and you will find many others who have close or similar stories and experiences. When writing my dissertation I read tens, if not hundreds, of books from authors I had never heard of prior to my process—authors whose words spoke to my life experiences and pain as if they had been walking alongside of me my whole life. Their stories, their insight, and their analysis of weight issues helped me, and like all other research, my writing was a reflection of their scholarly insight.

Conducting my research was a revelation that there is probably nothing that has not already been thought, said, or felt. However, very few of us ever put those universal thoughts or feelings onto paper, especially those of us who have not been affirmed intellectually, those who live on the margins of society. I now understand that by sharing my little bit of truth, by giving others the opportunity to share in my life experience, I have given voice to marginalized women—Black women and overweight people the world over. This is "connection," and connection is one of the ways that I have found purpose and meaning in my own life.

For me, the implications of SPN have been astounding, because I know that I am a part of a small community of scholars, People of Color, Women, Transnationalists, members of the LBGTQA community, those who are differently abled, and religious "minorities" who are on the cutting edge and changing the face of research not only at my university, but nationally. I find it painful to be at national conferences, in sessions where academic professionals and/or faculty members (especially those whose apparent identities would lead me to believe that they are members of marginalized communities), proclaim to a room full of impressionable junior faculty and young professionals what is the true scholarship. They define research so narrowly that it sucks the air out the room, creating an unspoken and quiet hopelessness for those who want to obtain a doctoral degree but who cannot bear the thought of writing another meaningless dissertation—those who wish to take a different path.

Their statements, which are thinly veiled as empathetic support, still emphasize how to play by the rules and get through a program and dissertation process, instead of challenging and changing the status quo. These professorial comments, as encouraging as they might seem on the surface, often shut down new ways of thinking and research freedom. They fail to question the oppressive history of research—for example, who was studied? How and why were they studied? Why is academically approved scholarship and research still controlled by a powerful few?

Research Is Meant to Be Read and Understood

But I dare anyone to read my dissertation and not be drawn into my research, sociological analysis, and personal reflection about body image and societal constructs related to weight. Unlike 99% of doctoral research that sits on shelves, never to see the light of day once it was approved and bound, when people ask me what I wrote my dissertation about, and when I describe my methodology, and when I share some of my analysis with them, they sincerely want to read it. More importantly, they are often moved by similarities between our experiences regardless of how much they weigh. In my humble opinion, my research is real, because it is practical and accessible for anyone and everyone who is struggling with weight issues or wants to think differently about the stereotypes connected to weight.

There was a time, not too long ago in our historical past, when education was only open to a select few, restricted by sex and gender, race, class, religion, and ability. But institutions of higher education have had to evolve and give access to people who have historically been marginalized within the academy. In turn, members of historically underrepresented and marginalized communities have answered the call and embraced academia, but we are no longer content just coming to "school" and getting an education in the traditional way that the dominant culture dictates. We are quietly and slowly breaking down academic barriers and creating our own methods of research within its fixed and rigid walls.

It is my opinion that the ultimate purpose of any educational experience is the development of intellectual liberation. The freedom to learn, research, write, and express one's self adds value to the institution and to the individuals who reside within it. It is time that Scholarly Personal Narrative be universally acknowledged and accepted as another, equally legitimate form of qualitative research. Providing space for scholars to write about things we are passionate about, or that are important to us as individuals, does not contradict research; it *is* research. Scholarly Personal Narrative helps individuals share their stories in universalizable ways that build resilience and authenticity, which in turn creates connections with others. I believe that genuine authenticity, expressed in personal narrative writing, is a form of intellectual and personal liberation.

Two SPN Reflections by Quarterlife Leaders in Higher Education

Essay #7 by Candace J. Taylor

Candace J. Taylor *is a Brooklyn-born, 30-year-old, West Indian American, first-generation, Queer-identified, feminist, womanist, social justice activist, educator, writer, reiki practitioner, doula, healer, environmentalist, historian, and soon-to-be yoga instructor. She has spent her entire professional career working as an advocate for underrepresented and marginalized students. Currently she works as the Coordinator for Programming & Leadership Development at the University of Vermont's Women's Center, which is housed within the Diversity and Equity Unit under the Chief Diversity Office.*

Candace is a graduate of both Smith College, with a B.A. in American Studies and Education, as well as from UVM, with a Master of Interdisciplinary Studies in Education degree. Her graduate thesis is titled The Birth of a Leader: One Mother's Transformative Journey of Leadership. *She is the mother of a very wise, adventurous, deeply loving, 8-year-old boy named David Justus, and she is grateful for the love and support of her wonderful partner, Tony. In her free time, Candace finds freedom and joy in her most sacred spaces: cooking, dancing, practicing yoga, and being in her garden. If you can't find her there, then she is most likely laughing out loud with her cherished community of friends and family.*

Uncovering the Mask:
Achieving Educational Freedom through Narrative

In order to holistically understand the multitude of ways in which Scholarly Personal Narrative has impacted my life educationally, professionally, and personally, I feel it's important to first learn a little bit about me and my personal journey and relationship within the field of education. All of my life I have fully and fundamentally believed in the value of education; it's a value that has been instilled in me from early on by my family. I loved school and worked hard to excel in it. My love for school ran so deep that when the end of the school year arrived I always felt lost. When my peers longed for summer vacations I dreaded them, eagerly awaiting the time when the doors of school would reopen and I could return to the routine of being a student. I loved reading some of the most memorable, great works of literature in English classes, running all kinds of exciting experiments and unearthing what goes on beneath the skin and beyond what the eye can see in Science classes. I loved remembering our past and drawing connections to our present in History and searching for the answer to all the equations that came before me in Mathematics. In the same way athletes prepare, focus, and dedicate themselves to their sport, as a student I did my best to prepare, focus, and dedicate myself to academics.

Learning was my life. Education was the key to happiness and freedom, growth, and betterment. Who wouldn't want that, to grow and be their best? Who wouldn't fight and give all they could to be free and happy? It's no wonder, then, that I have spent my entire academic career in undergraduate and graduate schools studying education as well as most of my professional career working in the field of education. Yet my relationship within this field has not always been positive. For better or worse, education has played a critical role in the formation of us all on a multitude of levels. Paulo Freire wrote: "No one is born fully-formed: it is through self-experience in the world that we become what we are" (1971, p. 1). This is the definition of socialization: taking the mounds of shapeless clay that we all enter this world as and over time and experiences slowly shaping and re-shaping ourselves into the form(s) we will occupy along the journey in life. The institution of education is one of the primary and most powerful systems of socialization in America. Its power resides in the systemic advantages it embodies historically, socially, economically, and politically. This permits our institution of education to largely impact the overall development of humanity's sense of purpose, meaning, leadership styles and practices, sense of self-worth and efficacy, and so much more. The stories and experiences that happen within the walls of our educational institution are directly linked to the future of our existence as a species and ultimately our society.

So much responsibility lies on the shoulders of our educational system, but currently it's structured in a way that is extremely limiting. The institution of education places more value and importance on teaching to a test, and standardizing knowledge and methodologies of instruction, than it does on experiencing the hidden richness that comes from the diverse perspectives and approaches to life and learning present in a learning community. Our educational system has become a metaphorical factory whose sole purpose is to serve as a socializing assembly line, pushing out pre-formed replicas and discarding any that do not come out exactly like the one before.

So when I say that I fundamentally believe in education, I fully understand the power of education to create change and form our society. And despite the work that I have put into having a pristine academic record, I am not someone who has felt an easy affiliation with the institution of education in America. In fact, I have often felt outside of this country's educational institution; its walls of glass give off the appearance of being open and permeable, yet even when I have embraced these walls, I have never been allowed inside. I have danced the dance for education. I have performed the part and even received the awards: national honor society, honor roll, merit scholarships, research assistantships, presidential scholars, honor societies, and the list goes on and on. Yet I experienced myself as an outsider.

Every step of the way along my educational journey I felt the need to fragment parts of my identity, personality, and parts of my inner self, carefully putting them into boxes in order to fit in and conform. This is not to downplay the very real power of peer pressure to impact a person's full participation within the institution of education. However, for me, I felt the most pressure to conform and be palatable from the educational institution itself. The pressure was often subtle but at times could be quite overt as well. I wanted so badly to be deemed a brilliant and strong student, a scholar and successful leader. I wanted to achieve this standing within the walls of education, because I could then be seen as good enough to become an educator and leader within the field as well as outside of it. However, I received the clear message that to achieve this I had to be a certain kind of learner, student, leader, thinker, writer, practitioner, and educator. As a relational person I struggled in classes all my life that were structured in a way that only permitted voice from a student when either called upon or uttered in the format of a focused question to the teacher (holder of all knowledge and wisdom).

I would have preferred to hear and share stories and learn not only from my teacher and the textbook but also from my classmates, to have the opportunity to learn about their lives and had a chance to share my life as well. As a feeler, with a strong emotional intellect, I was often distracted by the lack of space given to express the hurt and confusion I felt when I sat in classes that spewed out a false history that either completely minimized or outright excluded the role of people that looked like me on the development of this world. I would have favored having a space to express my anger and sadness, my confusion and questions without being seen as disruptive, unstable, or over-emotional. Instead, I clearly got the message that there was no room for emotion in academia, especially if I wanted to be a leader in academia; to behave otherwise was a sign that I was weak and not to be taken seriously.

As an external processer/storyteller who needs to talk out loud, to share and hear stories in order to understand and comprehend the world around me fully, it was hard for me to quickly and accurately problem-solve, critically think, or even ask questions, let alone answer them. I learned early that the only real acceptable times for students to be heard are when called upon or directly questioned by the teacher. I also realized that I could not succeed in this world being labeled as a deviant or troublemaker. I had seen up-close the lack of forgiveness or leniency bestowed upon those who didn't fit the social and/or academic norms within education and how that impacted their lives. I did not want to walk that road to nowhere, so I covered. Kenji Yoshino (2006) wrote that "Everyone covers. To cover is to tone down a disfavored identity to fit into the main stream...every reader of this book has covered, whether consciously or not, and sometimes at significant personal cost" (p. ix). So I worked extra hard to succeed within this model through covering, all while internalizing some of the messages that demonized those parts of me that didn't fit.

As a first-generation, American-born, Black woman growing up and living in poverty, succeeding in the institution of education, going on to graduate from an ivy league school and obtain my master's degree, I was supposed to have reached the golden land of success. While other families were investing in stocks and bonds, real estate, entrepreneurial endeavors, and property, my family was investing in me. I was the key to unlocking their prison of poverty and struggle. I was their chance at freedom. As I reflect back on this now, that responsibility was a lot to bear, but I did not care.

As a first-generation high school graduate, the college application process alone was like being told to climb Mount Everest without any climbing or hiking experience, no equipment, and an intense fear of heights. This did not stop my immigrant, single-parent mother from working a second job on the night shift at a gas station to pay for the college counselor that she heard was necessary to assure her child got into college. Although we could not afford a computer and printer, my grandmother and mother were hustlers in the best sense of the word. They watched the sales and saved up, so that when it came time to purchase a word processor on lay-away they could. That word processor enabled me to neatly type out each college application, because my mom read in the newspaper that typed applications were important to college selection committees. I saw how hard my family worked to invest in my education and me, and I fully knew my success was directly linked to them all.

I did not allow myself to be stopped when my own high school guidance counselor told me that I should not have applied to most of the colleges I applied to, especially Smith College, because I would not get in. I applied anyway, and when I received that acceptance letter, and all the ones that followed, I gracefully and confidently walked into her office, letter in hand, for her to announce on the school intercom that I, Candace Taylor, this little Bajun girl from the hood, got accepted to Smith College, and many others, with either partial or full merit-based scholarships.

Gloria Anzaldúa (1990) wrote the following in one of my favorite books, *Making Face, Making Soul: Haciendo Caras*: "The world knows us by our faces, the most naked, most vulnerable, exposed and significant topography of the body. When our caras do not live up to the 'image' that the family or community wants us to wear, and when we rebel against the engraving of our bodies, we experience ostracism, alienation, isolation and shame." Some of us are forced to acquire the ability, like a chameleon, to change color when the dangers are many and the options few. Some of us who already "wear many changes/inside of our skin" (Audre Lorde) have been forced to adopt a face that would pass.

It did not matter that I danced the dance, that I performed the part to a T, that in doing so I was metaphorically cutting, inflicting self-harm upon my inner self in order to be accepted by the norm. They could see beyond the masks; I still was an outsider, and any opportunity the system had to attempt to push me away from its glass walls and question my validity they did. Paulo Freire (1970) wrote in *Pedagogy of the Oppressed*:

> If the structure does not permit dialogue, the structure must be changed....Leaders who do not act dialogically, but insist on imposing their decisions, do not organize the people—they manipulate them. They do not liberate, nor are they liberated: they oppress.

I became disenchanted with our educational system, while fully having this intense belief infused into the foundation of my being that education had the power to create change and build a positive community, one radically different from our own now. It took a long time for me to be able to see them as different and separate things, that education itself did not have to look and feel like the way our educational system portrayed it to be.

Of all the famous names in education—Locke, Mann, Morrill, Dewey: those people that continuously make it on Education course syllabi across the nation— I consider Paulo Freire to be my educational hero. When I first read the works and radical wisdom of Freire, the fog began to clear. Education was no longer a mammoth structure with impenetrable glass walls. Education, learning, teaching were not just one methodology, one style, and attainable for just one kind of person. I began to realize that our educational system was a construct; its current structure and existence was a formation of those given the power and opportunity to create it, and because those that were given that power were not diverse, it was no wonder I did not fit. To take this a step further, I began to see that it was imperative for me and others like me, that have historically and systemically been silenced within education, to finally speak up and be heard. I began to research how education was practiced differently outside of our country's walls. I was happy to find that opportunity within the University of Vermont's Master of Interdisciplinary Education Program, and it is here, at this powerful and critical intersection in my educational career, where the introduction of Scholarly Personal Narrative takes center stage.

Scholarly Personal Narrative

Scholarly Personal Narrative (SPN) was created by Dr. Robert Nash, faculty member at the University of Vermont, and it consists of four components: pre-search, me-search, re-search, and we-search. Within these four components, writers must use the S, P, and N to illustrate and articulate the content of their manuscripts. SPN affirms that we all have a story to share that is worth hearing, can be learned from, and that is connected to others' stories. It's empowering, validating, and refreshing; it's broadening, opening and making room within academia to another way of knowing, understanding, and learning about the world we live in and are a part of shaping.

When I think of my personal journey within the field of education that I have shared thus far in this piece of writing, and the impact both my graduate college experience and the genre of Scholarly Personal Narrative has had on my life and perception of education, I am grateful. For a long time in my educational journey, I could not envision a way to be wholly authentic without being labeled a "trouble-maker" and essentially breaking the rules and jeopardizing my grades, scholarships, and academic standing. I was not afraid to share my voice and story in classes, but at the end of the day if I truly wanted to have a long-lasting impact after I left the walls of a classroom, I needed to find a way to have that same outspoken and outraged voice published and used in academic study. When I was introduced to Scholarly Personal Narrative I finally saw a road out of the silent forest of oppression into the open meadow of voice and truth and freedom.

My first graduate class at UVM, *Religion and Spirituality in Education*, with Robert Nash and Stacey Miller as the course faculty, was where I learned to write a Scholarly Personal Narrative. Unplugging myself from academia's metaphorical matrix to write in a format that actually inserted "me" and "I" into my research felt like an insurmountable task. I struggled…a lot. To be honest, it felt wrong, like I was doing something forbidden. But when I think about these feelings, truly think about them, I can't help but wonder—why? Why is inserting the "I" not important, *my* "I" so unacceptable? Do I not have any thoughts worth sharing? Could academia not learn something from someone like me? The truth is, I most certainly have something to say. I have come to see that writing, more particularly writing in this style of SPN, has become my act of political resistance.

Hence, slowly, SPN by SPN assignment, that first graduate class with Robert and Stacey broke down those walls that had been built over my entire academic career to reveal *me*, waiting amidst the rubble, somewhat bewildered but ready to use my voice for the very first time. In SPN, nothing matters more than my story, my voice, my take on scholarship and research, and this insight has been an empowering, life-changing gift. SPN has enabled me to reflect deeply, connect deeply, and come to a deeper sense of knowing and understanding. There is no more need for the mask, for playing the part, for dancing the dance to gain the approval of others while lying to myself. With SPN there is no more covering. SPN has given me permission to finally discover the wisdom and brilliance of my own life-story and to share it with others.

This is the power of SPN—its ability to connect and heal across difference, to expose what is unseen, to give power to the stories and voices of people and shatter the narrow historical perception of academic scholarship. SPN was born in the work of such womanist scholars as Audre Lorde, Gloria Anzaldúa, bell hooks, June Jordan—women-of-color scholars who have been inserting their narratives, and the narratives of our ancestors, into their scholarship for decades. SPN continues the work of these pioneers in academia on whose foundation I wish to add my narrative-brick, with love-filled and dedicated mortar.

Essay #8 by Vanessa Santos Eugenio

Vanessa Santos Eugenio, a Filipina American, is a higher education professional at the University of Vermont in the Career Services Office. She also serves as the Official Advisor for the Asian-American Student Union. She has been an educator in both private and public schools in Burlington, Williston, and Shelburne, Vermont. Vanessa graduated from the Early Education Program at the University of Vermont with her focus on using a student-centered approach to creating curriculum. She has specialized in creating language enrichment programs and working with anti-bias curricula with her students and fellow teachers to improve learning in inclusive environments, celebrating diversity and multiculturalism. She is also a local artist and the president of the co-op known as We Art Women. Vanessa is a tea enthusiast who performs Japanese tea ceremonies throughout the region. She utilizes two dynamic styles of writing—SPN and ESPN—on the topics of Religion and spirituality, the effects of fatherlessness on daughters, and theFeminine Amerasian Experiences. She is a co-instructor with Robert Nash for the Religion and Spirituality course at the University of Vermont. Her graduate work in Interdisciplinary Studies integrated self-care, mindfulness, and education.

Realizations at the Quarterlife: A Journey of a Leader

My Reflections on the Overall SPN Process

I strongly believe that some of the most exquisite pieces of SPN writing are full of the profound inner journeys an author takes. They are often some of the most emotionally charged learning that we, as humans, experience. Prior to my first encounter with SPN, I was trained in the mentality that writing was to speak to the facts, to the black and white. I found that my voice would get lost in a jungle of quotes. Papers became almost "voiceless." The reality is that life is full of gray area, and raw emotions, and it is that real emotion and first-hand experience that resonates with others. A person's story cannot be defined by someone else, but it can be an example, an encouragement, an inspiration to the reader. I believe that SPN is a wonderful medium to explore one's experiences and attempt to relate their truth to other people's truths.

When I first began writing about the topic of self as leader, I felt unsteady on how I identified with the title. Surely, I could recognize a few times in my life where I felt that others considered me to be a leader, but it was typically not my own self-identification. The term "leader" was given to me by others, and I felt that I needed to live up to the definition. I realized I spent a lot of time doubting where I was a leader based on my young age, my historical and cultural contexts, and various occupational roles I held. Through writing about my experiences and telling my personal story, I began to recognize where in my life I showed up as a leader. With a moving *Women & Leadership* course taught by Dr. Jill Tarule at the

University of Vermont, this journey became a deep, introspective, and emotional discovery about how I self-identified with who I am as a leader in my community and the styles of leadership I embody. I thought many leaders before and after me could relate to my experience, and I knew SPN would lend itself beautifully to the story of my journey that I wanted to tell. In the sections that follow, I will share excerpts from the final paper that I wrote for Dr. Tarule's course.

Writing without Losing My Voice

When I think about how one grows into being a leader, I am certain that no two people's journeys look alike. My path to self-definition has been a long, ongoing series of reflections. SPN writing has allowed me to take a deep look at my experiences to see how they have shaped who I have become. SPN has helped me to weave in the many identities I hold as a twenty-something, Asian American, immigrant woman, each of which is an integral part of who I am, and affects how I show up in the world as a leader. With SPN, I am able to integrate valuable quotes and references into the text, without losing my voice and experiences while I define myself. For example, here is an excerpt from a piece I wrote recently for Dr. Tarule's course that I mentioned earlier.

> *While I identify my cultural roots as an Asian American and was socialized to be feminine and obedient, I saw that through my experiences, being quiet or passive would not allow for change to happen. Learning to navigate the Western world and adopt attributes that did not directly align with the way I was brought up were, in fact, a healthy skill. As a result, I have recognized that I have a voice and that I have influence on others and can effect change at the systematic level by trusting in my skills and experiences. This course has given me the ability to identify my leadership style and be affirmed that my style choices and feminine characteristics and approaches to leadership are valued especially to the fields I have chosen to carve a career path in. An article called "Making a Difference", by Debra M. Kawahara, focuses on the various stories of several Asian American feminists and how they are able to successfully be leaders while holding values represented by both the Eastern and Western perspectives.*
>
> *I decided to research the notion that women's modesty can lead to non-promotion or recognition. Women continuously downplay their achievements as a result of socialization. This behavior leads to a catch-22, whereby women do not acknowledge their own achievements, but, instead, encourage and exemplify others' achievement. The outcome is predictably sad: Women do not get recognized for promotion or talents in groups or in the workplace. When I consider the way I had been socialized growing up, this theory supports the way I was raised to think of being a leader. As an Asian daughter in an immigrant family, I was taught never to bring attention to myself for fear of appearing egotistical or gloating. In my research, I studied Asian American female forms of leadership in the United States. All the data I found confirmed the Western stereotype that Asians and Asian Americans are "passive, unassertive, docile, and therefore lacking in leadership skills." Race and cultural values shape how Asian Americans show up*

as leaders in a predominantly White society along with its male-oriented paradigm of leadership. Traditional Asian values are "humility, harmony versus conflict, and the attention to group needs versus personal gains.

Throughout this excerpt, I speak from my personal experience as an Asian American woman who has internalized the values of modesty, humility, and quiet self-determination. I do not let the research component in my final paper (I have dozens of formal citations and quotations to support all of the generalizations I make) define my truths; rather I define my truths for myself, and I utilize the research as a secondary means of support for my claim. What this excerpt makes room for is allowing others to connect to me first as a person, a leader, and an Asian American woman; and then secondarily to me as a scholar exploring the qualities of modesty, humility, and self-determination. When I did the research, I sought out voices that reflected my personal definition and beliefs. I do not believe it is a coincidence that many of the references are the work of other Asian American scholars. This collective use of the "Asian-American femme" experience allows for the monolithic discourse of leadership to shift to a duolithic (my White counterparts *and* my non-White voice) discourse of who is a leader in the academy. SPN, when done effectively, encourages duolithic connections instead of monolithic separations.

Not Hiding Behind the Scholarship

When I work with and mentor students, I know they are often in a place of figuring out who they are and where they are socially located when they try to define leadership. I strongly believe that SPN writing lends itself beautifully to creating a safe space for students to express themselves, without hiding behind extensive referencing. So many students I know appreciate the opportunity to write as much with their inner, as with their outer, voice. What better way to define their own worth and validation? I, too, need to write in such a way as to validate my own voice. What follows is another excerpt from the final paper I wrote for the course I mentioned earlier.

My strongest self-identified role as a leader emerged when I studied to be an educator and when I was working in the field. I went to college with a decided major, based on previous assistance from teachers while I was in high school. I knew I wanted to make an impact on the future youth and to be a positive role model. Intrinsically, I knew I had good values, energy, patience, and excitement to learn and to teach.

During my time as an educator in the public schools, I primarily focused on Anti-Bias Curriculum and building Language Enrichment Programs in ASL, Spanish, Japanese, Mandarin, and other languages of interest to the students. I was given ownership by allowing my voice to be the "expert" voice regarding these types of educational initiatives. Some of this given power or leadership was based on the assumption that I had all of the answers or a clear vision on a topic that had not been integrated in the schools. For me, it was a source of passion and excitement, and I had a clear vision of how to establish and incorporate the curriculum into my classroom. My mentor teacher believed in my abilities and allowed me to take a lot of ownership and lead the process with our students. I am grateful for her trust in my abilities as a teacher. I am certain that this experience gave me a boost in confidence, not only in my abilities as an educator but as a colleague who could bring new ideas to the school.

I later took on a teaching position as a head teacher in an Early Childhood Enrichment Center. A male business owner who had owned the building the Early Childhood Enrichment Center was housed in had recently inherited the organization. I knew that I would be going into a new and exciting organization that was growing and changing because of the new leadership. I thought, for certain, I could make a change, a difference, and follow my passion of working with students. Within my first year I established the Language Enrichment Program and created the school's documentation handbook on policies for teachers and families. This experience was likely the only experience I have had where gender-dynamic differences in leadership were explicit and apparent.

It was not until a few months later that I realized my philosophy of education did not mirror the leadership's focus on profit and management. The focus was more on "the bottom line" and how much money each child brought in for the organization versus the focus being on intentional education to build a well-rounded curriculum for students. Educational decisions were made by money managers without consulting the staff. This disparity caused a large schism in the school between educators and the director. The philosophy of a top-down, money-driven structure of management was in dramatic contrast to a philosophy that focused on building a sense of community and teacher-student empowerment. There was a staff turnover of six teachers in less than five months as a result of management's retaliation against those teachers who advocated for educational change on behalf of what might be best for their students.

It was during this experience that I witnessed terrible injustice, and I just could not sit back and watch. My moral principles were involved, and I recognized the impact of how many management choices brought harm to the infrastructure of the organization. As a result, I sought to garner support from the teachers. I asked them not just for their opinions but also for solutions. As a result, together we constructed a formal proposal to bring to the director, and we were able to reach an agreement for a healthy work environment that could be mutually beneficial for management, teachers, and students.

While this writing may seem to reflect primarily a first-person account of my leadership journey, the implications that are gracefully added here allow me to freely write my experience as truth. My unencumbered writing allows for my voice and story to be the primary evidence that examines how one teacher took a professional-support risk to incorporate Anti-Bias Curriculum into a school system not entirely prepared for diversity advancement. This type of safe disclosure may encourage readers who are administrators to hear the impact of such risks. SPN in no way resulted in my experiencing any professional dilemma about this disclosure.

Discovering a Sense of Self-Pride through Validation and Self-Empowerment

While I was teaching, one of my student's parents approached me to join an art organization. I had been wanting to incorporate more artwork back into my life and thought a group would be a great way to become inspired. After a few meetings, I recognized that the group was experiencing hardship in communication and order given the co-op structure. After spending the first half of a year, I carefully watched and communicated with the group on what was working for them and what they thought could improve. After gathering information, building trust, and having faith in keeping the group together and active, I decided to propose a group structure based on previous organizations I had been in.

Leadership in the co-op came out of speaking up and offering my perspectives on how to move the organization forward. The more I went to meetings, I realized there were no systems in place for sharing power with others. One person really led the group and did all of the work. This had been creating quite a strain for her, and tension seemed to rise from group members. Documentation didn't seem transparent in a way that everyone felt they had access to it. I immediately wondered about what could be done, collaboratively, to help keep the group together and to feel autonomous while preparing for exhibitions.

Because of my time on executive boards during my undergraduate years, I thought the group could use some structure and a more formal way to document our work. I drew up proposals for executive positions with roles and responsibilities and brought it with me to a meeting. Everyone was quite receptive to the idea, and, as a group, we constructed what kinds of positions would be held and what kinds of responsibilities each position entailed. With that, we decided to build group expectations on sharing the workload in preparing positions, when meetings would happen, formulating an agenda, and specifying communication standards.

I then offered to create a web-based dashboard where all information could be held—documentation for shows, a calendar, loan agreements, contact information for organizations we had worked with, and contact information for all group members with a discussion board to boot! This process of structuring the organization took several meetings before we were able to build consensus. Everyone was included in the process and could share their ideas during that time. I facilitated and guided the conversation but never asserted my opinions alone. The group was highly appreciative of the end product and put the dashboard to good use once it was in effect, and it changed the way we handled our shows.

All great discoveries come from a deep inner journey.
—W. Brian Arthur

My pathways toward leadership have been non-linear, where I had mostly been encouraged into leadership roles at the start of my undergraduate experience, and eventually finding myself in positions of leadership as the result of speaking up or stepping up at the right time and place. During the times that I held positions of "power" and influence, I spent some time trying to figure out if I fit the definition of what a leader should be. I understood that a leader was one who was "directive," "assertive," who "spoke for others," and who "paved the way." I honestly thought that being a good leader meant having a good heart, a listening ear, and the ability to empower others and make change through sharing knowledge similar to my mentors.' I maintain firmly that these principles still remain true with the work that I do now, but the definition of "leader" has expanded based on my life experience and the definitions given in Dr. Tarule's *Women & Leadership* course.

My motivation for authoring this manuscript in the style of SPN was to give insight into my developmental process as a leader from a personal and deeply connected perspective. I detailed my journey, knowing SPN would allow me to be my whole and genuine self. I wrote clearly and freely about my personal experience over the years. Not only does this style of writing allow me to express the importance of my leadership journey to myself, but it also has a universal quality for many young leaders who are on a similar leadership path. I wanted to consider elements of race and cultural identity and how these socially affect me as an Asian American leader. I considered my growth and development from the time I began my undergraduate degree in Early Childhood Education and Human Development and Family Studies, and I examined leadership opportunities that were given to me or that I had self-selected. I researched the notion of "modesty" in females and Asian American Leadership Development in the United States. I explored the implications of cultural identity for people like me who work in predominantly White, male definitions of leadership.

As a result of this examination of my leadership history, I found that I can firmly identify myself as a leader, and I have found validation in my process with affirmation from the articles and discussions I experienced in the Women and Leadership course. My final paper for Dr. Tarule, as well as this SPN reflective essay, is just what I needed to re-examine my leadership style, persona, philosophy, and skill-set.

Here are the guiding leadership principles I choose to live by:

- Vulnerability
- Integrity
- Compassion
- Collaboration
- Leading by example
- Listening carefully and responding honestly
- Sharing power and knowledge
- Continuing to learn
- Responding to the concerns of others
- Respecting the official mission of the institution
- Being fully present at all times

11

Robert's and Sydnee's Closing Invitation to Our Readers

Dear SPN Readers,

> Every great story on the planet happened when someone decided not to give
> up, but kept going on no matter what.
> —Spryte Loriano

We hope that the SPN student reflections in Chapters Nine and Ten illustrate the principle that the shortest distance between two people is a story. All of our SPN writers testify to the healing, and consequent liberating, power of this type of personal writing. Healing moments can occur when transcendence comes out of misunderstanding—e.g., when great nations dispute, and people's stories are caught in the middle, and, of necessity, we are forced to listen to one another in order to reach peaceful resolution.

We are talking about scholarship that starts with the "I" and ends with the "We." SPN, in contrast to more "objective," distant forms of scholarship, is an evolving, intentional methodology in the academy. It starts with the singular self of the author as the primary source—a self with all of its vulnerability and resilience. For this reason, SPN is not for the squeamish. SPN writing requires the author to be authentic, transparent, purposeful, and unabashedly candid. The SPN writer is in complete control of the research instead of the other way around.

Both in this book, and as co-teachers, we have found ourselves to be less the omniscient experts on SPN and more the co-learners and co-facilitators. We believe, with all of our hearts and minds, that scholarship and personal narrative must overlap. We need to move beyond (but not exclude) the objectivist view of knowledge, and beyond the controlled, statistical studies, in order to meet the dynamic diversity needs of today's students. The personal narrative methodology allows for underrepresented, and multi-identitied, students to find the courage to speak to their fears, their hopes, and even to the dreams of their ancestors. SPN serves as a counter-narrative to the current objectivist bias in more traditional research literature by revealing singular, personal stories that have never been told before.

We hope, as you reach the end of this volume—our labor of love—that you have felt inspired, curious, intrigued, empathic, joyous, and reflective. We know that we do. We hope you have learned, questioned, played with, and are "down" with SPN. We do not want you to become SPN converts or SPN ideologues. Instead, we ask only that you give this writing methodology a chance. It could be a great authorial fit for you. And then again it might not. But you will only know this if you give it a try.

Each of us, as authors, has been trained to write in the traditional scholarly ways. Robert is a philosopher/analyst. Sydnee is a social worker/empiricist. Each of us is proud of our intellectual backgrounds, and we don't ever intend to abandon, or compromise, them. But SPN gives us the opportunity to deepen, enrich, and enlarge our disciplinary perspectives. Now we can be the "insiders" in our writing, testing out our research-hypotheses by examining them within the context of our own, personal lives. In this way, our research doesn't validate us; we validate the research. There is no liberation greater than this! Neither is there more insight about how to live an authentic life!

For both of us, SPN is not just a methodology or an outcome. It's a process. SPN writing has become a way for us to focus our personal cameras on what matters most—our stories. However, as with all good stories (you know the ones we mean, where you can't start another story until you can truly let go of the one that resonated so much with you), it's time for us, and you, to stop (not end) this part of the journey. It's time to let go of this book, and share it with others. SPN is really about "letting go." Letting go is the conventional SPN wisdom required to seek out personal truths and meaning. Letting go of the last written word in a manuscript is a writer's way of showing that the story does not end with a period but rather with an endless series of ellipsis points . . . or better still, a stream of question marks; or maybe even a perplexing string of *vice versas*. SPN manuscripts just *stop* . . . to be continued later; they do not *end*. Whatever, SPN is about letting go of the *exter-*

nal traditional writing rules and, instead, discovering the *internal* closeted words that cry out to be written simply because they matter. We believe that letting go is critical to honoring one's story.

We also hope you have found yourself embedded in these pages. As we mentioned, SPN is about the universalizable personal discoveries—those moments of truth when we realize we are not alone. For example, we are, indeed, connected to our Muslim neighbor's stories; and the stories of our trans-identified classmates; and the narratives of our domestically abused sisters and children; and the feelings of being "neither here nor there" of our international friends and scholars; and the "in-between" confusion of our bi-racial and multi-ethnic leaders; and even to the historical accounts of our forefathers and foremothers. Many of us have been marginalized. Many of us have been shamed for being on the fringes of the dominant society's expectations. And many of us have been estranged, even eliminated, from the mainstream dialogue. Sadly, many of us have rarely, if ever, experienced liberation from these socio-cultural vulnerabilities. SPN is a writer's gift that moves us from the margins to the center of our socio-cultural lives. SPN is each and every writer's "emancipation proclamation."

> If we would only listen with the same passion that we feel about wanting to be heard.
> —HARRIET LERNER

What makes SPN equally powerful is having a listening audience. This gives everyone a role in creating our individual, and collective, stories. If you have enjoyed reading our students' stories throughout the book, but perhaps are not yet ready to write yours, we encourage you to consider the following: Try being a mentor to others by inspiring them to talk about, or even write, their hitherto, untold stories of being discounted, de-valued, misinterpreted, and, most tragic of all, "disappeared." If you wonder whether you can do this kind of writing, we say—just do it! But if you really need further inspiration, read more SPNs like the ones we feature throughout our book. Most are available online at the University of Vermont.

> Sometimes the simple rhythm of typing gets us from page one to page two. When you begin to feel your own words, start typing them.
> —FINDING FORRESTER

Before we, your authors, can get to our own "rhythm of typing," however, the first thing we need to do is *to talk* with one another about key elements in our own stories—past, present, and future. We need to "feel" our own words. Sometimes this takes hours and even days. We talk about the ironies, paradoxes, and hard-won truths in our stories. We evoke from each other larger lessons and insights that might be of use to our students. We also talk about our students' stories and the individual (and common) themes that seem to emerge time and time again. We talk about the stories of our colleagues, our partners, our families, our friends, and even the stories of the strangers we might meet in a cafe, an airport or plane, at the super-market, or after a university-sponsored lecture.

When we are together as co-authors for many writing hours, we ask questions, we muse, we laugh and we cry, and we play. We press one another to dig more deeply in order to let the emotional "genie" (in Latin, the word means "genius") out of the bottle." Or, to change metaphors, we prod one another to open "Pandora's box" in order to deal more effectively with life's blessings and curses. If SPN accomplishes anything, like Pandora in the ancient Greek myth, it opens up the possibility of hope.

All of this is our way of sorting out the content of our writing before we put fingers to our keyboards. We do all of the above, because we know that some of our ideas need to be heard and validated by one another before we can commit them to the page. So, we want you to know that your voice deserves to be heard. And, while you may feel positioned on the margins, and perhaps you might even feel that it is an insurmountable task for you to write your story in an academic environ-ment, please know that there is a growing number of educators who value schol-arship that features personal narrative. Remember the wise words of Lao Tzu, "A journey of a thousand miles begins with a single step." And that single step could be for you to just listen for a while . . . both to your own inner voice as well as to the indomitably courageous voices of others.

> It takes courage to grow up and turn out to be who you really are.
> —E.E. CUMMINGS

And we would add to cummings' quote that it takes vulnerability and courage *to write* about who we really are. Throughout its history, higher education has system-ically, and systematically, discouraged the personal stories of its student constituen-cies—many of whom are first-generation college attendees. As a consequence, academe has tragically muted the stories of that vast, interconnected, generational community of others that has had such a profound impact on each and every one of us and our students. Not a single student has ever come to either of us without a history—without a culture, a family, a legacy, a complex amalgam of intersect-ing, sometimes competing, identities; or without hopes and dreams, fears and night-mares, achievements and failures.

And, so, at this time, we challenge you to stretch out, to "bend low" toward what is missing in the academy. Remember that the meaning of "profound" is actually to "bend low" in order to "stretch high." SPN helps each of us to become aware of all our untold, underrepresented stories—many of which have been relegated to the "abyss" for much too long. The payoff of being "profound," then, is to understand that it is only by exploring the bottom, that we create the very real possibility of moving forward. And, moving forward means that, in our writing, we have the oppportunity to help others to do the same.

We ask: How, in the process of unearthing your stories, are you *standing by*, rather than *standing for*, or *standing on top of*, those who are also on the margins? How are you helping those silenced SPN writers to bend low toward their own stories? This is the call of action in SPN writing. This is where SPN ends up whenever it is successful. It answers the three basic questions we must always address in undertaking any type of personal narrative scholarship: What? So What? Now What?

Thus, we invite you to join us in the process of liberating the voices of those who are marginalized, disenfranchised, and underrepresented. This invitation, of course, comes with one non-negotiable precondition: Each one of us must first be willing to listen to the call of our own repressed, and suppressed, voices.

With Gratitude and Humility,
Robert & Sydnee

Afterword

Jacob Diaz, *Learning to Trust My Voice*

Perhaps the most difficult challenge for our students, though, is to believe deep down that, indeed, their lives do signify.
—NASH AND VIRAY (2012)

Before you tell your life what you intend to do with it, listen for what it intends to do with you. Before you tell your life what truths and values you have decided to live up to, let your life tell you what truths to embody, what values you represent.
—PALMER (2000)

I am honored to author this reflective afterword for such a compelling book that is much needed in today's times. It is important because the gift of SPN is that it creates space for the experiences in our lives to be held up to the light and honored for their brilliance. Our life experiences originate from within each of us as authors attempting to understand the complexities of not only our own lives but also our respective places in a complex society. In true SPN fashion, I feel I should share with you a bit about who I am and describe how this method has helped me to believe in myself and trust that my life "signifies," as both Nash and Viray highlight in this book.

I am a fourth-generation Mexican American who identifies as Chicano, a first- generation college student who was raised in San Diego, California. I am the oldest of three sons, and my parents are from Corpus Christi, Texas. I have always loved being in school, and I think it is one of the reasons I now serve as Vice President for Student Development at Seattle University, which is a Jesuit institution located in the Pacific Northwest. For the first 7 years of my formal schooling, I felt alive and excelled academically. I really enjoyed learning and, thanks to my parents, felt the freedom to enjoy an amazing childhood. Something curious happened to me in the seventh grade, however. I remember vividly being placed in "advanced" classes and feeling "smart" as a result. I found all of the courses to be challenging in a constructive way, except for one. My pre-algebra class seemed to be a language I just couldn't understand. I am not sure why to this day, but it all seemed out of reach for my brain to process the information. And yet there I was showing up each day trying my best to learn and to feign interest when I felt myself tuning out because I just didn't connect with what was being taught.

After about two weeks in the class, we took our first exam, and I knew that I had done poorly, to say the least. It was a Friday, and over the weekend I hoped that somehow I did better than I thought; but Monday would reveal the true reality. There I was on Monday morning anxiously awaiting the receipt of my grade, and the teacher began calling out each student's name and grade and asked them to sit in a certain seat according to the grade they received on the exam. The student receiving the highest score sat in the front left seat in the classroom, and the remainder lined up behind this student until all seats were filled. I immediately grew anxious and began to sweat, praying that my name would be called sooner rather than later. I knew that I had done poorly, but how poorly would remain to be seen. It seemed like forever until my name was called, and when it was I found myself in the second or third row from the right toward the back of the classroom. I felt ashamed. I wanted to hide, but I couldn't. I wanted to be in the front row with the "smart" people. I wanted to run but felt trapped by the authority of the teacher. I didn't feel smart anymore. Maybe all the grades I had gotten before were gifts from the teacher and not accurate. Maybe I was dumb?

I carried these thoughts and feelings with me throughout my high school years, and, looking back, I realize that I performed according to what I believed. I wasn't a poor student, nor was I an academic star. I was in the middle of the pack. (At least I saw myself that way.) I decided to immerse myself in athletics and tried to play football and was a wrestler in high school. Through these outlets, I made great friends and felt like I mattered. I thought the classroom setting was a way to participate in these activities, but certainly not a way to advance myself.

My high school years passed by, and graduation crept up on me. I had completed the requisite credits to receive my high school degree and was ready to launch into the next stage of life. I didn't think college was for me. That place was for smart people and, if you looked at my grades, you'd see that I didn't exactly excel. I remember friends being called into the guidance counselor's office to talk about college, but that permission slip never did come my way. As a result, I thought that the school administrators had reviewed my grades and decided that I wasn't smart enough for college. This confirmed the negative perception I had of myself for some time. I knew I was a hard worker, for this is one of the many lessons my parents instilled in me, so I decided that what I would do was become a commercial fisherman. I figured that my love for ocean fishing and a job on a boat would be the ideal thing for me. It is ironic that once I began working on a boat I learned quite a few lessons about myself. I learned that I loved being around people and working with them, and that while I didn't see a long career in the commercial fishing business for myself, I wasn't sure of what I would do. I was confident, however, that somehow I would figure it out.

Discovering My Self-Doubt Monster

We ourselves, driven by fear, too often betray true self to gain the approval of others.
—PARKER J. PALMER (2000)

After my 4-month stint as a commercial fisherman, I returned home. Thankfully my parents took me back, although it was under two conditions. First, I would work, and second, I would have to go to school. The first one was easy, especially given my recent experiences on the fishing boat. But the second one paralyzed me with fear. How could I excel in a college course when I had a hard time completing high school? Given the conditions I was under, I went to my local community college and enrolled in one course. Ironically, it was pre-algebra! But this time I did much better. The professor was great, and I started to tentatively believe that maybe I could learn and enjoy the classroom like I had in elementary school. It took me 4 years before I transferred to the University of California, Santa Barbara, where I majored in English Literature. I recall vividly wanting to prove to the world that I could succeed in college. Deep down, I thought that if I achieved a degree I would no longer be seen as dumb and that others would approve of me.

I received an outstanding education at UCSB. It took place both in and out of the classroom, and, thankfully, there were many advisors and mentors along the way who continually reminded me that persistence and hard work would pay off and that I was smart enough to succeed. It was during my time as an undergraduate that I began to see the inequities that existed in higher education. I began to see myself as a racial being who had to wrestle with my own internalized oppression. I also noticed that there were not many people who looked like me in either faculty or administrative roles, and I decided then and there that I wanted to change that. I wanted to make it easier for college students like me to succeed in college. I often wondered why there were not more Latinos at my university, given the large numbers that I knew lived in California. Where were we?

Discovering My Calling

> Some journeys are direct, and some are circuitous; some are heroic, and some are fearful and muddled. But every journey, honestly undertaken, stands a chance of taking us toward the place where our deep gladness meets the world's deep need.
> —PARKER J. PALMER (2000)

> Beginning with a cohort of 100 students, only 55 Chicanos...will graduate from high school, compared with 83 White students and 72 Blacks. Of the 100, only 22 Chicanos...will enroll in an institution of higher education, compared with 38 Whites and 29 Blacks. Only seven Chicanos...out of 100 will complete college compared with 23 Whites and 12 Blacks.
> —MARISA DE LOS SANTOS (CITED IN DIAZ, 2004)

While at UCSB, I was an involved student. I served as a resident assistant in the halls, a peer advisor in the Chicano/Latino/a support services area, and even helped to co-teach a course for first-year students that was aimed at assisting their transition to university life. It was due to this involvement that I found a home in the university where I could match my desire to change the academy with a passion for helping students succeed in college. I had learned that to enter this noble profession required graduate training, and this is what took me out to the University of Vermont where I would pursue both a master's degree and a doctorate.

As I moved through my graduate education, I discovered that I wanted to understand how Chicanos like me had persevered in college within traditionally White collegiate environments. What had kept them pressing forward? What worked for them? How did they do it? I wanted to contribute their stories to the educational literature, as I had identified a void that I thought was important to fill. The more I learned about Chicano college students, the more I saw myself in them, and I felt a call to dive more deeply into my own life-narrative. I wanted to understand why I had persevered and to offer my story to fellow Chicanos in the hope that it might be helpful to their success in college.

Admittedly, the idea of having my dissertation be an SPN was scary. My self-doubt arose loudly, and I questioned whether the academic community would dismiss my dissertation and as a result dismiss my life story as not being credible enough for public consumption. Would the dissertation dutifully honor my proud Chicano community? Would it finally put to rest the notion that I wasn't smart enough to be in college in the first place? Would I finally be accepted?

Learning to Trust My Voice

> What a long time it can take to become the person one has always been. How often in the process we mask ourselves in faces that are not our own.
> —Parker J. Palmer (2000)

My soul was drawn to SPN, while my intellect wanted to run in the opposite direction. I was afraid of what I would unearth and at the same time excited to make a contribution to the literature that was unique and innovative. I needed to narrativize in writing my own journey in higher education as a Chicano, and this is where I began. I wish I could say that writing an SPN dissertation was comfortable. On the contrary, it was the most challenging and thought-provoking writing I have ever done. For every page I wrote for public view, I estimate there were probably three or four pages that went into another file on my computer. Every author's style is different. I learned through the SPN journey that my writing took me to places that I could never have foreseen. In my case, seeing the wound created by the self-doubt I carried was simultaneously difficult and liberating. The more I wrote, the more confident I became.

At times it was like I was being written—the words flowing from my heart and mind through my hands and onto the computer screen. There were other days when the writing came much slower, but I noticed that when I would veer off of my authentic SPN voice into safer territory, my writing would become laborious. Through "butt to chair," as Robert, my advisor, would often remind me, my SPN voice began to take shape. I began to trust again. It was akin to becoming reacquainted with an old friend. For me, I was becoming reacquainted with the learner in me and the belief that each and every student has within them all that they need in order to excel in life. The primary function of education, in Socrates's sense, is to draw pre-existent wisdom and knowledge *out* of the student, and not merely to dump it in.

Conclusion

> Why would anyone want to embark on the daunting inner journey about which Annie Dillard writes? Because there is no way out of one's inner life, so one had better get into it. On the inward and downward spiritual journey, the only way out is in and through.
> —PARKER J. PALMER (2000)

> Until we enter boldly into the fears we most want to avoid, those fears will dominate our lives.
> —PARKER J. PALMER (2000)

I think this is the point of SPN and, in particular, the role it can play in the lives of marginalized people. For me, SPN unleashed the humanity in my spirit in a way that I can best describe as liberating. I began to feel and think of myself as a scholar; without qualification, for the first time in my life I felt like my story mattered, and I did not need to rely upon the validation of others to prove it to me. While some years have passed since I completed my dissertation, I often recall the SPN journey with gratitude. As a man of color in higher education, I find that racism continues to rear its ugly head and impact access to higher education in numerous ways. As a high-level administrator, I find peace in knowing that I can see my life for what I understand to be true, and take it from there. The extraordinary power of SPN is evident in this book. I know that for me Scholarly Personal Narrative writing has been a gift for my soul, and I hope my story returns this gift to the lives of others.

*Jacob Diaz is Vice President for Student Development at Seattle University. His SPN dissertation, *Marginalized Narratives in the Academy: One Chicano's Story of His Journey in Higher Education*, won the prestigious Doctoral Student Scholar of the Year Award in 2004 at the University of Vermont.

Bibliography

Allison, D. (1995). *Two or three things I know for sure*. New York: Penguin Books.

Anderson, R. (2001). Embodied writing and reflections on embodiment. *Journal of Transpersonal Psychology, 33*(2), 83–98.

Anzaldúa, G. (1990). *Making face, making soul: Haciendo caras*. New York: Aunt Lute Books.

Atwood, M. (2002). *Negotiating with the dead: A writer on writing*. New York: Cambridge University Press.

Banks, W. (2003). Written through the body: Disruptions and "personal" writing. *College English, 66*(1): 21–40.

Black, A.M. (2001). *Modern American queer history*. Philadelphia: Temple University Press.

Brown, B. (2010, December). *TedX: The power of vulnerability* [Audio Podcast]. Retrieved from http://www.ted.com/talks/lang/en/brene_brown_on_vulnerability.html

Bruner, J. (1977). *The process of education*. Cambridge, MA: Harvard University Press.

Bruner, J. (1990). *Acts of meaning*. Cambridge, MA: Harvard University Press.

Casagrande, J. (2010). *It was the best of sentences, it was the worst of sentences: A writer's guide to crafting killer sentences*. Berkeley, CA: Ten Speed Press.

Chang, H. (2008). *Autoethnography as method*. Walnut Creek, CA: Left Coast Press, Inc.

Clark, R.P. (2006). *Writing tools: 50 essential strategies for every writer*. New York: Little, Brown.

Clark, R.P. (2010). *The glamour of grammar: A guide to the magic and mystery of practical English.* New York: Little, Brown.

Cohen, J.A. (2005). The mirror as a metaphor for the reflective practitioner. In M.H. Oermann & K. Heinrich (Eds.), *Strategies for teaching, assessment, and program planning.* New York: Springer.

DeSurra, C., & Church, K. (1994). Unlocking the classroom closet: Privileging the marginalized voices of gay/lesbian college students. Retrieved from http://www.eric.ed.gov/ ERICWebPortal/contentdelivery/servlet/ERICServlet?accno=ED379697 (temporarily disabled; see link for more information).

Diaz, J. (2002). *Marginalized narratives in the academy: One Chicano's attempt to re-narrate his journey in higher education.* Unpublished doctoral dissertation, University of Vermont, Burlington.

Dillard, A. (1990). *The writing life.* New York: HarperPerennial.

Du Bois, W.E.B. (1903). The talented tenth. In L.F. Goodchild & H.S. Wechsler (Eds.), *The history of higher education* (2nd ed., pp. 551–561). Boston: Pearson Custom Publishing.

Dumond, V. (1993). *Grammar for grownups: A guide to grammar and usage for everyone who has to put words on paper effectively.* New York: HarperPerennial.

Freire, P. (1970). *Pedagogy of the oppressed.* New York: Herder & Herder.

Frankl, V. E. (1959). *Man's Search for Meaning.* Boston: Beacon Press.

Friedan, B. (2001). *The feminine mystique.* New York: W.W. Norton. (Original work published 1963)

Goldberg, B. (2002). *Beyond the words: The three untapped sources of creative fulfillment for writers.* New York: Jeremy P. Tarcher/Putnam.

Gornick, V. (2001). *The situation and the story: The art of personal narrative.* New York: Farrar, Straus and Giroux.

Graff, G., & Birkenstein, C. (2006). *"They say/I say": The moves that matter in academic writing.* New York: W.W. Norton.

Haley, A. (1976). *Roots.* Garden City, NY: Doubleday.

Haroian-Guerin, G. (Ed.). (1999). *The personal narrative: Writing ourselves as teachers and scholars.* Portland, ME: Calendar Islands Publishers.

Harper, H. (2006). *Letters to a young brother: Manifest your destiny.* New York: Gotham Books.

hooks, b. (1989). *Talking back: Thinking feminist-thinking black.* Boston, MA: South End Press.

hooks, b. (2000). *Feminist theory: From margin to center.* London: Pluto Press.

Hunter-Gault, C. (1992). *In my place.* New York: Vintage Books.

Kane, C.H. (1988). *Ambiguous adventure.* London: Heinemann.

Kornegay, L. (2012). *Leading to change the world: One African American woman's journey into positions of leadership in predominantly white institutions.* Unpublished doctoral dissertation, University of Vermont, Burlington.

Lamott, A. (1994). *Bird by bird: Some instructions on life and writing.* New York: Random House.

MacLeod, J. (1995). *Ain't no makin' it: Aspirations & attainment in a low-income neighbor-hood.* Boulder, CO: Westview Press.

McCullough, D. (2003). Climbing into another head. In M. Arana (Ed.), *The writing life: Writers on how they think and work.* New York: Public Affairs.

Melone, T. (1962). *De la négritude dans la littérature Négro-africaine.* Paris: Présence Africaine.

Menand, L. (2010). *The marketplace of ideas: Reform and resistance in the American university.* New York: W.W. Norton.

Miller, S. A. (2009). *310: One university leader's critical reflection of body image through the lens of transformational learning.* (Doctoral dissertation). Retrieved from University of Vermont library. http://library.uvm.edu/dissertations/index.php?search_type=item& bid=1740845

Moraga, C., & Anzaldúa, G. (Eds.). (2002). *This bridge called my back: Writings by radical women of color* (3rd ed.). Berkeley, CA: Third Woman Press. (Original work published 1981)

Nash, R.J. (2004). *Liberating scholarly writing: The power of personal narrative.* New York: Teachers College Press.

Nash, R.J., & Bradley, D.L. (2011). *Me-search and re-search: A guide for writing scholarly personal narrative manuscripts.* Charlotte, NC: Information Age Publications.

Nash, R.J., & Murray, M.C. (2010). *Helping college students find purpose: The campus guide to meaning-making.* San Francisco, CA: Jossey-Bass.

Nunez, A.M. & Curraro-Alamin, S. (1998). Statistical Analysis Report. /First-Generation Students: Undergraduates Whose Parents Never Enrolled in Postsecondary Eduation. /June, 1998. http://nces.ed.gov/pubsearch/pubsinfo.asp?pubid=98082

Obama, B. (1995). *Dreams from my father: A story of race and inheritance.* New York: Three Rivers Press.

Palmer, P.J. (2000). *Let your life speak: Listening for the voice of vocation.* San Francisco, CA: Jossey-Bass.

Park, R.E. (1928). Human migration and the marginal man. *The American Journal of Sociology, 33*(6), 881–893.

Pascal, B., & Tourneur, Z. (1942). *Pensées de Blaise Pascal.* Paris: J. Vrin.

Pipher, M.B. (2006). *Writing to change the world.* New York: Riverhead Books.

Rhodes, R. (1995). *How to write: Advice and reflections.* New York: Willam Morrow.

Strober, M.H. (2011). *Interdisciplinary conversations: Challenging habits of thought.* Stanford, CA: Stanford University Press.

Strunk, W., & White, E.B. (2000). *The elements of style* (4th ed.). Needham Heights, MA: Allyn & Bacon.

Taylor, M.C. (2010). *Crisis on campus: A bold plan for reforming our colleges and universities.* New York: Alfred A. Knopf.

Tieger, P.D., & Barron-Tieger, B. (2001). *Do what you are: Discover the perfect career for you through the secrets of personality type.* New York: Little, Brown.

Welch, S. D. (1999). *Sweet dreams in America: Making ethics and spirituality work.* New York: Routledge.

Welch, S. D. (2000). *A Feminist Ethic of Risk.* Minneapolis, MN: Augsburg Fortress Press.

X, M. (1965). *The autobiography of Malcolm X.* New York: Random House.

Yoshino, K. (2006). *Covering: The hidden assault on our civil rights.* New York: Random House.

Studies in the Postmodern Theory of Education

General Editor
Shirley R. Steinberg

Counterpoints publishes the most compelling and imaginative books being written in education today. Grounded on the theoretical advances in criticalism, feminism, and postmodernism in the last two decades of the twentieth century, Counterpoints engages the meaning of these innovations in various forms of educational expression. Committed to the proposition that theoretical literature should be accessible to a variety of audiences, the series insists that its authors avoid esoteric and jargonistic languages that transform educational scholarship into an elite discourse for the initiated. Scholarly work matters only to the degree it affects consciousness and practice at multiple sites. Counterpoints' editorial policy is based on these principles and the ability of scholars to break new ground, to open new conversations, to go where educators have never gone before.

For additional information about this series or for the submission of manuscripts, please contact:

> Shirley R. Steinberg
> c/o Peter Lang Publishing, Inc.
> 29 Broadway, 18th floor
> New York, New York 10006

To order other books in this series, please contact our Customer Service Department:

> (800) 770-LANG (within the U.S.)
> (212) 647-7706 (outside the U.S.)
> (212) 647-7707 FAX

Or browse online by series:
> www.peterlang.com